STIGMA STORIES

STIGMA STORIES

RHETORIC, LIVED EXPERIENCE, AND CHRONIC ILLNESS

Molly Margaret Kessler

THE OHIO STATE UNIVERSITY PRESS
COLUMBUS

Library of Congress Cataloging-in-Publication Data
Names: Kessler, Molly Margaret, author.
Title: Stigma stories : rhetoric, lived experience, and chronic illness / Molly Margaret Kessler.
Description: Columbus : The Ohio State University Press, [2022] | Includes bibliographical references and index. | Summary: "Building on previous research into stigma within rhetoric and blending it with health communication, disability studies, narrative medicine, and sociology, this book takes a rhetorical approach to studying stigma as emergent within the lived experiences of stigmatized chronic conditions-specifically chronic gastrointestinal conditions"—Provided by publisher.
Identifiers: LCCN 2021059180 | ISBN 9780814214916 (cloth) | ISBN 0814214916 (cloth) | ISBN 9780814282106 (ebook) | ISBN 0814282105 (ebook) Subjects: LCSH: Stigma (Social psychology) | Gastrointestinal system—Diseases. | Chronically ill—Social aspects. | Chronic diseases—Social aspects. | Sociology of disability. | Rhetoric—Social aspects. | BISAC: LANGUAGE ARTS & DISCIPLINES / Rhetoric | SOCIAL SCIENCE / Sociology / General
Classification: LCC HM1131 .K47 2022 | DDC 305.9/08—dc23/eng/20220202
LC record available at https://lccn.loc.gov/2021059180
Other identifiers: 9780814258330 (paper) | 0814258336 (paper)

Cover design by Susan Zucker
Text design by Juliet Williams
Type set in Adobe Minion Pro

CONTENTS

PREFACE

ON JANUARY 19, 2019, Seven Charles, a ten-year-old Black boy from Kentucky, killed himself. Left home alone for just an hour while his father, Donnie, was at church choir practice and his mother, Tami, left to run a few errands, Seven was tasked with completing a list of chores. The type of boy who followed the rules, Seven promptly finished his homework and left it for his mother's review on the kitchen table. He then cleaned his room and began to fold and put away his laundry. But sometime in the middle of this last chore, Seven stopped, leaving laundry scattered on his bed. He then entered his closet, where his mother would later find him unresponsive. What started out as a normal day for the Charles family turned out to be one of their worst.

Although Seven's death came as a complete shock to Tami and Donnie, they have worked to piece together an explanation in the days and months since his death. According to his parents, Seven had been verbally and physically bullied several times by classmates and his adult bus driver in the months preceding his death. As Tami described, Seven wasn't just teased. He was the target of racist harassment, and he was ostracized for a medical condition.[1] Born with an imperforate anus (a condition in which the anus is either

---

1. I do not mean to downplay the role that racism played in Seven's experiences. My retelling of Seven's story attempts to follow stories shared in the many of the interviews that Seven's parents have given in the wake of Seven's death, which emphasized the bullying Seven experienced because of his ostomy and GI conditions.

blocked or missing), Seven underwent twenty-six surgeries by the age of ten, an average of two surgeries each year of his life. Along with these surgeries, Seven lived most of his childhood with an ostomy—a surgically created opening on the abdomen that allowed Seven to excrete digestive waste into an ostomy bag affixed over the opening.

Seven didn't want his classmates to know about his conditions or the fact that he needed an ostomy to go to the bathroom, so he did his best to hide them and prevent any leaks at school. However, sometimes his ostomy bag leaked digestive waste when it wasn't fully sealed against his abdomen or when it needed to be emptied. According to his parents, Seven occasionally experienced these leaks at school, which his classmates noticed and teased him about. "Kids at school and on the bus would make fun of the smell that stemmed from his condition," Tami explained (Wheatley, 2019).

Eventually, Seven was able to undergo ostomy-takedown surgery that closed the opening on his abdomen and enabled him to defecate anally. However, as his body adjusted to functioning without an ostomy, sometimes Seven struggled with fecal incontinence and subsequently continued to face bullying. Like the leaks of his ostomy bag, the leaks Seven experienced due to fecal incontinence were uncontrollable, though this didn't deter the bullies. Seven and his parents did their best to prevent and limit any accidents, but sometimes they still happened. And even when the leaks were managed, the bullies did not go away. Tami remembered, Seven "just wanted to be normal, that's all" (Kim, 2019).

Tami and Donnie eventually turned to school officials for help, asking them to open an investigation and reprimand the students who were harassing Seven. Though the school agreed to investigate, Seven's parents felt that the situation had escalated beyond repair and therefore found Seven a new school for the next academic year. Tami also secured different transportation to school so that Seven could avoid taking the bus after even his adult bus driver made comments to Seven about his conditions and related smells. Tami would later recall how she had told Seven he just needed to make it through the school year and he would be able to start over at a different school. Despite these interventions and the promise of a fresh start at a new school, Tami lamented, Seven "just couldn't take the bullying any longer" (Ross, 2019).

Though no one will ever know for sure, Seven's parents have publicly and repeatedly pointed to the bullying their son experienced as a powerful contributing factor in his death. It is difficult—impossible even—to imagine what Seven, at just ten years old, endured. A congenital chronic condition, an ostomy, leaks, fecal incontinence, over twenty surgeries—Seven overcame significant medical hurdles. A "miracle child," his mother called him (Shanklin,

2019). On top of his medical challenges, Seven went to school, a place where he should have been able to make friends, experience the wonders of baking soda volcanoes, and get lost in the pages of a chapter book, and was, instead, outcast. It's obvious in listening to the stories that Tami and Donnie have shared since Seven's death that many of the people Seven interacted with at school failed to see the miracle of his life. Instead, although Seven was among millions of people around the world who are born with or develop chronic conditions, particularly related to the gastrointestinal (GI) tract, others saw him as abnormal, and, worse, they made him feel unworthy of life. In other words, Seven was stigmatized.

•

Seven's story demonstrates just how real and powerful stigmas are and just how urgently we need to resist them. Seven's story also reminds that acknowledging the very existence of stigma, particularly related to GI conditions, is a critical first step in eradicating this kind of stigmatization and preventing the bullying and harm that Seven endured. This book is one attempt to inoculate against the fear, mystery, and consequent stigmatization of ostomies and chronic GI conditions by studying and sharing the lived experiences and stories of people like Seven. The stories and experiences of people like Seven, if we take the time to really listen to them, can help destigmatize chronic GI conditions by providing more nuanced pictures of what it is like to live with a GI condition and inviting others to embrace empathy over fear and stigmatization. Stigmas often emerge from ignorance or misunderstanding, and they maintain power in silence; thus, this book provides one platform where the stories and experiences with chronic GI conditions, and stigma, can be made visible and heard. In doing so, this book is a call to both listen and speak up.

I'm advocating for the kind of careful listening that Krista Ratcliffe (2005) has outlined: "a stance of openness that a person may choose to assume in relation to *any* person, text, or culture" (p. 17). Ratcliffe's rhetorical listening is both relevant and instructive for the work I attempt to do throughout this book and that I invite readers to do along with me. Such listening is active; it takes cognitive, emotional, and intellectual work. Rhetorically listening to stories like Seven's requires us not only to hear others' experiences but to reflect on our own and our own potential participation in perpetuating stigmas, be it through silence, accident, or intention. We must rhetorically and reflectively listen if we want to ethically engage with each other's lived experiences, particularly in the contexts of health and medicine, and, in turn, eradicate stigma. Just as Seven's story demands that we rhetorically listen to his story and others like it, it also demands that we reject stigmatization as a constant in the world or as somebody else's problem. Stigma's emergence isn't isolated to interpersonal interactions; that is, we cannot assume that if we aren't bullying others ourselves or if discriminatory comments aren't coming from us, then we are off the hook. Stigma, as I'll dive into in the coming pages, is at once personal, interpersonal, and societal. Therefore, it is the responsibility of each of us to acknowledge our own complicit and/or active roles in either perpetuating or eradicating stigma in all its manifestations.

We'll never fully know the reasons for Seven's death, but if stigma played even the smallest of roles, I hope this book can advance a critical conversation regarding the seriousness of stigmatization, why stigmas exist, how they are kept alive, how they can be relinquished, and how doing so is a shared, social project. In the coming pages, I set out to do the complex work of raising awareness, encouraging more nuanced understanding, and improving the lived experiences of those struggling under the rhetorical and experiential weight of stigma.

But what, exactly, is stigma? This is a question that has many answers and, yet, often no answer at all. Stigma is one of those odd things that is difficult to define, yet somehow easy to spot, feel, or know. Like other related forms of social and structural oppression, stigma can be overt and explicit, but most often it emerges in implicit and ambiguous ways that make it not only hard to define but difficult to identify, bound, and uproot. Stigma's simultaneous obviousness and elusiveness initially piqued the curiosity that led to the research presented in this book, but it is the experiences and stories I have heard (and lived) regarding stigma that kept me coming back, digging deeper and harder to understand what exactly stigma is, what it does in the world, why and how it persists. Although many researchers have worked to answer these questions (and to such work this book is certainly indebted), stigma continues to harm its targets—disabled people, Black, Indigenous, and people of color (BIPOC), those who don't fit current standards of beauty/thinness/fitness, the elderly, immigrants, neurodivergent people, the poor. Really, the list of stigmatized identities and embodiments is far too expansive for anyone to capture fully; any difference from countless norms can provoke stigma. Because it affects so many people for so many reasons, this book sets out to build and expand our understanding of stigma.

Given the difficulty in defining and studying stigma *and* its widespread nature, this book aims to chip away at this complex phenomenon by narrowing in on the stigmatization of chronic GI conditions. I am focused on ostomies and chronic GI conditions in this book for a variety of interrelated reasons. Conditions and experiences related to the digestive system are an ideal case for rhetorically theorizing stigma because these conditions sit on the edge of several boundaries. They are invisible, until they become visible (visually, auditorily, or olfactorily). They occupy the junction of the natural (all living things excrete) and the taboo (but what they excrete is unacceptable). And they enable us to consider how some medical technologies, experiences, and interventions fall within the accepted realm of the normal (contact lenses, cardiac implants, appendectomies) while others (excreting waste into a pouch through an opening on the abdomen) are considered abject.

GI-related stigma is not necessarily the most important or far-reaching stigmatization (though some might argue that it is), but the stigma surrounding digestion and related entities, practices, and biomedicalized conditions is as pervasive as it is pernicious. Seven's story provides an especially painful and severe example of GI-related stigmatization, but stigma is often micro and mundane. I don't need to look far or try very hard to demonstrate this. Take, for example, how Western society has developed a range of mitigation euphemisms to avoid directly talking about GI-related things and practices. We say things like *going to the bathroom, number two, the porcelain throne, doodoo, potty, ladies'/men's rooms*. This is of course just a handful of examples. Most often, when GI topics must be discussed, we find ways to talk around them, buffering our discursive (and sometime material) proximity.

Don't get me wrong: this book is not an attempt to dismantle stigma by advocating for a complete abandonment of our polite approach to bathroom topics. I imagine I'm not alone in my preference for saying "I have to go to the bathroom" during a meeting rather than getting any more specific or concrete. This book *does* look, however, at the practices that enable us to avoid, make invisible, and, in turn, stigmatize GI-related conditions. Specifically, I suggest that this inculcated aversion to all things GI evidences widespread fear, shame, and distaste that often leads to, if not precipitates, stigmatization. GI-related stigma no doubt exists, and it inflicts emotional, social, physical, and mental harm across the GI community. Indeed, it is far-reaching and deep-seated. Accordingly, GI conditions and the lived experiences that accompany them are an important and rich site for studying stigma. My hope in narrowing in on GI-related stigmatization is not only that I can deeply examine and theorize stigma in ways that will help address the specifics of GI-related stigma, but also that this specific contribution will motivate and inform additional research into stigma for other conditions, lived experiences, and identities.

Additionally, I focus on GI-related stigma because it is important to me and to the communities in which I live and that I hope to serve. I know Seven's story because it was shared widely and mournfully within my personal IBD (inflammatory bowel disease) community. In particular, I live with

Crohn's disease, a chronic autoimmune disease that affects the entire GI tract. As much as I write this book from my academic positionality, I write this book from my identity as a person living with Crohn's disease and, relatedly, as a person who has faced bullying and stigmatization for it. My teenage years, in particular, are scored by experiences with bullying related to my Crohn's. My own lived experiences and stories serve as compass, counterpoint (and mostly unwanted) companion as I captured, analyzed, and retold the stories you'll hear in the coming pages. I work throughout this book to make this undeniable positionality present when it is relevant or has something meaningful to add to various discussions.

However, whether or not it's explicitly presented on each page, my patient-researcher perspectives are there. As I conducted the research that guides this book and wrote each sentence you'll read, I was repeatedly overwhelmed with flashbacks of strangers' hurtful comments in public bathrooms as I dealt with my own uncontrollable symptoms. I relived instances when employers reprimanded me for having to run to the bathroom more frequently than my legally sanctioned fifteen minutes every four hours and when healthcare providers mercilessly told me that I would never be normal or live a normal life. Too, I researched, wrote, and edited this book from hospital beds, clinic exam rooms, and bathrooms as frequently as from my desk. My own experiences undoubtedly shape my arguments in ways I've accounted for and in ways I have yet to realize.

Perhaps most relevant among my own lived experiences with the stigmatization are those I've experienced within our own academic community, which have both motivated this work and nearly led me to quit several times. In anonymized reviews of my work, much of which has been revised for inclusion in this book, colleagues have scoffed at my academic interest in GI conditions and ostomies because they are "disgusting," peer reviewers have made "poop jokes" in response to article drafts and conference proposals, and one reviewer even went as far as to close a review noting that all my project did "was make [them] think about diarrhea." Such comments, both wildly unhelpful and mostly unsurprising, frequently left me upset and eager to give up on this research altogether. Often I've wondered whether these colleagues realized the impact their actions would have on me. But then I think about the stories I've heard from other people with GI conditions or ostomies, particularly those about the painful life-altering and life-ending implications of stigmatization, and I quickly fall short in mustering the empathy and interest required to ask questions about rhetorical intention. Stigma doesn't require intent; it has rhetorical implications regardless.

My positionality and the experiences that come with it have impacted everything from the research questions I asked and the ways I collected data to the ways I analyzed, interpreted, and now share my findings. The coming chapters explore these method/ological influences in much more detail, but what's perhaps most important now is that I believe my personal perspective isn't a bias I needed to overcome to do this research or a limitation I needed to continually suppress in order to do high-quality work. In contrast, it is the very reason I am well suited to conduct this research.[2] My expertise as a rhetorician of health and medicine and my lived experiences as a person with Crohn's disease complement and amplify each other. And they've motived me to find ways that my trained and experiential insights can help theorize and challenge the stigma associated with these conditions.

To this end, I see this book as both a response to and an invitation for discomfort. Rhetorician Caroline Gottschalk Druschke (2017) has argued that rhetorical studies, particularly of science, technology, and medicine, "needs discomfort" to intervene in the spaces and issues that matter most to us (p. 3). "We need—now—to engage with people and things, potentially make fools of ourselves, and labor with others to do the work that most matters to us, our field, and our world" (p. 3). My rhetorical investigation into stigma thus takes up Druschke's call. Facing the discomfort surrounding GI conditions and ostomies by tracing the rhetorical tendrils of stigma might be uncomfortable at first, but grappling with that discomfort is an act of care for people who have been stigmatized, as much as a step toward transformative and destigmatizing change. Therefore, I begin this book with an invitation to get uncomfortable, to lean in if and when you find yourself uncomfortable reading about poop, ostomies, and digestion. This work is important for those with ostomies and GI conditions, but, as is clear, the pervasiveness of stigma extends well beyond the contexts presented in this book. My work in the coming pages is therefore both specific and broad—grounded in ostomies and GI conditions but relevant and illuminating for a host of conditions affecting millions of people. My hope is that this book, as a starting place, will help uproot stigma and instill care, empathy, and justice in its place.

---

2. Here, I follow the lead of many feminist and disability studies scholars who have argued that research and knowledge are always situated and partial (see Haraway, 1988; Harding, 2009) and who have thus pointed to the value in being entangled as both insider and outsider (see Ginsburg & Rapp, 2013; Molloy et al., 2018).

ACKNOWLEDGMENTS

THIS BOOK is the product of endless support, encouragement, and kindness from colleagues, friends, and family. People from so many parts of my life helped make this book possible in both tangible and intangible ways. I know that these acknowledgments are incomplete, but I hope everyone who supported me in this process knows how much I value you and wish to celebrate you now and always. I'm astonishingly lucky to have so many wonderful people in my life.

First, to all my research participants and all those living with chronic GI conditions whose stories I studied for this book, I am forever grateful. I hope the publishing of this book is a small gesture of thanks, and I hope my research does make a difference for our community. The research participants who became inspiring friends throughout this process are irreplaceable. Special thanks to Alicia Aiello for your friendship, kindness, and collaboration; it's such a pleasure to know and work with you.

This research has taken most of the last decade to reach this point; therefore, I'd be remiss to not thank those who have taught and guided me along the way. Thank you to Chuck Schuster for being an early advocate and mentor for me. To Dave Clark and Bill Keith—it is a privilege to know, learn from, and be mentored by the two of you. I'm so grateful for all the laughs along the way, too. The most special of thanks to Scott Graham. From taking my first rhetoric class with you and researching alongside you on your innovative projects to caravanning with you to my first conferences and learning the ropes of publishing through your mentorship, I don't know how I could thank you enough. I'm deeply grateful that you invested in me all those years ago and are still friends with me now.

Thank you to those who were kind and generous to me in my earliest years in the discipline, especially Lora Arduser, Kristen Bivens, Marie Moeller, Jenell Johnson, Kenny Fountain, Lauren Cagle, Catherine Gouge, Jeff Bennett, Kenny Walker, Kim Emmons, Zoltan Majdik, and Ashley Mehlenbacher. That you remembered my name, invested in my work, and made me feel like I was part of the rhetoric of health and medicine (RHM) and Association for the Rhetoric of Science, Technology, and Medicine (ARSTM) communities, especially in my earliest years in the field, is something I will always appreciate. Along these same lines, I'm so grateful to Emily Winderman, Avery Edenfield, and Jen Malkowski for the camaraderie that I know I can always count on from each of you.

Thank you to those who read earlier versions of this project when it was incomplete and probably nonsensical and who generously offered brain power to this project throughout its development. Special thanks to Tara Cyphers at The Ohio State University Press—your editorial guidance and patience were instrumental in moving this project forward—and to the journal *Rhetoric of Health and Medicine* for allowing reprints of portions of "The Ostomy Multiple: Toward a Theory of Rhetorical Enactments" to be included in chapters 1, 2, and 5. Many thanks to Sarah Singer, Lily Campbell, Janene Davison, Adam Hubrig, and Leslie Anglesey, whose feedback at the 2020 RHM Symposium was extremely helpful and insightful, and to the two anonymous reviewers whose feedback was not only extremely constructive but also generous and encouraging.

Thank you to my colleagues and friends at the University of Memphis, especially Shanna Cameron, Liz Lane, Will Duffy, Darryl Domingo, Terrence Tucker, and Loel Kim. Our time together was too short but was the best way to begin my career. I learned so much working with each of you. Thank you also to all my colleagues at the University of Minnesota, especially Tom Reynolds, Mary Schuster, Pat Bruch, Donald Ross, Barb Horvath, and Ann Hill Duin. I'm delighted to know and work with you, and I will forever appreciate your smiles and notes of encouragement over the last five years. Particular thanks to Lee-Ann Kastman Breuch, who helped me realize the significance of stories and whose confidence in this project enabled me to keep going. To the most cheetah of all cheetahs, Amy Lee, your mentorship came into my life just when I needed it most. I can't possibly capture my gratitude for you and our friendship. Ben Trappey and Mike Aylward, our work together has been tremendously helpful and generative as I've thought about what stories do in health and medicine, and it's a pleasure to work together and learn from you both. Deepest thanks also to the bright and awesome students who helped bring this project to fruition, especially Alex Finely, who designed the incredible image that serves at this book's cover, Celeste Musick, and the wonderful students of my Fall 2019 RHM seminar—Danielle Stambler, Jackie James, Emily Gresbrink, Luke Shackelford, Brain Le Lay, Jessa Wood, Stuart Deets, and Tina Shirk. I have learned so much from each of you; thank you for being the scholars, teachers, and all-around incredible people you are.

I have absolutely no doubt that this book would not have seen the light of day if it weren't for a handful of truly incredible people who met with me whenever I needed to bounce ideas or reminders to just keep writing, picked up the phone when I was in tears over a rejection or writer's block, took me to happy hour and coffees between writing sprints, texted me hilarious videos when I needed it most, read random chunks of writing with brutal and wonderful honesty, sent me facemasks and sweet notes of encouragement, and just simply became the academic family I didn't know I needed. For these gifts of generosity and immense kindness, thank you to Lisa Melonçon, Cathryn Molloy, and Blake Scott, who have both pushed me as a scholar and championed me and my work, and to Rachel Presley, Katie Fredlund, and Dani DeVasto, three of the fiercest and funniest women whom I admire so dearly. Your friendship and mentorship have meant the world to me, and this book would not have been possible without each of you, truly.

To the village who kept me alive and reminded me that my worth extends beyond this book, there are no words to express my gratitude, but I'll try anyway. A long overdue thanks to Paul Galuska—Mr. G.—you gave me confidence as a student and writer so many years ago. I've no doubt your encouragement set me on a path to become a writing professor and to being able to write this book. The fab five (that name will never get old), Molly Budlong, Chelsea Tauer, Chloé Husnick, and Kaylee Olund—you are my people, and the laughter you add to my life is invaluable. I'm so thankful that we've always stuck together. Emily Browne, who always answers when I call, boosts my confidence, and plays some seriously inspirational recorder and bagpipes—you are an absolute treasure, and I am unbelievably grateful for space camp and bad henna tattoos. The deepest thanks to Leah Schroepfer, Jeanne Knapkavage, David Kufahl, Beth Anne Card, Mike Connaker, Sarah Card, and Dave Card. What a gift it is to call you family and to have you all rooting for me. All my thanks and love to Margaret Knapkavage and Jean Kessler, my grandmothers, who are true models of strength, independence, and resilience.

I can't possibly say how grateful I am for my parents, Joe Kessler and Lori Kessler, who raised me to be relentless in the pursuit of my dreams, to speak up for myself always, and to do everything in kindness, and for my beautiful sister, Casey Kufahl, who is my forever role model. The patience the three of you have shown me for the last twenty-nine years is truly the work of saints. I've counted on you for ER trips, hospital stays, countless scans, tests, and appointments, and never once have the three of you complained or hesitated. You always pick up when I call, ready to listen, console, or hype me up. The sacrifices you have made in service of my wild dreams are not lost on me. The three of you light up my life, and I'm honored to share with you any success that comes my way.

Finally, Danny, the joy of my life and the steady calm in my chaos. This book was seriously made possible by the countless hours you spent brewing coffee, helping me think through ideas, reading drafts, listening when I was frustrated or excited about a new idea, cooking meals, taking care of Sadie and Luna, supporting me so I could keep working when I was sick, and watching Disney movies and reruns of *Friends* with me. This book is for you.

CHAPTER 1

Studying Stigma

A Rhetorical Approach to Stories and Lived Experience

SIX IN TEN ADULTS in the US live with at least one chronic condition, according to the Centers for Disease Control and Prevention (CDC, 2019a). In other words, over half the US population lives with at least one long-term, likely incurable, condition (CDC, 2021b; National Center for Chronic Disease Prevention & Health Promotion, 2012). Such conditions vary widely but include cancer, addiction, diabetes, obesity, Alzheimer's disease, and autoimmune conditions, among many others. Despite research demonstrating an already staggering prevalence of chronic conditions in the US, the number of Americans affected by chronic conditions is only estimated to rise. According to one report, "between 2000 and 2030 the number of Americans with chronic conditions will increase by 37 percent, an increase of 46 million people" (Anderson, 2010, p. 7; see also Wu & Green, 2000). The prevalence of chronic conditions alone is startling; however, concerns don't end there. As a category, chronic conditions disproportionately account for 75 to 90 percent of the overall healthcare costs in the US each year, an estimate that lands somewhere between two and three trillion dollars annually (Buttorff et al., 2017; CDC, 2019b; Wu & Green, 2000). More importantly, chronic diseases have consistently been the leading cause of both death and disability in the US (Kochanek et al., 2011, 2019; Murphy et al., 2017; Xu et al., 2010, 2018).

Concomitant with the rise of chronic conditions has been, unfortunately, a rise in those affected by stigma.[1] The list of stigmatized conditions is extensive; thus, examples of stigmatization are abundant. In the time I have been writing this book, the morning news alone has featured several stories about "fighting stigma" for a range of conditions. Posttraumatic stress disorder, postpartum depression, anxiety, and obesity are just a few of the stigmatized health and medical topics that have recently made major headlines. With little exception, stigma persists for an expansive list of chronic conditions. Put simply, stigma is an all too common feature of lived experience for so many people.

According to social psychologists Valerie Earnshaw and Diane Quinn (2012), "approximately half of adults are living with a chronic illness, many of whom feel stigmatized" by their condition (p. 157). Stigma, most commonly defined as "an attribute that is deeply discrediting" (Goffman, 1963, p. 3), has been considered to have three main categories: physical deformities, character blemishes, and affiliations with racial or religious identities (Goffman, 1963). Most chronic conditions fall into the first type, so-called[2] physical deformities, as chronic conditions transform healthy bodies into ill, often disabled, ones. However, many chronic conditions are also stigmatized because they are seen as character blemishes, such as those that are viewed as preventable and/or associated with deviant behavior like HIV and sexual promiscuity, diabetes and unhealthy eating, or lung cancer and smoking.

Stigma, in other words, is central to living with a chronic condition for many people. Indeed, stigma surrounding chronic conditions is nearly as pervasive as chronic conditions themselves, and its negative consequences are felt deeply by many living with them. Research has demonstrated that because of stigma, people living with a range of chronic conditions experience embarrassment (Conrad et al., 2006), shame (Malterud & Ulriksen, 2011; Rosman, 2004; Saunders, 2014), a sense of internalized dirtiness (Manderson, 2005; Simbayi et al., 2007), decreased sense of self-worth (Hamilton-West & Quine, 2009; Kato et al., 2016), and discrimination (Conrad et al., 2006; Kılınç & Campbell, 2009). Stigma not only leads to decreased quality of life for those with chronic conditions but also "worsen[s] preexisting health disparities" (Courtwright, 2009, p. 91) and "likely acts as [a barrier] to care access" (Earnshaw & Quinn,

---

1. See Charmaz (2000), Joachim and Acorn (2000, 2016), and Earnshaw and Quinn (2012).

2. I include *so-called* here because I want to trouble and reject the language Goffman used to theorize stigma. Disability studies scholars have recognized the value of Goffman's foundational work while also challenging the insensitive and often ableist language he used (see Brune et al., 2014).

2012, p. 159). Further, researchers have found that stigma commonly "disrupts" finances, food practices, familial and social relationships, and the sex lives of those with chronic conditions like diabetes and gastrointestinal diseases (Aikins, 2006; Manderson, 2005). As communication studies scholar Dennis Owen Frohlich (2016) summarized, stigma "may be more difficult to manage than the physical symptoms" for people with chronic conditions (p. 1413). What seems abundantly clear overall is that millions of people not only suffer from chronic conditions but also endure stigma and its far-reaching effects.

Given the significant and myriad impacts of stigma, research into lived experiences with stigma and chronic conditions is both necessary and urgent. Recognizing this, and following the work within my disciplinary home, rhetorical studies, that has addressed chronic conditions (Arduser, 2017; Bennett, 2019), I set out nearly a decade ago to investigate lived experiences with chronic conditions, particularly focusing on the stigma that pervades such experiences. As somebody who studies persuasion and who lives with a chronic condition, I wanted to understand how persuasive practices inform and complicate people's experiences with chronic conditions and stigma. To prioritize a deep rather than broad examination of stigma, I narrowed my focus to chronic GI conditions for a variety of academic and personal reasons. Research-wise, GI diseases are among the less popular areas within health and medicine studied by rhetoricians.[3] GI diseases understandably have a tough time competing for academic and public attention with public health crises like the COVID-19 pandemic or more prevalent conditions like cancer, diabetes, or mental health conditions. Studying GI conditions struck me as a way to address an understudied area and to build out the capacity and scope of my home field, the rhetoric of health and medicine (RHM), the specialized area within rhetorical studies that attends to the persuasive, meaning-making dimensions of health and medicine such as patienthood, clinical care, biomedical practice, public health policy, and embodied experiences (see Scott & Melonçon, 2018). At the same time, personal experience motivates my focus on GI conditions because I live with a chronic GI disease.[4] I was diagnosed with Crohn's disease in my late teens; therefore, I have firsthand experience with stigmatization related to chronic GI conditions in my own personal,

---

3. However, there are a handful of scholars whose lead I follow in studying or discussing GI conditions, experiences, and materiality, including Yergeau (2018), Vidali (2010, 2013), and Hubrig et al. (2020).

4. For additional discussions that have guided my own research on the value and complexity of researching a health and medicine topic with which the research has a personal connection, see Molloy et al. (2018) or Ginsburg and Rapp (2013).

professional, and social interactions, relationships, and healthcare. For example, when faced with surgical decisions recommended by my healthcare team, I refused to undergo surgery at the age of nineteen because I was terrified that I would wake up with an ostomy bag on my abdomen. In the years since, I have often contemplated that decision and grappled with why I was so strongly motivated by my then fear of ostomies.

My complex firsthand experience with a chronic condition sparked my interest in why and how stigma is such a powerful force. However, in March 2015 my research was suddenly catalyzed when I opened my Facebook account to an overwhelming flurry of sad, confused, and angry posts about a woman named Julia who had cancer and an ostomy. Quickly, I discovered that Julia was a participant (effectively, a spokesperson) in the CDC's Tips from Former Smokers campaign, a nationwide public health campaign designed to decrease smoking across the US. As a participant in this campaign, Julia joined over thirty other "real people" who were sharing "real stories" about "living with smoking-related diseases and disabilities" with national public audiences primarily through thirty-second television commercials (CDC, 2020a). One of these commercials featured Julia, a middle-aged Black woman who developed colorectal cancer after years of smoking. In her commercial, Julia detailed her experiences with colorectal cancer, chemotherapy, and surgeries. Of her experiences, she poignantly told viewers, "What I hated most was the colostomy bag" (CDC, 2015a).

Let me pause here to provide some necessary context. A colostomy bag is a small bag or pouch worn on the abdomen over a surgically created opening called an *ostomy*. Through this opening, an end of the small or large intestine[5] (called a stoma) is exteriorized on the abdomen (see figure 1). People with ostomies—often referred to as ostomates[6]—wear an ostomy bag to collect waste as it is excreted through this opening. The term *ostomy* is commonly used metonymically to refer to the ostomy, stoma, and ostomy bag, and I use this shorthand throughout this book.

---

5. There are also two other common types of ostomies: urostomies and gastrostomies. Urostomies are surgically created openings in the abdomen through which urinary waste is excreted. Gastrostomies are surgically created openings in the stomach. My focus in this book, however, is on gastrointestinal ostomies for the lower GI tract: colostomies and ileostomies.

6. While the term *ostomate* is used within biomedicine to refer to anyone who has an ostomy, the term has also gained particular rhetorical traction as an activist identity for those living with ostomies. As I've described elsewhere (Kessler, 2016), many people living with ostomies choose to self-identify as ostomates as an activist and celebratory identification with their ostomies. Many others, however, create material and discursive distance between themselves and the ostomy by identifying as someone with an ostomy or as someone who wears an ostomy.

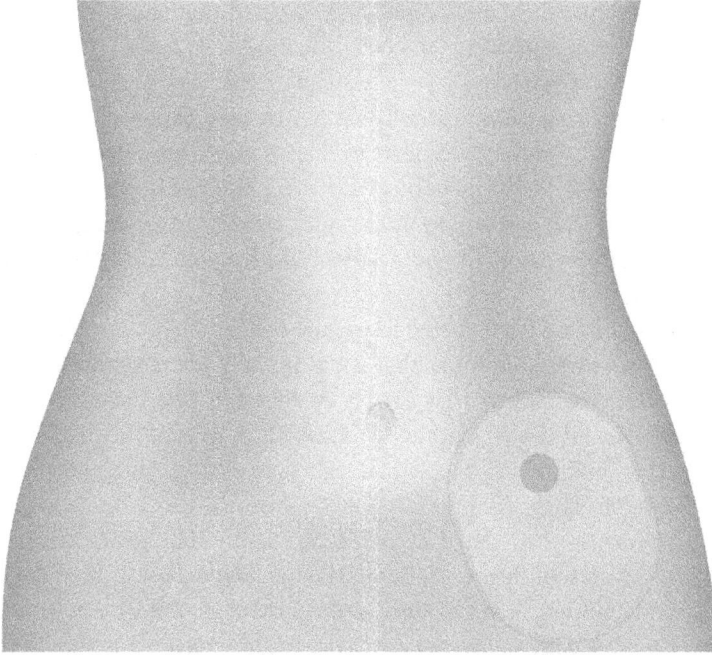

FIGURE 1. The stoma or end of the intestine (the dark circle beneath the pouch) is covered by an ostomy pouch that is adhered to the person's abdomen in order to collect fecal waste known as "output."

Ostomy surgery, as Julia learned firsthand, is necessary when all or part of the colon, rectum, and/or small intestine is removed because of injury, scarring, or disease like cancer or inflammatory bowel disease (IBD). An ostomy enables the evacuation of waste when these digestive organs have been damaged, removed, and need to heal after injury or surgery. About 100,000 new ostomies are created annually in the US, adding to the estimated 750,000 people who already have ostomies (United Ostomy Association of America [UOAA], 2016). For many people, ostomies are permanent, placing them in the category of chronic conditions. For others, ostomies are considered temporary, which means that after weeks, months, or even years, the ostomy can be surgically reversed, enabling the person to evacuate waste through the rectum and anus. That said, even when ostomies are temporary, research has suggested that many of the lived experiences are similar to those with chronic conditions (Follick et al., 1984). In Julia's case, her doctors found a large cancerous tumor in her colon, so she underwent surgery to remove it. Along with that tumor, part of Julia's colon needed to be removed, which meant that she needed an ostomy to excrete digestive waste.

Julia's story for the Tips campaign mentioned that she underwent surgery but primarily emphasized the colostomy bag she "hated" (CDC, 2015a). Throughout her commercial, Julia explained that she hated her ostomy because she was constantly worried that her ostomy bag would come loose and leak (digestive waste). These fears led her to isolate herself at home where she could deal with her ostomy privately. By emphasizing her extremely negative experiences with her ostomy, Julia's story served as a warning to viewers: if you don't want to end up like Julia—that is, with an ostomy—then you must quit smoking.

Julia's commercial itself offered important insight into the very lived experiences with chronic conditions that I was initially interested in investigating, but it's the controversy that quickly surrounded Julia that serves as one key impetus for this book. Within just a few short days of the public release of Julia's story, over 10,000 people had signed a petition calling for the CDC to remove Julia's video from the national airwaves (Rund, 2015). In addition, several national health-related organizations sent public letters issuing the same call. The reason? Stigma. Thousands of people, many of whom live with chronic GI conditions and ostomies, argued that Julia's story not only mischaracterized life with an ostomy; worse, it *spread stigma*.

I initially saw these responses and critiques on my own social media accounts but quickly discovered that the backlash against Julia's story was much bigger than my own networks. Across the responses, people shared their own stories about life with ostomies and chronic GI conditions such as cancer, Crohn's disease, ulcerative colitis, short bowel syndrome, and irritable bowel syndrome. Notably, these stories were drastically different from Julia's. They praised ostomies as lifesaving surgeries and technologies. They celebrated the lives that were enabled and empowered through ostomies. And they resisted Julia's stigmatizing depiction of ostomies that suggested ostomies always leak and are universally disabling (Burns et al., 2015).

As it unfolded, I followed this controversy closely and became increasingly captivated by the different ostomy stories being shared and the central role stigma played across them. Stigma seemed to be both perpetuated and challenged within these stories, so I began to hypothesize the role stories played both in sharing lived experiences with chronic conditions like ostomies *and* in de/stabilizing stigma. Julia's story highlighted the negative shift she experienced in the meaning of her life, self, and body once she had an ostomy. For Julia, experiences with leaks and social isolation negatively influenced her sense of self and ostomy, so much so that she hated her ostomy more than any of her other cancer-related experiences. In contrast, the stories shared by people protesting Julia's commercial focused on the experiences made possible by ostomies like leaving the hospital after long stays or eating favorite foods again. These experiences, unlike Julia's, positively shaped the meaning of ostomies. Across the stories, I noticed that as people develop, are diagnosed, and live with chronic conditions, the meanings of themselves, their bodies, and their conditions are often transformed in profound ways through a diverse mix of influences at work within individuals' lived experiences including cultural expectations, norms, material forces, and structures (e.g., bathroom location and access, medical technologies, pharmaceuticals, feces), public and private stories, language used by healthcare providers, and many others. The preliminary insights I gleaned from this controversy steered my research into chronic conditions and stigma toward ostomies and chronic GI conditions as well as the stories people tell about their experiences with such conditions. Before Julia's commercial aired, I was already invested in GI-related chronic conditions because of my own lived experiences with Crohn's disease; however, Julia's story and its responses confirmed chronic GI conditions as an important site for rhetorical study.[7]

Consequently, I began trying to map the controversy surrounding Julia onto the research literature on stigma across fields including RHM. Previous research in sociology, nursing, and social psychology affirmed that ostomies and related GI conditions, like other chronic conditions, are highly stigmatized (see, e.g., Frohlich, 2014; Smith et al., 2007). Research within RHM has also indicated that the rhetorical theorization of stigma is both a priority of the field and an important area for future work, with research to date demonstrating that stigma is a highly rhetorical phenomenon, affecting a speaker's credibility and agency.[8] However, I was left wondering how exactly Julia's story spread stigma. What about her story of her own experiences propelled stigma? How could ostomies, described by many as lifesaving, be so stigmatized and feared that the CDC thought they could persuade people to quit smoking? What could these stories tell us about stigma's rhetoricity and life with chronic conditions? In attempting to answer these initial questions, I realized that stories like the ones shared by and in opposition to Julia's have much to tell us about the nexus of stigma, chronic conditions, lived experiences, and persuasion. Therefore, this book begins with the idea that the stories people tell about their experiences with ostomies and chronic GI conditions are rich sites for exploring how stigma, specifically surrounding chronic conditions, is rhetorically perpetuated and challenged.

---

7. See also Vidali (2010, 2013).
8. See, for example, Johnson (2010) and Molloy (2019).

Rhetoric of Stories, Stigma, Lived Experiences

Stories in health and medicine are powerful. They help us navigate illness, build communities, and make sense of our lives and experiences with disease, death, and acute issues. Researchers from fields ranging from narrative medicine and medical sociology to literature and RHM have long been drawn to the power and role of health and medical stories. As Siddhartha Mukherjee (2010) wrote in *The Emperor of All Maladies,* "Medicine . . . begins with storytelling. Patients tell stories to describe illness; doctors tell stories to understand it" (p. 390). However, stories are more than a starting place; they are one way in which medicine is done and experienced. In one of my favorite lines about the importance of stories in health and medicine, Dr. Lewis Mehl-Madrona (2007) explained the rhetorical work stories do for healthcare providers: "When people don't believe our stories, they won't follow our treatments. Instead of using terms such as *noncompliance* or *lack of adherence,* we could just say the story we told didn't go over very well" (p. 7). Listening to symptoms, reading CT scans and blood workups, diagnosing, treating: each of these culminates in a story for and about patients that drives how they interact with their bodies and with medicine. Indeed, stories are central to the practice and experience of disease, illness, and medicine, both within and beyond the sphere of Western biomedicine.

In the public sphere, stories do important, complex, value-laden work as they "document and catalogue experience" with illness so that it can be shared and reported to others (Segal, 2012, p. 298). Moreover, stories, particularly about embodied conditions, provide templates for understanding our own bodies and experiences. That is, they generate roadmaps that help us navigate what it is to be diagnosed and endure treatment for cancer, be a person with autism, take metformin or birth control, or undergo an MRI. When we've heard others' stories, we can use them to frame our own health and medical encounters.[9] As Arthur Frank (2010) put it, stories "work with people, for people, and always stories work *on* people, affecting what people are able to see as real, as possible, and as worth doing or best avoided" (p. 3; emphasis original).

Similarly, Jeff Bennett (2019) has pointed out that "narratives, anecdotes, and myths are decisive in their ability to energize a patient's feelings, guide medical deliberations, and arrange classificatory hierarchies" (p. 9). In other words, stories are persuasive; they inscribe a "hierarchy of values" (Segal, 2012,

---

9. Here, I'm drawing on M. Remi Yergeau's (2018) discussion of how narratives (in their case, narratives about autism) "structure" as they "mediate" experiences in the world (p. 9). I also am building on discussions within narrative medicine that, in particular, inform my thinking here. See Mehl-Madrona (2007), Frank (2010), and Charon (2006).

p. 298), and, as Julia's story shows, they can call listeners to action.[10] Julie-Ann Scott (2018) summarized that "telling, listening, and interpreting stories enables human beings to share experiences, to access how life is lived through bodies other than our own" (p. 4). Stories tell us how to make sense of and give order to a variety of conditions, diseases, and medical tests; how to define wellness, health, and sickness; what it is we might expect as we navigate our embodied selves and lives.

Accordingly, rhetoricians of health and medicine have been drawn to the persuasion and power of stories in health and medical contexts (see, e.g., Arduser, 2014; Bennett, 2019; Berkenkotter, 2008; Johnson, 2014; Segal, 2012; Yergeau, 2018). Stories are not only a valuable mode of rhetorical activity; they also enable us to engage with people, conditions, and experiences on the terms of the storytellers themselves (Frank, 2010; Jones, 2016; Mol, 2002). For these reasons, this book is focused on exploring what I call *stigma stories*—stories that rhetorically engage, promote, or resist stigma—in order to "access how life is lived" through bodies with chronic conditions (Scott, 2018, p. 4). Understanding and studying stigma stories first requires some important definitional work regarding stories, stigma, and my approach for understanding and studying each individually and together. I've so far outlined the rhetorical work that stories do within the expert and public spheres of health and medicine, but that doesn't entirely explain what exactly a story is. In the next sections, I take time to unpack stories and stigma, and then I situate those concepts within my own approach grounded in RHM and disability studies.

Story

Experts spanning many disciplines agree that stories are highly powerful and valuable; however, what counts as a story or how to identify one if you see or hear it is another matter altogether. In general, we have an intuitive sense of *story*; it's a term we use in everyday life to describe a variety of discursive and sometimes material events. Because stories are everywhere, we categorize them into a variety of kinds and types (e.g., fictional, nonfictional, news, histories and herstories, and, of course, genres of stories like comedy, tragedy, quests). These categories help us set expectations and find our way through different kinds of stories. Too, we often read stories not only for content but

---

10. The Tips from Former Smokers campaign was and continues to be highly successful in its smoking-cessation efforts. This campaign is why Julia's story was shared.

also for stylistic and literary elements like allegory, tone, characters, diction, or metaphor.

While genre and stylistic categories provide one way to make sense of stories, I'm more interested in *what* stories do in the world. Therefore, I approach stories as rhetorical objects[11] or entities that participate in meaning-making and that are entangled with contexts, practices, time, space, culture, matter, and power. Figuring stories as rhetorical objects is an important first step for delineating stories as data for my research into stigma; however, the parameters of (stigma) stories—that is, where a story starts and stops, how to know what a story is and isn't—take additional consideration, as many fields have worked to concretize the characteristics of stories. Notably, in the interest of scope, my discussion of stories is limited to a handful of theorizations of stories specifically in the contexts of health and medicine.[12]

Among these, the field of narrative medicine is perhaps most relevant beyond my own field of RHM. Narrative medicine is "defined as medicine with narrative competence to recognize, absorb, interpret, and be moved by the stories of illness" (Charon, 2006, p. vii). In other words, narrative medicine has emerged and taken residence as a field complementary to medicine itself: specifically, a partner field that situates narrative as a central part of medicine's knowledge, practice, and ethics. In part, narrative medicine developed in response to the acknowledgment that patients' stories of what it is like to *live with* a condition had much to offer biomedicine's understanding and practice of medical care. Placing patients' stories within biomedicine has led narrative medicine to ground itself interdisciplinarily in fields like literary studies and methods like narratology in an effort to meaningfully engage with stories.

For those who employ narratology and literary frameworks to conduct narrative medicine work, stories are defined by core features, a mix of which needs be present for something to qualify as a story. For example, Frank (2010) delineated a basic structure or set of story features: abstract, orien-

---

11. For more on rhetorical objects, and the ways in which they are not exclusively discursive, see David Grant (2017). In "Writing Wakan: The Lakota Pipe as Rhetorical Object," Grant examines the Lakota pipe as a rhetorical object and demonstrates the mix of agential forces that are at play within a rhetorical object—material, discursive, experiential, human, animal, social, historical.

12. In addition to the specific theories/approaches to stories I mention in the text, Natasha Jones's (2016) work on narrative inquiry for technical communication and human-centered design also broadly informed my thinking about stories. Properly and fully discussing Jones's work is beyond the scope of what I could cover in this chapter; however, for those interested in a feminist and technical communication approach to stories and narrative, I highly recommend Jones's treatment of narrative inquiry.

tation, complicating event, resolution, evaluation, and coda. These features likely show up in the stories I collected and share throughout this book; however, these features did not guide my data collection or analysis as I engaged stigma stories. Frank further articulated several "capacities" or recognizable elements that enable the work of stories, what they do and how they do it; thus, these capacities provide another framework under which I may have delimited stigma stories. These capacities include trouble, character, point of view, suspense, inherent morality, resonance, symbiotic, shape-shifting, truth-telling, imagination. Noting that not all capacities need be present to qualify as a story, Frank clarified that several must be engaged in order for a story to, well, be a story. Again, while I find this characterizing helpful, I didn't operationalize or limit my story-gathering by these capacities. In retrospect, I wouldn't be surprised to find that these capacities define the stigma stories shared in these pages; however, in the selecting and studying of stigma stories, capacities or particular literary features did not drive my approach because my focus was on the lived experiences that were shared within stories and how those experiences animated how ostomies and chronic GI conditions were made to mean within specific life events and moments.

Much like Frank, Rita Charon (2006), considered a founder of narrative medicine, has focused on broad elements that characterize a story or narrative, including "a teller, a listener, a time course, a plot, and a point" (p. 3). Charon's definition leaves the scope of "story" or "narrative" expansive, which matches her sense that stories and narratives[13] are both discrete, with a clear scope (e.g., a patient's story about how she broke her leg), and broad, meta, and layered over the course of many small stories, interactions, and experience (e.g., a patient's story, usually presented over many interactions and stories, that explains their attitude toward medicine). In accordance with Charon's definition of story, narrative medicine is frequently focused on clinical encounters and the treatment/care of patients within the bounds of biomedical relationships and stories shared between patients and healthcare providers. While certainly there are stories specific to patient–provider interactions and the physical bounds of clinics and hospitals, the stories shared in this book reach outside the parameters of biomedicine proper. This is in part because experiences with chronic illnesses, GI-related or otherwise, and stigma seep into

---

13. Across scholars who study stories in the contexts of health and medicine, the terms *stories* and *narrative* are used in a variety of ways. Sometimes the terms are interchangeable; sometimes they refer to distinct entities. In my case, I draw on Harrington's distinction between story and narrative, which positions stories as "living, local, and specific" and narratives as "templates" or "resources from which people construct the stories they tell" (Harrington, 2008, pp. 24–25).

every corner of individuals' lives, including but moving far beyond the boundaries of biomedicine and interactions with healthcare providers.

Accordingly, Mehl-Madrona's (2007) work on narrative medicine is helpful for me in that it is expansive in its understanding of borders and contours of medicine. In particular, Mehl-Madrona's Indigenous approach to stories and healing sees both stories and medicine as far-reaching, crossing cultures, spaces, time, experiences, and entities. Much like Charon, Mehl-Madrona is committed to the field of narrative medicine and its focus on stories as a way to expand the purview and practice of medicine so that it more fully considers the humanistic dimensions of medicine, treatment, and care. However, unlike Charon, Mehl-Madrona has not defined or confined stories by particular literary or textual features like plots or characters, though he does provide some characteristics that align with Charon's and Frank's focus on stories' literary elements. Instead, Mehl-Madrona approached stories as a way to exceed the limitations of Western biomedicine and its focus on statistics, randomized controlled trials, pharmaceuticals, and Western ways of knowing. This isn't to say that Mehl-Madrona outright rejected the philosophy and practices of Western biomedicine; rather, he saw it as *one* way of doing and knowing health and healing, not *the only* way. Stories, for Mehl-Madrona, united Western biomedicine with individuals' lived experiences, cultures, language practices, knowledges, and belief systems and place Western medicine among a constellation of relevant entities that inform our understandings of health and medicine.

Thus, stories are a way to connect what often appears as disparate or conflicting approaches to bodies, afflictions, and healing. Mehl-Madrona (2007) explained that healthcare providers and healers "treat by telling a story" (p. 6). Narrative medicine has presented one pathway to avoid divorcing lived experiences from healthcare and to place biomedicine among agents within the experience and process of illness and care. Even when it comes to a medical fact, Mehl-Madrona "prefer[red] to call that an explanatory story rather than a fact, because it reminded [him] that there are other ways to put together the same observations and even better stories that could emerge over time" (p. 11). Stories, therefore, connect and describe experiences, embodiments, responses to treatment, dialogues about a condition or ailment, biomedicine's diagnostic tools and procedures, and all other factors that give way to an illness's presentation, symptoms, and cures. Mehl-Madrona's approach to stories guides my own, particularly in its willingness to be open to the variability of stories, its commitment to lived experiences, and its acknowledgment that stories are among the most fundamental units of meaning-making within health and medicine.

The conceptions of stories presented by narrative medicine scholars serve as both foundation and context for my own work in stories. In particular, I agree that stories are central to health and medicine and that such stories often have consistent features (though I'm not focused on mapping those features). However, unlike these narratology and narrative medicine scholars, I approach stories from a rhetorical perspective, particularly one guided by praxiography and multiple ontologies theory (as I explain more later in this chapter and in chapter 2), which necessarily means that my definition of and approach to story departs from narrative medicine and narratology in important ways.

Stories, in my conception, are defined less by features and more by the work they do. As Frank (2010) has described, despite his taxonomies for stories, "stories are too lively and too wild to be tied up" (p. 1). Thus, treating stories as rhetorical objects allows flexibility in the boundaries and features that define a story and, in turn, orients me toward the events and experiences shared by storytellers through their stories. Experiences and meaning-making drive the boundaries of a given story, and, depending on the experience(s) shared, and the meaning made from that experience, stories can take many shapes, include diverse elements, and vary in length and scope. For example, some of the stories in this book take the form of several textual paragraphs in a blog post, while others are Instagram posts with a handful of photos, a few lines of text captioning, and a series of hashtags. Other stories show up in interviews with people living with ostomies and chronic GI conditions, in news articles, on TV shows, and in public health campaigns. To be clear, some of these stories are from actual patients' lives while others are fictionalized stories told in public media. I chose to include this diverse mix of stories because they all influence the meaning-making that happens in the public sphere about ostomies and chronic GI conditions; thus, they all participate in the de/stigmatization of these conditions. In my search for stories, I explored any spaces and ways that shared lived experiences with ostomies, chronic GI conditions, and stigmatization.

Rather than get caught up in finding the beginning, middle, or end of stigma stories or identifying characters or plots, I focus more on understanding the lived experiences being shared and how those experiences worked to make meaning about ostomies and chronic GI conditions. This often meant that stories were bound by particular events (e.g., a hospital visit, an interaction at a grocery store, a first date), but sometimes stories expanded across multiple moments. In either case, I listened for how and where the storytellers drew boundaries around their own experiences and explained how particular event(s) were meaningful in their lives. This open approach to stories was, of course, messy and perhaps sometimes inconsistent in the size or shape of data collected, but it allowed me to be both flexible and inclusive in my effort to understand *how* meaning is made about ostomies and chronic GI conditions, particularly how they were made to be stigmatized in space and time. In this way, the messiness was a strength rather than a limitation. It prevented me from layering preconceived ideas about where lived experiences and meaning-making started and stopped, and it allowed the storytellers to be actively involved in generating the data, findings, and insights presented throughout this book.

Too, stories, in my approach, are both material and discursive and include a variety of agential, rhetorical entities—human, nonhuman, social, political, discursive—at work within stories.[14] That is, stories are always emergent through a range of entities that take shape as material, discursive, political, and social as they are practiced or experienced in space and time. What I'm getting at here is that although stories show up in this book as textual (by virtue of this book being textual itself), the stories are always more than text in that they present lived experiences that are fully material and always embodied. In taking this position toward stories, I'm also drawing on Cheryl Mattingly's (1998) work on the narrative structure of experience. Stories, Mattingly has argued, are "informant accounts" that provide "access [to] events" and "a way to learn something new about [the storyteller's] experiences and beliefs" (p. 7).

Treating stories as informant accounts and thus storytellers as informants helped me approach interview participants, writers of blog posts, or social media influencers, as present and active agents throughout my research and write-up, rather than as passive data points made invisible in the name of objectivity or rigor. This further contributes to my positioning of stories as rhetorical objects not only in data collection and analysis but in presentation as well. The informant storytellers and their stories show up throughout the book as fully as possible and in the storytellers' own words as much as possible. In this way, I honor their lived experiences and stories on their own terms (which, as I explain later, is central to the work I do here) and continually position stigma as something *done in practice,* not *inherent* in ostomies or chronic GI conditions. As I show, this focus on events and stories as informant accounts is imperative to positioning stigma not as an inherent characteristic but as rhetorical itself.

---

14. Here I'm drawing on the work of new materialist scholars like Kim TallBear (2017) and Karen Barad (2003, 2007).

Stories about life with a stigmatized condition or identity provide a way to unearth how, where, and why meanings, like stigmas, emerge and take hold. Indeed, stigma stories grant access to lived experiences and events that might otherwise be inaccessible or invisible; at the same time, they allow storytellers themselves to articulate how lived experiences were (made) meaningful. While perhaps mutable and messy as units of analysis, stories are poised for a rhetorical study of stigma because stigma too isn't static or straightforward; the flexibility and openness of stories is conducive to studying a phenomenon as elusive as stigma. Stories, when approached as experiential and rhetorical, are a prime way to understand how stigma emerges and becomes powerful. As rhetorical objects, stories are not just representations of lived experiences; they are themselves a piece of those experiences. Part of having an ostomy or chronic condition is having to tell people about it, to live through and with the stories that share experiences and make meaning. Paying attention to stories rhetorically means listening to them as accounts of how people navigate the material-discursive practices and norms that define and often exclude and oppress people and their embodied selves.

As Malea Powell (2012) has importantly shown, stories are both about us[15] and of us; the stories we choose to tell, in turn, tell us who we are, what we are about, and where we are going (p. 389). Stories, Powell further reminded us, "constellate," coming together in place and through time to make meaning among interconnected experiences and events (p. 388). In this way, stories are epistemological—they reveal our ways of knowing and the ideologies and entities rooted in those practices. And they are ontological—they drive our ways of being in the world and what we do both as individuals and in communities (Powell, 2012). Powell's work is illustrative for my definition of stories in that it positions stories as essential spaces of meaning-making. Powell observed that stories "matter," "have an effect," and are "real" (p. 390). In these ways, stories are not only spaces to share events and experiences but spaces of potential transformation. They help illuminate practices and values that often become so engrained that they become invisible, and this illumination helps us track our present and more actively determine our future. Building on Powell, this approach to stories enables me to understand what it is like to live with an ostomy and chronic GI condition and face stigma, how stigma is done within specific practices, and how it is being countered. Those same stories, thus, point to the paths and practices that can transform stigmatizing

---

15. I choose to use ambiguous collective personal pronouns here deliberately. The *we* is flexible and responsive. We might be people with ostomies and chronic GI conditions. It could be rhetoricians or scholars interested in health and medicine. We could be Americans or all of humanity. All these collectives fit the point I'm trying to make here.

experiences and the very rhetorical ecologies that enable those experiences to be possible and become powerful.

Consequently, theorizing stigma through stories is both explanatory and interventional. In other words, in theorizing stigma through stories, I am deliberately aligning with rhetoricians J. Blake Scott and Catherine Gouge's (2019) suggestion that theory-building, especially in RHM, is not only "inventional" but "an act of care." Theorizing stigma through stories and lived experiences enables me to study how stigma shows up in the lives of people with chronic GI conditions and, in doing so, helps me find ways to "thoughtfully attend to and car[e] for" the embodied, lived experiences shared within those stories (Melonçon & Scott, 2018, p. 12). Thus, the kind of theory-building I aim to do through stigma stories is about finding ways to privilege and attend to what impacts "those with the most at stake" (Scott & Gouge, 2019, p. 191). This book undertakes such work by privileging the stories and experiences of the millions of people living with ostomies and chronic GI conditions and by drawing from those experiences and stories to theorize stigma in ways that will hopefully impact those living with chronic GI conditions by helping to destigmatize. In turn, I hope the theory-building and analysis reported in the coming pages is generative for future work that can privilege the millions more with other stigmatized chronic conditions.

Stigma

With this conception of stories in mind, my next step in foregrounding stigma stories is defining stigma itself, which, like stories, evades easy or clear definition. Of course, extensive research has investigated stigma, both within and beyond rhetorical studies, and, as I've already explained, my project is grounded in RHM but also guided by previous work in disability studies. However, to fully situate my rhetorical approach to stigma, I begin with sociologist Erving Goffman. Goffman's (1963) seminal book *Stigma: Notes on the Management of a Spoiled Identity* occupies a central role in most contemporary conversations regarding stigma. As I've mentioned, stigma, according to Goffman, is "an attribute that is deeply discrediting" (p. 3). While this basic definition from Goffman is often operationalized in contemporary stigma research (a problem I elaborate on later), Goffman offered a more nuanced theorization of stigma, centered on the relational processes like conversational encounters that stage stigma (p. 13). Goffman argued that the emergence and management of stigma occur in interactions between what he called "normals" and "stigmatized." With a focus on these interactions, Goffman suggested that stigmatization occurs when any attribute deviates from what has been socially deemed normal.[16] Difference and stigma become interchangeable in Goffman's theory; any difference from the normal naturally warrants and facilitates stigma.

Building on Goffman's stigma theory, disability studies scholars have advanced the concept of stigma, particularly by resisting the idea that stigma is inherently synonymous with difference and by questioning how particular characteristics become stigmatized (see Coleman, 1986; Garland-Thomson, 1997). According to much work in disability studies, stigmatization is a relational and highly contextual process used to "categorize differences and impose some kind of meaningful order on experience" (Garland-Thomson, 1997, p. 31). More specifically, scholars have argued that stigma is a social process that "infuses negative value" by identifying particular objects, bodies, persons, identities, and characteristics as different and problematic (Garland-Thomson, 1997, p. 31; see also Coleman-Brown, 1986; Kafer, 2013; Wendell, 2001). Stigmatization, Rosemarie Garland-Thomson (1997) has summarized, "is an interactive social process in which particular human traits are deemed not only *different*, but *deviant*" and through which concepts like *neutral, normal,* and *legitimate* are defined, enforced, and calcified by dominant social groups and systems (p. 31; emphasis added). In essence, stigmatization deems some entities normal, and others undesirably different (Kafer, 2013). Thus, stigma is not inherent but a meaning-making activity that gives order and value, is enabled by power, and propels fear, repulsion, and avoidance (Coleman, 1986; Coleman-Brown, 2017; Garland-Thomson, 1997; Kafer, 2013; Wendell, 2001).

Consequently, rhetoric, as a study of meaning-making and power, has much to offer theorizations of stigma. In alignment with disability studies frameworks of stigma, rhetoricians have forwarded similar stigma theories that focus on the processes in which difference has been conflated with problematic deviance (Johnson, 2010; Rothfelder & Thornton, 2017). Jenell Johnson (2010) has argued that a rhetorical approach to stigma is one that examines "stigmatization as a dynamic social process rather than an individual attribute" (p. 462). Moreover, rhetoricians have positioned stigma as a "rhetorical phenomenon" (Rothfelder & Thornton, 2017, p. 362) and as "an object of rhetorical criticism" (Johnson, 2010, p. 462). Stigma, rhetorically understood, is a "social force enacted through language and rooted in culturally and historically contingent values" (Johnson, 2010, p. 462). Thus, a rhetorical study

---

16. Goffman (1963) argued that "normal" tends to mean White, healthy, heterosexual men (p. 128). For more discussion on this, see Garland-Thomson (1997, p. 3).

of stigma, informed by disability studies, searches for the processes by which stigma is made possible and powerful as well as the processes by which stigma is fought. This has predominantly led rhetoricians to focus on the relationship between stigma and credibility and to consider how being stigmatized impacts a stigmatized individual's ability to be heard, valued, trusted (Johnson, 2010; Molloy, 2015). For example, Johnson studied the "rhetorically disabling" effect that stigma had when the public learned that Senator Thomas Eagleton (the running mate of 1972 US presidential candidate George McGovern) had previously been treated for depression, which was credited for McGovern's loss to Richard Nixon. Cathryn Molloy (2015, 2019) has also illustrated how stigmatization works to discredit people with chronic mental illnesses. Molloy (2015) concluded that "stigma takes potential rhetors out of the polis altogether and renders them less-than-fully-human" (p. 159). Additionally, as M. Remi Yergeau (2018) demonstrated, neurodivergent individuals are frequently stigmatized and dehumanized because their words and actions are cast as unintentional and involuntary (p. 10). Yergeau showed that under such logics, the stigmatization of neurodivergence doesn't simply negate credibility; it positions neurodivergent people outside the realm of rhetoricity or meaning-making altogether.

While I recognize stigma's key rhetorical role in establishing or negating credibility for rhetors, I'm most interested in extending this previous rhetorical work on stigma by focusing more specifically on the "dynamic processes" and practices in which "differentness" is made to mean undesired, abject, disgraced, and deviant (Johnson, 2010). As the coming chapters demonstrate, for people living with ostomies and chronic GI conditions, stigma doesn't always negatively affect a person's ability to speak or to be considered credible or trustworthy. In fact, in some stories I explore in this book, stigma actually bolsters the *ethos* of people living with ostomies and their stories. Most often, though, stigma discredits the very existence of people living with ostomies and related conditions or, as Molloy (2015, 2019) described, renders these people "less-than-fully-human" (2015, p. 159). Examining the stories and lived experiences of those with ostomies and chronic GI conditions, I argue, productively expands our understandings of the rhetorical processes and power of stigma.

Accordingly, I advance a rhetorical approach that positions stigma as both part and result of meaning-making practices, especially stories about living with ostomies and chronic GI conditions. In this sense, stigma is enmeshed in material-discursive rhetorical systems composed of persuasive practices like the way people talk to each other, tell stories, experience bodies, and engage the world. Stigma is not just a look of disgust or condescending comment; it's the absence of a bathroom on every floor and the internal cringe that crawls up your spine reading about poop. Indeed, stigma is a complex, insidious force. Powerful, interlocking, and dominant systems, namely twenty-first-century Western biomedicine but also ableism, sexism, racism, ageism, colonialism, and classism, have led us to believe that there is an optimal, normal, way for our bodies to be.[17] Under these logics, human bodies should perform, look, and exist in particular ways—we should have four limbs; we should grow tall, but not too tall; we should weigh enough, but not too much; we should be White,[18] but if we aren't, we should act White; we should eat through holes on our faces and shit through holes no one else should ever see. These expectations—what scholars across disciplines have called *norms*—drive the actions, thoughts, words, and expectations we use to order ourselves and others. When norms are not upheld, stigma emerges to make us toe the line. Stigma, in other words, is enacted when these complex and interlocking material-discursive rhetorical systems attempt to (re)assert stability, stability that privileges and demands the dominant norms and ideals.

RHM, Disability Studies, and Stigma Stories

As a rhetorical project, this book traces how ostomies and related chronic GI conditions are stigmatized. That is, how such conditions—through and within material-discursive systems—are *made to mean* discreditable, undesirable, disgusting, unworthy, subhuman. How does stigma operate rhetorically? What meaning-making practices de/stigmatize chronic conditions? What role do stories play in those meaning-making practices, and how can stories help in studying stigma? How might rhetoric help us trace, understand, and challenge stigmas surrounding ostomies and GI conditions, as well as other conditions, technologies, and experiences with health and medicine?

In attending to these questions, I study stigma through people's lived experiences as shared within stories. Thus, I am also forwarding a particular

---

17. While I could cite any number of scholars here from across disciplines, I refer readers to Alison Kafer's *Feminist, Queer, Crip* (2013) as a primer for considering the variety of scholarship that has interrogated the relationships between these systems and their effect on bodies.

18. Throughout the book, I capitalize both *Black* and *White* in reference to race. In doing so, I'm trying to give presence to these categories as rhetorically significant. I'm also trying to resist suggesting that White is the norm when, really, it is "a specific social category" that brings with it clear social and material privileges (Ewing, 2020). At the same time, I capitalize *Black* to honor and recognize the "personhood, culture, and history" of Blackness (Mack & Palfrey, 2020).

rhetorical approach for studying lived experiences in contexts of health and medicine, as well as chronic conditions, through stories. Although research, particularly in health communication,[19] sociology,[20] and nursing,[21] has theorized and explored stigma, I argue that rhetoric, particularly RHM, can provide important insight regarding health-related stigmas and chronic GI conditions, including ostomies, because rhetoric is not just a diagnostic or critical tool. RHM is committed to both making and adapting knowledge, often in an effort to intervene or ameliorate (Scott & Melonçon, 2018, p. 6). Or, as Caroline Gottschalk Druschke (2017) put it, "rhetoric is our means of negotiating life in common" (p. 3). The tools of RHM can not only help acknowledge and understand stigma but also help (re)negotiate our life in common so that stigma can be overcome altogether.

As a way to "make sense of the world," (Koerber, 2000, p. 61; see also Druschke & McGreavy, 2016), rhetoric is a rich tool for understanding the processes and practices by which both norms and stigmas materialize, circulate, change, and collapse. Specifically, rhetoric examines the persuasive practices that create meaning in the world, meaning that is in flux, highly contingent, and contextual (Bitzer, 1968; Johnson, 2014; Teston, 2017). For my research, rhetoric offers explanatory power for making sense of stigma, especially as stigma is established, documented, navigated, and shared within stories. As rhetorician Judy Segal (2005) has outlined, RHM "illuminat[es] and recast[s] problems in health and medicine" by mapping how meaning is made in health and medical contexts (p. 1). Moreover, rhetoric's attunement to power (Dolmage, 2014; Johnson, 2014) is especially useful for understanding stigma in the contexts of chronic conditions. Rhetoricians recognize persuasion and power as intimately intertwined. In other words, RHM and rhetorical studies more broadly examine "power in action, particularly the power of meaning" (Johnson, 2014, p. 12). In line with this conception of rhetoric, the study of stigma that unfolds in this book focuses on the practices and processes in which particular conditions, identities, technologies, and bodies are staged and made to mean undesirably different through powerful, persuasive actions.

Importantly, though, when I say that stigmatization is enacted through rhetorical processes, I am not only referring to interactions between individuals, as Goffman might have it. Instead, drawing on both RHM and disability studies, I am committed to exploring how a variety of practices, systems, and logics (e.g., ableism, medicalization, sexism) enable stigmatization. Central to

19. See, for example, Smith (2007, 2014).
20. See, for example, Kelly (1992) and Scambler (2004).
21. See, for example, Garcia et al. (2005) and Joachim and Acorn (2000).

distinguishing stigma as a rhetorical process is accounting for the distinctions and relationships among stigma, disease, disability, medicine, and systems of power. As I discussed at the outset of this section, disability and stigma have often been framed as interchangeable, in part because disabilities are so frequently and compulsively stigmatized. Conflating disability with stigma or assuming that being disabled automatically warrants stigmatization is highly problematic, and it highlights the complex nuances that must be recognized between disability, illness, stigma, and medicine. Untangling these relationships, especially in the context of chronic GI conditions, provides necessary groundwork and is essential to the theory-building project of this book. Therefore, in the next paragraphs, I take a step back to first explore tensions between disability studies and biomedicine by offering a short overview of the medical and social models of disability and, relatedly, by discussing the nuances between disability, impairment, and illness. Then, I elucidate how these models play out for a rhetorical study of stigma related to chronic GI conditions and ultimately position my theory-building work at the intersection between political/relational models of disability and RHM.

While there are many models for theorizing disability, the medical and social models of disability are especially relevant to my theorization of stigma. These two models provide an important foundation for understanding the relationship between disability and stigma, and they also help me tease out the nuances between chronic illness and disability. For starters, the medical model is perhaps the most pervasive understanding of disability. Despite its name, the medical model does not simply refer to the way medical providers and experts approach disability; instead, it is "the positioning of disability as an exclusively medical problem and, especially, the conceptualization of such positioning as both objective face and common sense" (Kafer, 2013, p. 5). In other words, the medical model positions embodied difference as abnormal, problematic, stigmatizing, and unequivocally in need of fixing. That is, it places disability and illnesses as *problems within individuals* that can and should be solved through Western medicine. Within a medical model, those with disabilities and illnesses are expected to perpetually attempt to (re)solve their embodied differences and to normalize because, ultimately, the goal of Western medicine is to prevent, minimize, invisibilize, overcome, and ideally eradicate disease/disability. As Susan Wendell (2001) explained, the "identification [of disability with illness] contributes to the medicalization of disability, in which disability is regarded as an individual misfortune, and people with disabilities are assumed to suffer primarily from physical and/or mental abnormalities that medicine can and should treat, cure, or at least prevent" (p. 17; see also Oliver, 1996). In this medicalized view, illness and disability become definitional opposites of normal and, as Goffman (1963) reminded us, anyone or any body that is not "normal" is "deviant" and thus at risk of stigmatization. Bodies and minds that deviate from what has been deemed "normal" are cast as diseased, disabled, deficient, and in need of the remedies that medicine can provide (Kafer, 2013).

Importantly, disability studies scholars and disability activists have shown that the medical model can be an extremely harmful way to conceptualize disability. The idea that Western medicine itself can or should attempt to normalize bodies is a fraught endeavor that problematically figures those with embodied differences (read: most all of us) as undesirable, inadequate, and in need of fixing. This isn't to say that all of Western medicine is inherently villainous; rather, its underlying ideologies help create a rhetorical environment conducive to the stigmatization of disabled and different bodies. When people with illness and/or disability refuse to or cannot be cured and consequently fail to normalize, stigmatization often results. All of this is to say that the relationship between illness, disability, and stigma is influenced extensively, and often negatively, by paradigms of Western medicine.

In response to the medical model of disability, disability studies has advanced the social model, which both argues that disability is not a medical condition to be treated or cured and focuses on the cultural, social, physical, political, and economic forces that oppress people with embodied differences. In other words, the social model of disability "names systems of oppression as the problem, not individual bodies" (Clare, 1999, p. 106). Similarly, Tom Shakespeare (2017) outlined that the social model "defines disability as a social creation—a relationship between people with impairment and a disabling society" (p. 196). The social model ultimately refutes the idea that disabilities are problems within individuals and further rejects the idea that normalization and Western medicine are the most impactful and legitimate ways to address the discrimination and marginalization of disabilities. The social model, alternatively, pivots the site of the problem and the site of intervention away from individuals and toward the ableist systems and structures that create the disability.[22]

This turn toward the social model, which centers the ableist systems and structures as the source of the marginalization, discrimination, and stigmati-

---

22. Buildings that lack wheelchair ramps are a canonical example of structures that create disability. According to the social model, for people who use wheelchairs, it is not their wheelchair that prevents them from entering but the building itself. This is an obvious example. The social model extends in more complicated ways to disabling systems like policies and laws, social attitudes and dominant culture, and access to social services, employment, education, and healthcare.

zation of disability, has been highly useful for illuminating problems with the medicalization of disability. However, central to the social model of disability is the separation of disability and impairment—a distinction that becomes especially troublesome in the context of chronic conditions (Kafer, 2013; Wendell, 2001). *Impairment* refers to particular embodiments or conditions that affect a person (e.g., Crohn's disease or paralysis), while *disability* is conceptualized as the result of systems (both discursive and material) and ideologies that construct some identities and embodiments as not only different but problematically different.[23] As Kafer (2013) has explained, in the social model framework, "impairments aren't disability, social and architectural barriers are" (p. 7). This distinction between impairment and disability has emerged, in part, in resistance to the idea that all disabled people are sick or diseased. Disability studies scholar and activist Eli Clare (1999) has argued specifically against the impulse "to think of disabled people as sick, diseased, or ill people" (p. 105). He further contended:

> Of course, disability comes in many varieties. Some disabled people, depending on their disabilities, may indeed have pressing medical needs for a specific period of time or ongoing basis. *But having particular medical needs differs from labeling a person with multiple sclerosis as sick, or thinking of quadriplegia as a disease.* The disability rights movement, like other social change movements, names systems of oppression as the problem, not individual bodies. In short it is ableism that needs the cure, not our bodies. (pp. 105–106; emphasis added)

In short, advocates of the social model argue that disability is more than a diagnosis or impairment, and that disability itself does not require medical but rather social intervention.

Ultimately, while the social model has been productive in displacing individualized and medicalized understandings of disability, it has made the placing of chronic conditions, specifically, within or outside of disability studies a tricky task (Erevelles, 2014; Kafer, 2013; Wendell, 2001). The social model's distinctions between disability and illness are rooted in the medical model's medicalization of disability and the stigmatization and harm that medicaliza-

---

23. At the risk of being read here as arguing that disability is always perceived as a negative identity or embodiment, I want to clarify that many disabled people reclaim and embrace their disability identity as an act of resistance and empowerment. In such instances, disabled people often still recognize that their disabilities are created through social and structural systems, but they simultaneously celebrate their disabled identities as a means to highlight, resist, and deconstruct those systems.

tion has enabled, not in a desire to exclude those with medical conditions from the landscape of disability justice. Rejecting medicalization and normalization brought on by the social model of disability has been an important step in acknowledging social and structural ableism; however, it leaves those with chronic conditions at a precarious crossroads between medicine and social systems, between impairment and disability. Kafer (2013) has argued:

> Asserting a sharp divide between impairment and disability fails to recognize that *both* impairment and disability are social; simply trying to determine what constitutes impairment makes clear that impairment doesn't exist apart from social meanings and understandings . . . the social model with its impairment/disability distinction erases the lived realities of impairment; in its well-intentioned focus on the disabling effects of society, it overlooks the often-disabling effects of our bodies. (p. 7)

Further, Wendell (2001) suggested that the social model of disability is predicated on the "healthy disabled . . . whose physical conditions and functional limitations are relatively stable and predictable for the foreseeable future" (p. 19). Building the social model of disability on the experiences of healthy disabled people is problematic because it pits illness against disability and elides "those disabled people whose bodies are highly medicalized because of their suffering" (p. 18). These individuals, according to Wendell, evidence the limitations of a strictly social model of disability:

> Some people with disabilities *are* sick, diseased, and ill. Social constructionist analyses of disability, in which oppressive institutions and policies, prejudiced attitudes, discrimination, cultural misrepresentation, and other social injustices are seen as the primary causes of disability, can reduce attention to those disabled people whose bodies are highly medicalized because of their suffering, their deteriorating health, or the threat of death. Moreover, some unhealthy disabled people, as well as some healthy people with disabilities, experience physical or psychological burdens that no amount of social justice can eliminate. Therefore, some very much want to have their bodies cured, not as a substitute for curing ableism, but in addition to it. (p. 18; emphasis added)

Although the social model has demonstrated that disability is not fully a diagnostic category, scholars like Kafer and Wendell have pushed back on the idea that disability, as an identity or embodied, is *entirely* socially constructed.

The tensions that emerge between disability and impairment raise important questions for my investigation into chronic GI conditions and stigma. Where do chronic GI conditions and ostomies fit within these models and tensions surrounding disabilities? And what does the answer mean for my study of chronic GI conditions and stigma? Under either the medical or the social models, chronic GI conditions are not neatly or easily categorized as disabled. Some with chronic GI conditions may find medical treatments that allow them to manage their conditions both medically and socially, while others are never fully able to control symptoms or disease, in which case both medical and social consequences typically emerge. Too, many chronic GI conditions are marked by periods of flares and remission, which essentially means that there are symptomatic periods (flares) and asymptomatic periods (remission). This ebb and flow defines living with most chronic conditions but has also prompted disability studies scholars to further question whether chronic conditions should be included under the umbrella of disability (Erevelles, 2014; Kafer, 2013; Wendell, 2001). Under the medical model, this ebb and flow does not readily poise chronic GI conditions to be considered disabilities socially, medically, or legally.[24] The physical manifestation of disease is extremely significant when it comes to socially classifying chronically ill bodies. Those whose conditions are invisible to outsiders are perhaps least likely to be deemed disabled through social or structural means, which can protect them from stigmatization but also exclude them from the benefits of disability communities and activism. At the same time, ostomies' relationship to disability is complicated in other ways. Unlike some chronic conditions, ostomies require daily management that is not always considered disabling but often is. Further, many people with ostomies also have comorbid chronic conditions such as IBD or cancer that, when compounded with managing an ostomy, can have a profoundly disabling effect. Under a medical model of disability, ostomies and most chronic GI conditions are considered a disability; however, the fluctuating nature of flares/remission as well as the individually specific experiences with ostomies trouble the idea that these those with ostomies are disabled under social models. And, regardless of these models, many people living with ostomies and chronic GI conditions do not identify as disabled, while perhaps just as many embrace disability identities.

---

24. In the US, Crohn's disease, one of the two primary types of IBD, is included in the Social Security Administration's list of qualifying conditions for disability protections and benefits. However, the qualifying criteria for Crohn's disease are very narrow. Although it wasn't a primary part of my research for this book, an unanticipated finding was that many people with IBD, while too sick to earn livable wages, struggle to receive disability benefits because they do not sufficiently meet one of the five strict criteria.

Ostomies and chronic GI conditions consequently occupy a liminal space between the medical and social models of disability, which has repercussions when considering stigma. Both social and medical systems participate in the meaning-making of ostomies and chronic GI conditions. For instance, contemporary medicine frequently frames ostomies as a "last resort" or final option in a long series of treatment options. Social systems pick up, extend, and exacerbate these medicalized understandings of ostomies as last resorts, and thus stigmatize and stage them, the rerouted digestive system that comes with an ostomy, and the alternative way of evacuating waste, as problems that need to be corrected or hidden. Additionally, some people with ostomies feel empowered to engage in activities that were impossible prior to receiving an ostomy, especially in cases where preostomy disease rendered a person hospitalized, while others find going out in public with an ostomy to be embarrassing or humiliating. In either of these cases, it is not simply the medicalized experience of having an ostomy that enables or prevents disability, nor is it solely social systems; instead, the entanglement of medicalization, socialization, and individual preferences, experiences, attitudes, and histories participates in the sense of dis/ability.

Acknowledging the complexities surrounding both the medical and the social models of disability, I follow Kafer (2013), who offers a third model, the political/relational model, a "friendly departure from the more common social model" (p. 7) that both contends that "the *problem* of disability no longer resides in the minds or bodies of individuals but in the built environments and social patterns that exclude or stigmatize particular kinds of bodies, minds, and ways of being" (p. 6; emphasis added) and honors the embodied realities and impairments. To do so, the political/relational model "position[s] disability as a set of practices and associations that can be critiqued, contested, and transformed" (p. 9). I rely heavily on Kafer's political/relational model because it attends to the social dimensions of disability while deliberately acknowledging the embodied, lived realities that become deeply intertwined with political and social spheres. Additionally, the political/relational model serves as a model for my theorization of the stigmatization of chronic GI condition, which works to move stigma outside individuals and into social, material, discursive, political spheres, while being careful to not lose sight of the physical, often medical, realities of living with chronic GI conditions.

The political/relational model of disability, when combined with RHM, offers a nuanced lens through which I can explore the lived experiences of and the stigmatization of chronic GI conditions and ostomies. Specifically, Kafer's political/relational model of disability aligns with and facilitates my interest in the practices and embodied experiences of stigma. By situating disability itself as "a set of practices," this model helps me situate having an ostomy and living with a chronic GI condition as a set of practices that stage and give meaning to those conditions, the people who have them, and their experiences. Moreover, a political/relational model attends to the lived experiences of people living with embodied differences and recognizes the detriments of situating impairment/disability along the binary of physical/social. Kafer (2013) has suggested that "what we understand as impairing conditions—socially, physically, mentally, or otherwise—shifts across time and place, and presenting impairment as purely physical obscures the effects of such shifts" (p. 7). Thus, a political/relational model positions disability as a collective affinity (see Scott, 1989) that

> encompasses everyone from people with learning disabilities to those with chronic illness, from people with mobility impairments to those with HIV/ AIDS, from people with sensory impairments to those with mental illness . . . because all have been labeled as disabled or sick and have faced discrimination as a result. (Kafer, 2013, p. 11; see also Linton, 1998)

Expanding disability to include this wide-ranging collective extends the reach of disability studies, potentially motivating more people to be extends in and committed to political and social change. Additionally, the more expansive approach to disability forwarded by a political/relational model enables me to sidestep the complex issue of whether ostomies and chronic GI conditions should or need to qualify as disabilities and instead recognizes that critical and activist possibility is opened by inclusivity and by being able to locate my work in this book within both RHM and disability studies. This is not to say that I am arguing that all ostomies and chronic GI conditions are always disabling, nor that all people living with ostomies or chronic GI conditions embrace a disability identity. Instead, I recognize that my examination of stigma through ostomies and chronic GI conditions is richly informed by a political/relational model of disability and, hopefully, has much to add to ongoing conversations at the intersections of RHM and disability studies. Finally, Kafer's political/relational model is explicitly intersectional, which helps attune my study to the multifaceted ways that stigma is enacted at the compounding intersections of disability, gender, sexuality, race, and age. Together, these foundations catalyze my rhetorical investigation of stigma and my efforts to intervene in the stigmatization of ostomies and chronic GI conditions.

In the remainder of this chapter, I elucidate my approach for studying the rhetorical processes of stigma. Specifically, I introduce my praxiographic methodology (Mol, 2002) for capturing and analyzing stigma stories (explored more fully in chapter 2). Then, in the spirit of methodological openness,[25] I outline my data collection, which included participant observations, ethnographic interviews, and textual artifacts. In these discussions, I take special care to detail the methodological choices I made, particularly as I collected stigma stories online. Finally, I preview the forthcoming chapters.

Studying Stigma Stories

Throughout the coming chapters, I present analyses from a multiyear exploration of experiences with stigma, chronic GI conditions, and ostomies. This research included a variety of qualitative approaches, which I outline in this section, to gather stigma stories. These stories have much to say about what it is like to live with a chronic condition and about the complex processes and systems that de/stabilize stigma. Each chapter, then, shares stories about how living with an ostomy and/or chronic GI condition is done by people, and how a key part of life for these people is dealing with stigma. These stories have much to teach us rhetorically, medically, and socially, and I share them with caution and respect, in the hopes that sharing will empower ostomates and people living with chronic conditions to challenge stigma and provide more robust and ethical understandings of the rhetorical processes of stigma. I explore many stories that demonstrate stigma's looming presence and impact, but I also explore how many people living with chronic GI conditions are fighting to change the public understanding of what it's like to live with an ostomy or chronic GI condition. Through these stories, I trace how stigma is done in practice and, subsequently, how ostomies and chronic GI conditions are made meaningful, stigmatized or otherwise, and how these meanings become powerful.

While I've so far argued that stigmatization is a rhetorical process, I haven't been clear about what ramifications that has for how I conducted the research that undergirds this book and my arguments. Importantly, when I argue that stigma is a rhetorical process, I do not mean to suggest that stigma is locked in discourse. Nor do I mean to imply that I explore the language *about* stigma, which places stigma as separate from language that describes or reports it. Thus, this book makes an argument about *how* we should study stigma and lived experiences rhetorically. Specifically, I outline and apply a

---

25. Scholars within RHM, in particular, have called for more explicit and thorough discussions of method/ology in our publications. For one such example, see the introduction to *Methodologies in the Rhetoric of Health and Medicine* (Melonçon & Scott, 2018).

methodology for studying stigma through a rhetorical engagement with lived experiences (see chapter 2 for this full discussion). Accounting for the *lived experiences* or *practices*—terms I use interchangeably throughout this book—that are involved in stigmatization has two important consequences.

First, focusing on practices places stigma as active, something enacted in practices, rather than an inherent quality. Stigma, in this formulation, moves from potential to kinetic energy—from something held in, inherent in, or attributed to certain entities to rhetorical power in motion, emergent within practices and events. In other words, the rhetorical approach to stigma I advocate is one that highlights that stigma is not an ontological precondition of ostomies, GI diseases, feces, mental illness, obesity, disability, skin color, ethnicity, sexuality, or otherwise—a claim that persists across stigma research where stigma is defined as an inherent attribute. As rhetoricians know well, meaning is not fixed but is always in the process of being made. My work, therefore, is grounded in previous arguments that rhetoric is a "verb," a "performance," or a "becoming" (Teston, 2017, p. 2). This kind of rhetorical approach to stigma allows me to trace the "processes of becoming" in which stigma emerges, becomes powerful, and is countered (p. 2).

Second, foregrounding experiences shared within stories enables me to account for the range of rhetorical work that stages stigma, which includes but is often not limited to discursive practices. Stigma is not just experienced discursively. As stories throughout this book show, stigma's meaning is made through embodied, material, psychological, social, and discursive practices. My emphasis here on rhetorical practices and lived experiences, as I elucidate in the coming chapters, is important. I suggest that RHM focus on the practices that enact stigmas, as well as the lived experiences and practices of those who are stigmatized—first as a means of identifying stigma's sources, and then as a means of changing, intervening in, and upending stigmatizing practices. If our eye is on intervention, I argue, we must focus on the practices in which we see stigma being done and, just as importantly, being undone.

To capture experiences of stigma and other lived experiences with ostomies, I rely on the work of other RHM scholars who have centered rhetoric as embodied and lived in experience. Lisa Melonçon and Erin Frost (2015) remind us that meaning-making (as well as knowledge-making) emerges from diverse sources including traditional biomedical resources, online patient communities, and, I would add, embodied, lived practices (p. 9). After all, our embodiedness "is our means of making sense" of discourse and action (Fountain, 2014, p. 13). Indeed, Fountain (2014) argues (and I agree) that rhetoric and meaning are embodied: "bodies, objects, and discourses, mutually articulate each other through embodied rhetorical actions that give these objects their meaning" (p. 194). Furthermore, as Candice Rai (2016) aptly summarized:

> We might think of rhetoric—not simply as razzle-dazzle style or verbal bullshittery—but also as intimately tied to suasive public narratives and shared material conditions, *as a force that not only orders our lives but also animates our bodies.* Gets under our skin. Puts things into motion through and beyond human will. Emerging from and wedded to the coconstitutive interactions of language, people, things, matter, and all other presences and forces in the world . . . a theory of persuasion that (includes but also) extends beyond a concern for symbols, symbolic content, argument, language, rational logic, and human intention. (p. 7; emphasis added)

This version of rhetoric is especially apt for investigations of lived experience within the purview of health and medicine because, as RHM knows well, a diverse range of entities—bodies, fatigue, stethoscopes, stool samples, cells, pathology reports, cultural attitudes, patient–provider encounters, belly gurgles, medical charts, to name just a handful—make up the lived experience and meaning-making that occurs within "the networks, ecologies, and activity systems that shape health-related discourse and its effects" (Scott et al., 2013, p. 1). Accounting for rhetoric as embodied and material-discursive becomes especially important for studying lived experiences generally and lived experiences with stigma more specifically (a point I further explore in the next chapter).

Consequently, as I've mentioned, I collected and analyzed stigma stories as "informant accounts" (Mattingly, 1998) that "tell about events" and embodied experiences (Mol, 2002, p. 20). I treat stories as reports of how chronic conditions and stigma are experienced and done in practice (Mol, 2002, p. 15).[26] That is, I study stigma praxiographically, as it is enacted or done in practices and shared through stories. Praxiography—an ethnography of practices—was developed by the anthropologist and philosopher Annemarie Mol to study how atherosclerosis, an arterial disease, "is enacted in multiple practices and how, on account of those practices, it has many realities, not one" (Pender, 2018, p. 14). Praxiographic work foregrounds practices because, as Mol argues, practices stage reality. Therefore, I adapt praxiography for my investigation into stigma stories as a way of attending to lived experiences and of situating stigma as a rhetorical process instead of a static object (my approach to prax-

---

26. Although I discuss my praxiographic approach in chapter 2, a brief overview of my methodology serves as framing at this point.

iography is detailed thoroughly in chapter 2). In other words, I listen to and analyze stigma stories for the practices presented within them and how those practices tell us something about how stigma is done or countered in the lives of those living with ostomies and chronic GI conditions.

RHM scholars have recognized praxiography's utility and have adapted it for a variety of different projects. For example, praxiography, grounded in multiple ontologies theory, has been deployed to better understand pain medicine (Graham, 2015; Graham & Herndl, 2013), lived experiences with mental illness (Molloy, 2015), genetic risk (Pender, 2018), health policy deliberation (Card et al., 2018; Teston et al., 2014), and vaccines (Lawrence, 2020). Mol's praxiography and related multiple ontologies theory have been particularly useful in helping rhetoricians of health and medicine move toward ontological inquiry that studies the practices that stage entities and realities. This move toward practices and ontology, as RHM scholars have illustrated, allows our work to examine "a constellation of diverse practices" (Teston et al., 2014, p. 162) in order to understand how "differently situated material activities . . . produce different objects" (Graham, 2015, p. 31). Within a praxiographic approach, stigma comes into being and disappears in practices; subsequently, ostomies and chronic GI conditions are also staged and made to mean undesirably different, through particular practices.

Put simply, praxiography and its RHM adaptations provide an important foundation for examining complex lived realities like chronic conditions and stigma. Stigma is enacted in a range of material-discursive and embodied practices, and praxiography provides a useful methodology not only for capturing these diverse practices but for understanding how these practices enact (or counter) stigma. Accordingly, throughout this book, I examine stigmatizing practices that enact ostomies and chronic GI conditions as undesirable or abject, as well those practices that stage these conditions and associated identities differently (i.e., not stigmatized) through stories about those practices. As later chapters show, stigma is not inherent in ostomies; instead, particular practices stage the ostomy as stigmatized, as deviant and different, and other practices stage the ostomy quite differently. In any case, I argue that practices enact both stigma as well as ostomies and chronic GI conditions in particular and meaningful ways.

In chapter 2, I detail and justify my praxiographic approach to stigma more fully; however, here I'd like to outline my approach to data collection. Praxiography, as an extension of ethnography, was initially developed and deployed through extensive physical observations of practices as they occurred in space and time. However, as I've made clear, the focus of my research has been on stories and the experiences shared within them. I gathered many stories for this research through ethnographic means including participant observations and interviews. I conducted over 200 hours of participant observations at an annual event, which I attended twice, for women living with chronic GI conditions and ostomies. Approximately sixty women attended each of these three-day events, which gave me the opportunity to listen to many stigma stories. At these events, attendees spent time discussing various topics presented as important to living with these conditions, including diagnosis, treatments, exercise, work, dating, sex, relationships with caregivers, and mental health. In these discussions, many stories were shared about the day-to-day experiences and challenges of life with chronic GI conditions, and many stories were shared about experiencing and navigating stigma.

To follow up on the stories I heard during participant observations, between 2015 and 2020 I interviewed twenty people living with ostomies and/ or chronic GI conditions. These sixty- to ninety-minute semistructured interviews asked participants about stigma, as well as day-to-day life, care, and treatment. Interviews were conducted using a mix of convenience, and then purposive and snowball, sampling to assemble a robust and diverse group of interview participants (Koerber & McMichael, 2008). That is, during the first wave of interviews ($n = 9$), which took place between 2015 and 2017, I deliberately recruited a convenience sample from attendees of the event at which I conducted my participant observations. During a second round of interviews, conducted between 2018 and 2020, I used purposive sampling to strengthen the diversity of my original interview sample ($n = 9$). I also used snowball sampling during this second wave of interviews to identify additional participants ($n = 2$).

Note that much of the data collected throughout my research and thus informing the claims I make throughout this book are from women. My ethnographic observations were at any event *exclusively* for women, and because I recruited half my interview participants from that event, many of them were women ($n = 15$). Therefore, as I incorporated my third data-collection method (outlined next), I was committed to collecting stories from as many identities as possible. The skewed representation of women in my data certainly impacts my findings in ways that I've worked to account for and no doubt in ways I've failed to see. That is not to say, however, that my findings are somehow less valid. They are situated and incomplete (Haraway, 1988); the claims in this book are not intended to be generalizable, anyway. In fact, listening to the stories of women with ostomies and IBD helps illuminate the intersectional ways that gender impacts stigmatization. Nonetheless, the gendered skew in my data reflects an important phenomenon within the ostomy and chronic GI communities. Women, at least from my view having studied these communities for nearly a decade, tend to be more vocal, particularly in public, online spaces. This is not to say that men are absent; there are many men sharing their stories and experiences online (for two well-known examples, see Greenly, n.d.; Powers, 2020). But as one man I interviewed told me, "Women just seem to be far more willing to talk about their experiences." Thus, throughout this book and especially in chapter 5, I work to account for the gendered dimensions of the stories and experiences shared.

Additionally, the stories in this book are skewed toward White perspectives. This is partly a result of the space in which I conducted my initial observations that then led to my interviews. That event at the time was mostly White. White individuals are also represented more in my research because of my own ignorance at the outset of this research nearly a decade ago. When I began this work, I thought I was focusing *only* on ostomies, chronic GI conditions, and stigma, leaving other identities and embodiments as outside the scope of my research. In fact, I thought I was conducting good work precisely because I isolated those particular phenomena. There was other research, after all, that looked at Black experiences with chronic GI diseases or how gender impacted quality of life for people with ostomies (as just two examples). I now know how privileged and uncritical that perspective was, and I worked through additional rounds of data collection to correct this harmful oversight. Specifically, in my second round of interviews, I recruited specifically to diversify the storytellers, perspectives, and lived experiences represented in my data set. I also took this more careful approach in collecting online stories, which I detail more in the next several paragraphs. Acknowledging the messiness and mistakes I made and worked to correct through my research process is important in enabling readers to situate my findings and in being accountable and ethical as a researcher.

Finally, I collected hundreds of stories online from a wide range of sources including blog posts, social media posts, news articles, and listicles.[27] This third data-collection strategy, as I begin to explain here and elaborate in the next chapter, allowed me to engage with the rich stories that were being shared publicly about living with an ostomy or chronic GI condition and stigma. Because stigma is a social, relational, and rhetorical process, many of the practices that give meaning to ostomies—stigmatizing or otherwise—emerge in the public sphere. As Phaedra Pezzullo and Robert Cox (2017) defined it, the public sphere is

---

27. A listicle is a relatively new web genre of articles that are organized by list. For example, the following are listicle titles: "Top 10 Things You Should Know About Ostomies" or "5 Pictures That Show Wisconsin Is the Best State."

> the realm of influence that is created when individuals engage others in communication—through conversation, argument, debate, or questioning— about subjects of shared concern or topics that affect a wider community. The public comes into being in our everyday conversations as well in more formal interactions . . . and the public sphere is not just words: visual and nonverbal symbolic actions, such as marches, banners, and photographs. (p. 21)

Indeed, just as a range of practices stage stigma, a diverse array of public, rhetorical artifacts and spaces participate in those practices. In fact, stigma for ostomies and chronic GI conditions is so public and familiar that it is a fixture in popular culture, a reference that can be used off the cuff to evoke disgust or distaste. For example, in 2013 comedian Jim Carrey, frustrated by gun-legislation press coverage, called Fox News "a media colostomy bag that has begun to burst at the seams" (Huffpost, 2013). The popular lifestyle television channel TLC has even gone so far as to include ostomies in their UK series *Too Ugly for Love?*, a show that chronicles folks with conditions and medical experiences that have deemed them romantically unlovable. And, one evening in the middle of working on this book, I tuned in to a new episode of the *Match Game* remake, where the actor and show host Alec Baldwin randomly quipped: "I have a colostomy bag I could show you" in a sarcastic response to other celebrities on the show jokingly wearing body enhancers (e.g., padded bras and underwear). These are but a few quick examples. The pages of this book share many such public stories.

To find these public stories, I immersed myself in the public ostomy and chronic GI condition discourse through my existing network and quickly expanded that network as I discovered new websites, organizations, and communities pertaining to ostomies, chronic GI conditions, and stigma. In doing so, I was able to identify a variety of platforms and artifacts for inclusion in my research. This strategy, for example, was how I was first introduced to Julia's commercial within the Tips from Former Smokers campaign. In the early years of this research (around 2016), I also set up a series of Google Alerts using terms like *ostomy, stigma, IBD, colorectal cancer, chronic,* and *gastrointestinal disease.* Ultimately, I collected and analyzed over 300 artifacts[28] from a variety of spaces, including organizational websites like Uncover Ostomy, the UOAA, Ostomy Connection, and The Mighty; news articles from national and regional outlets; social media campaigns including #GetYourBellyOut,

---

28. I stopped actively collecting online public stories when I felt I had reached data saturation. See Charmaz (2006) and Creswell and Creswell (2014).

#WorldOstomyDay, and #BagsOutForSeven;[29] and blogs and posts by high-profile figures in the ostomy and GI communities such as Jessica Grossman, Gaylyn Henderson, Sam Cleasby, and OstomyGuy.

These online stories presented a way for me to reach a wider range of perspectives and stories and to more fully understand and calibrate the stories I observed and listened to firsthand through participant observations and interviews. However, online research, particularly about health and medical topics and experiences, requires special caution and ethical consideration. Too, a praxiographic approach in digital space presents unique challenges that have gone relatively unexplored. This is, in part, because a key tenet of Mol's (2002) original praxiographic approach is physical place, as she argued that different places stage objects differently (p. 55). For example, the atherosclerosis staged at home tended to be different from the atherosclerosis staged in the pathology lab. However, S. Scott Graham and Carl Herndl have argued that Mol's original emphasis on place can be adapted. Theorizing pain praxiographically, Graham and Herndl (2013) write:

> Mol (2002) is quite physical in her sense of "site of practice" as a "where"—as a physical location of a set of practices—an understandable move considering her focus on atherosclerosis distributed through different spaces in a hospital. But the idea of specific physical sites of practice is less useful in our inquiry into pain medicine. We could easily say that the diagnosis occurs in the examination room, but that would be a somewhat myopic view. Diagnosis occurs equally in a variety of locations, for example, the examination room, the laboratory, the library, the Internet. Pain management is a spatially distributed practice . . . we will refer to "pragmatic regimes of engagement" or "pragmatic regimes," an all-encompassing term, for example, action, practice, habit. In short, *a pragmatic regime of engagement is a way of interacting with the world from which emerges orders of value and agency attributed to people and objects.* (p. 114; emphasis added)

These pragmatic regimes are especially important for praxiographically accounting for language and meaning-making. As Graham (2015) later explains, regimes of practices "are sites of doing, and doing includes the practices of speaking, writing, visualizing, and representing" (p. 35). Consequently, I studied the practical regimes of stigmatization as well as the sharing of stigma stories publicly online to investigate "spatially distributed" stigmatizing experiences and practices. I collected and analyzed, for instance, several

---

29. Capitalization of each word added for accessibility.

posts on a website called The Mighty, an online community where people share stories about chronic conditions and disabilities through written and video formats. Posts on The Mighty rhetorically operate as a regime of practice in that a particular web space is a "site of practice," and they provide a particular "way of interacting with the world" through which meaning, value, and agency emerge and are attributed to the stories, experiences, and people that are shared through the site (Graham & Herndl, 2013).

However, conducting praxiography in digital regimes of practices opens the metaphorical floodgates for data. For instance, the social media campaign #GetYourBellyOut, which aims to fight stigma and empower people living with ostomies and chronic GI conditions, has hundreds of thousands of posts alone (I discuss this campaign more in chapter 5). If I wanted to treat patients as their own ethnographers, study the practices in which stigma is staged (or dismantled), and do so in the public digital domain, I needed to find ways to bound my study. Drawing on McKee and Porter's (2012) heuristics for online research proved especially useful from my digital praxiographic work. Specifically, McKee and Porter suggest that researchers consider the following dimensions when conducting writing research online: public versus private, data identification, degree of interaction, topic sensitivity, and subject vulnerability. These metrics, they argue, should be used to guide researchers' decision-making processes regarding online research and consent. Thus, I considered each of these dimensions as I collected digital artifacts.

- **Public versus Private.** I focused exclusively on digital posts that were expressly public. This included blog posts; news articles; social media posts that were participating in campaigns designed to reach broader, public audiences; and public advocacy sites that solicited and featured the stories of people living with ostomies and chronic GI conditions. None of the data analyzed for my research required a password or even an account to access; no data collected were protected by membership of a social media or advocacy group. I took special care to ensure that anything I treated as a praxiographic report of a person's lived experiences was specifically meant for public viewing.
- **Data Identification.** Much of the data I collected is easily identifiable online. In fact, I deliberately included data that were identifiable because many of the blogs and websites I analyzed for this project explicitly state the goals of public education and awareness. Therefore, I chose to only include data where I felt identification was acceptable, if not promoted. Blogs or posts that seemed particularly private and sensitive, even though

they were posted publicly, were excluded from the data set. Such artifacts included those that discussed highly specific personal information (e.g., identifiable information about location, age, or health-related information) and artifacts that were posted publicly but that appeared to be intended for a smaller, more personal network of people (e.g., posts that discussed other people in an identifiable way).

- **Degree of Interaction.** Unlike digital research in forums and private groups, my research focused entirely on publicly published data such as blog posts, news articles, and social media posts that were part of public campaigns. Therefore, I did not interact with the vast majority of the authors who composed the stories I've included as data. That said, I do personally know a handful of the people whose writing or posts were included in the data set, because I am an active member of the chronic GI community as a patient and researcher. In these instances, the authors were already aware of my research, and none expressed a desire for their writing to be excluded.

- **Topic Sensitivity.** Stigma and other experiences with chronic conditions are often highly sensitive experiences. This actually served as a reason for me to turn to digital spaces for data collection (as I explained earlier in this chapter). Collecting artifacts posted publicly online offered me a way to engage lived experiences but to limit my research to the stories people wanted to share. Rather than asking people to expose every aspect of their lived experiences with me, I relied on what people had already decided was shareable information.

- **Subject Vulnerability.** Sharing personal health experiences and information, like experiences with chronic conditions and stigma, is a highly vulnerable act. Therefore, as I've repeated, I focused on the stories and experiences that people independently chose to share publicly. As McKee and Porter (2012) point out, technological knowledge should be considered when evaluating subject vulnerability (p. 253). That is, researchers should be mindful that some people may post publicly online but may not be fully aware of what "public" means in an online space. By limiting my data collection to spaces like blogs, news outlets, and social media campaigns, I worked to ensure that I collected artifacts written by people who were indeed aware of the extent to which their stories would be accessible by the public.

These principles guided my data collection as I worked to identify and select stories of people's experiences and practices with ostomies, chronic GI conditions, and stigma.

Thus, I drew on multiple forms of data collection to crystallize[30] lived experiences with ostomies, chronic GI conditions, and stigma in a meaningful and robust way. Calibrating the stigma stories shared across these spaces enabled me to develop a strong understanding of many lived experiences with ostomies, chronic GI conditions, and stigma.

Preview of Chapters

The chapters of this book trace the rhetorical practices taken up and embodied within stigmatization and its resistance by the diverse stakeholders involved. To lay the groundwork for my analysis, chapter 1 begins by exploring how stigma[31] has been studied and by outlining what a rhetorically grounded approach adds to these conversations. In this chapter, I point to key tensions in contemporary stigma research and consequently carve out space for my own rhetorical theory and approach for studying stigma, which, as I've alluded to in this chapter, focuses directly on capturing lived experiences. Chapter 2 argues that a rhetorical praxiography approach to stigma stories enabled me to rhetorically listen to people as ethnographers of their own lives (Mattingly, 1998; Mol, 2002) while calibrating those experiences with others' experiences, as well as my own experience as a person with Crohn's disease. Thus, chapter 2 makes an ethical case for studying stigma stories praxiographically. To do so, the chapter details my praxiographic analysis of stigma stories articulating different stagings of stigma in the lived experiences of people having ostomies and chronic GI conditions. In doing so, chapter 2 sets the stage for the analyses that follow in chapters 3, 4, and 5 that examine how stigma is enacted and countered, as well as how ostomies and chronic GI conditions are staged through lived experiences shared in stories. Readers within RHM, in particular, will find the methodological discussions in chapter 2 useful, as I build on previous RHM scholarship to extend praxiography's utility for RHM.

That said, I've written this book with this diverse readership in mind in hopes that each might find useful takeaways. Discussions in this book are

---

30. Crystallization, as theorized by Laura Ellingson (2009), is akin to triangulation. Crystallization as a technique brings together multiple forms of data to crystallize phenomena. I use *crystallization* here instead of *triangulatation* because crystallization explicitly recognizes that all data is partial and situated. Furthermore, crystallization values stories and lived experience, further making it apt for my study of stigma.

31. As readers will see, I discuss work on ostomy stigma in particular, but much of this work has been done from a biomedical perspective. Therefore, I also draw on and discuss research on health-related stigmas, more generally, that has been done within health communication, anthropology, health psychology, and nursing.

valuable for RHM but also for patients, healthcare providers, publics, and larger-scale institutions such as the CDC and the UOAA. Patients, healthcare providers, researchers, publics, and institutions—each of these broad groups is embroiled in the de/stigmatization of ostomies. In order to combat stigma, this wide range of diverse stakeholders must be involved. This work is already underway at organizations such as the UOAA and the Crohn's & Colitis Foundation of America, each of which has content that focuses on recognizing and overcoming stigma. I hope to enrich these conversations through the addition of rhetorical research and insights.

In contrast to the antistigma and ostomy-positive goals of the aforementioned advocacy organizations, I show how other public institutions utilize stigma (deliberately or not) as a rhetorically powerful tool. For example, chapter 3 shows how one of our nation's most trusted sources of health information—the Centers for Disease Control and Prevention—relied on stigma as part its most recent antismoking campaign, Tips from Former Smokers. More specifically, chapter 3 returns to Julia's story to analyze how particular stigma stories do the very work of rhetorically staging stigma. Alongside Julia's, I review several other public ostomy stories that have been accused of spreading stigma. I argue that one thing these stories share is the way they draw on experiences with leaks and disability to stage the ostomy as a worst-case scenario or last resort and, in so doing, precipitate a visceral public audience (Johnson, 2016; Winderman et al., 2019) and propagate stigma. Moreover, this chapter extends current RHM theorization of stigma by showing how stigma can actually enhance rhetorical credibility when stories and experiences align with pre-existing stigma.

Importantly, it is not only my analysis that contends that stigma is staged in these stories. Instead, as chapter 4 shows, thousands of people responded to the CDC's stigmatizing ostomy message by highlighting how their ostomy experience diverges from what Julia described in her CDC materials. These responses, as I alluded to earlier in this chapter, told drastically different ostomy stories—stories that resisted stigma through sharing empowering experiences with the ostomy such as leaving the hospital, returning to "normal" life, and falling in love. Chapter 4 calibrates the responses to Julia with stories collected during interviews and participant observations to show that these and other stigmatizing public ostomy stories are indicative of common ostomy experiences. Central to these stories and the experiences shared in them is an ostomy that is enacted as lifesaving and positive. These more bright-sided stories illustrate that the stories we often hear in the public sphere about ostomies (presented in chapter 3) do not provide a full account of what living with an ostomy is or can be. Putting both negative and positive stories (and those in between) in dialogue in chapter 4 also helps show how listening to stigma stories requires an attunement to the intersecting identities and experiences that inform ostomy experiences.

In addition, the analyses across chapters 3 and 4 trouble current best practices in health-messaging campaigns for relying on stigma, demonstrate the central to the divergence between Julia's experience (as promoted by the CDC) and the experience of those who protested her, and highlight the value of stories in countering stigma. In other words, the analyses in chapters 3 and 4 show how different stories energize or dismantle stigma by sharing different experiences. The insight of these chapters is especially valuable for public institutions like the CDC, as I examine how, despite its admirable antismoking efforts, the organization could have benefited from more thoughtful consideration of multiple audiences and the risks of deploying scare-tactic strategies. Additionally, scholars focused on health writing, health communication, public health, and strategic communication will find value in this chapter's discussion of empirically validated health-messaging strategies.

Chapter 5 examines the role of visual practices (e.g., displays) and norms regarding gender and sexuality in stories that stigmatize ostomies as well as those counter that stigma. In the same way that leaks and lack of control are cited as experiences that disable and stigmatize people with ostomies, as we've seen so far in Seven's and Julia's stories, visual displays or lack thereof are commonplace for enacting and countering ostomy stigma. In particular, chapter 5 reviews cases such as #GetYourBellyOut, an international antistigma ostomy-empowerment campaign where people posted pictures revealing their ostomies; television network TLC's series *Too Ugly for Love?*, which included people with ostomies; Bethany Townsend, an aspiring model championed for posting pictures of herself in a bikini with her ostomy; and Sam Cleasby, a famous blogger in the ostomy and chronic GI communities, who posted boudoir-style photos on her blog and was criticized for "sexualizing disability." Through a discussion of these diverse cases, chapter 5 argues that stigmatizing practices work to police who is allowed to reveal their ostomy, when, and how, which often disciplines people into concealing their ostomies. Further, this chapter examines how destigmatization is caught up in complex ways with the idea and process of normalization. Specifically, it suggests that certain people (i.e., those who fit particular societal standards for sexual attractiveness) are applauded as heroes for revealing their ostomies, while others (i.e., those who misfit such standards for sex appeal) are stigmatized even further for exposing their ostomies, attempting to sexualize disability, or otherwise existing with an ostomy.

Chapter 6 concludes the book by elucidating key takeaways of a rhetorical investigation of stigma for four primary stakeholders: (1) researchers in RHM, (2) people living with ostomies and other chronic conditions, (3) healthcare providers, and (4) public institutions such as the CDC. Primarily, I suggest that the careful tracing and analysis fostered by a rhetorical understanding of stigma illuminates pathways of intervention on many scales: from the micro level of day-to-day interpersonal encounters to nationwide communication stemming from institutions and organizations to the mundane, often implicit cultural biases we unconsciously agree to and propagate each day. I argue that this book not only provides a rationale for placing stigma within the bounds of caring for chronic conditions (including but not limited to ostomies and GI disease) but also might serve as an initial guide to the types of themes and lived experiences that warrant discussion within those care encounters. Specifically, this final chapter generates important takeaways for patient–provider interactions, as stories shared herein suggest that healthcare providers often play a critical role in shaping the lived experiences of people with ostomies and chronic GI conditions. This is significant because our current medical culture, at least as experienced by the ostomates voiced in this book, tends to position many lived experiences, including stigma, outside of health and medical care related to ostomies and GI conditions. In other words, healthcare providers typically treat disease and malfunctioning bodies instead of people. As one MD put it, "As doctors we've become more powerful at manipulating the manifestations of disease, but I don't think we've become any better at understanding how to care for the people who have disease" (Spaeth, 2015). If (as has been one goal of the patient-centered care movement) healthcare providers treat people, then stigma falls squarely within the bounds of treatment and patient–provider encounters, not pushed to the periphery as secondary or separate treatment. To help make this argument, the chapter briefly discusses ways that healthcare providers are aiming to combat stigma through embodied simulations, wherein providers wear an ostomy bag for a day to gain embodied insight into ostomates' lived experiences. In addition to takeaways, I take time, in chapter 6, to reflect on the experience of writing this book as both researcher and patient, outsider and insider. As a way of looking forward, chapter 6 summarizes how this book lays the groundwork for future work on stigma toward chronic, often unapparent, conditions, as well as future work on lived experience specifically in health and medical contexts.

Taken together, these chapters trace the diverse and complex rhetorical practices that stage ostomy stigma and the counterrhetorics that have emerged to powerfully push back. Each chapter works to carefully unravel the ways that ostomies are made to mean in public discourse by considering the values, histories, cultures, and practices that have sustained stigma for decades. In doing so, each chapter tells many stories. Stories of pain, shame, and embarrassment. Stories of resistance and standing up to bullying. Stories of just trying to survive. These stories and the people who live and share them deserve our attention and our action. In sharing them throughout this book, I hope to foster empathy, awareness, and a chance for all of us to recognize our implicit and explicit participation in one of our most insidious cultural monsters: stigma.

CHAPTER 2

Listening for Stigma

Praxiographic Solutions and Stigma in Practice

When I was first diagnosed during my senior year of high school, I didn't really understand what was happening, and more than anything, I wanted to pretend that nothing was. Of course, left to its own devices, my disease became virtually unmanageable, which in terms of my daily life meant that I had next to no control over how frequently or urgently I needed to use the bathroom. One day, about a month after my diagnosis (and effectively a decade into having untreated symptoms), I sat in sixth-hour, senior-year Spanish class and was struck by the horrifying feeling that I needed to get to a bathroom right away. I quickly excused myself from class and literally ran down the hall to the bathroom, where I whipped open a stall door, unaware of anyone else in the room. Sheer panic and anxiety had taken over. Fight or flight initiated. But thank god, I had made it. I hadn't had an accident at school yet, but this wasn't the first close call. Although I was learning to anticipate when this urgency would suddenly appear, this whole autoimmune disease thing was still pretty new. I tried to discreetly relieve my angry intestines, knowing there was little I could do to control this situation. The memories of just that stress and fear alone would be enough to haunt me a decade later, but the story doesn't end there.

From the false privacy of the bathroom stall, I heard laughter. In my rushed entrance, I hadn't noticed two other girls in the bathroom, fiddling with their makeup and skipping class. Not just any two girls, either—two of the most popular and, of course, most notoriously mean girls in my high school. I had friends and was well liked, but these girls were well beyond my social stratum. And they were witnessing the wrath of my disease in full force. "Oh my god. What the hell is going on in there?" "That is DIS-GUS-TING." "Should we go call a plumber?" All but paralyzed with shame, I flexed every muscle in my body, hoping to silence it long enough for the girls to leave. I slowly picked my feet off the floor, hoping I had done so quietly but quickly enough that the girls didn't notice my shoes, an easy way for them to identify who was hiding behind the bathroom stall door. I held both my breath and my tears and waited for the snickering to stop. Why me? Why a digestive disease? Why did they have to be in here? After what felt like hours, the two left the bathroom, but not without a final "*I can't believe a girl could be so gross.*"

This is a story that I've no doubt many people with gastrointestinal (GI) disease and ostomies would find relatable. It illustrates an unfortunately familiar experience for people with ostomies and GI disease: body uncontrolled in public space, stigma fully unleashed. Bathroom stories, like this one, are a hallmark of the lived experience of people having these conditions. Indeed, bathrooms present a complex space for marginalized bodies (Booth & Spencer, 2016; Kafer, 2016). I've heard many such stories in my time working on this research: stories of panicked searches for public bathrooms; of accidents in shopping malls because a cashier refused access to employee bathroom, the only bathroom nearby;[1] embarrassment when a stranger assumes that a man is using the female bathroom because they see feet facing *toward* the toilet instead of away, when really an ostomate was just emptying her pouch. And stories like the opening one of just trying to survive a day with unruly intestines. As most GI patients will tell you, hell hath no fury like an inflamed bowel. Bathrooms become our lives.

Importantly, too, this story demonstrates some of the different ways in which stigma emerges in practices and experiences. It can emerge through nasty comments and harsh whispers and through expectations and anxiety. But, of course, this is not the only stigma that people with GI diseases or ostomies have come to know. Many people I've spoken with for this project have

---

1. Refusal of bathroom access is such a rampant problem that states have begun passing the "Restroom Access Act," also known as "Ally's Law," which requires that public places allow people with particular medical conditions, like IBD or ostomies, to use private or employee-only restrooms (Crohn's & Colitis Foundation of America, n.d.). The law is named after Ally Bain, a woman living with Crohn's disease, who was denied bathroom access at a clothing store while out shopping with her mom. Ally has spearheaded this legislation to ensure that people with medical needs are granted the right to bathroom access.

described the materialization of stigma in a variety of instances and ways. In their experiences, stigma emerges among stares at the local pool or eye rolls in line at the grocery store, within biased attitudes at a job interview or doctor visit, at dinner when a date abruptly excuses himself after he learns of the ostomy hidden beneath his date's clothes, or simply in the decision to act as if someone or something doesn't exist. Making stigma all the more dangerous is that it often manifests in subliminal ways. Indeed, stigmatization can be "overt" or subtle," and "it can manifest in interaction, avoidance, social rejection, discounting, discrediting, dehumanization, and depersonalization of others" (Bos et al., 2013, p. 1). Stigma is everywhere, somewhere, and nowhere all at once.

As Cathryn Molloy (2019) put it, stigma is "the steady hum . . . that casts its shadow over the lived experiences of bodies and minds" (p. 54). The insidious, shadowy nature of stigma presents a variety of challenges to researchers aiming to capture and understand it, despite the "enormous array" of research conducted (Link & Phelan, 2001, p. 365). Across the academy, the methods for studying stigma are as diverse as the fields conducting the research. Stigma has been studied as a psychological, interpersonal, sociological, political, physiological, rhetorical, and economic phenomenon (Johnson, 2010; Vickers, 2000). For instance, stigma has been examined physiologically, through changes in hormonal response, heart rate, and muscle contraction (Graves et al., 2005; Himmelstein et al., 2015[2]); socially, as reported through interviews and surveys and observed in social spaces (Hughes & Romo, 2020; Molloy, 2019; Rohde et al., 2018); and textually, as documented in tweets or archives (Johnson, 2010; Kosenko et al., 2019). No doubt, all these approaches have afforded key insights into stigma.

However, based on my own lived experience with GI stigma and my preexisting knowledge of the ostomy and GI communities, I knew at the outset of this study that stigma doesn't neatly fit into any one definitional or methodological box. Molloy (2019), citing Pescosolido et al. (2013), argued that stigma "originates in social relations, is diffuse in everyday life, and is

---

2. Himmelstein et al. (2015) claim to study physiological responses such as cortisol stimulation as a "consequence of" stigma rather than as stigma itself. However, I argue, perhaps in conflict with their stated argument, that they study stigma *as* changes in cortisol. For instance, to study stigma, they informed participants that they "aimed to examine hormonal responses to shopping" (p. 369). Further, their findings suggested that participants who perceived themselves as overweight were more likely to experience changes in cortisol when responding to what the researchers deemed as a stigmatizing scenario. They did not ask participants whether they felt stigmatized; instead, they focused only on changes in cortisol as an indicator of response to stigma. Therefore, it seems that their conception of stigma and consequently their method for studying it were physiological, at least in part.

extremely difficult to combat" (p. 40). Stigma is physical, social, experiential, textual, emotional, and embodied, as scholarship has shown—but these dimensions of stigma do not emerge in isolation. Stigma is all of these, and probably more, *at once*. Simultaneously physical, social, embodied, discursive. Therefore, at the outset of this research, I had to answer: what method/ologies within or beyond RHM enable me to capture the diverse rhetorical practices that enact stigma and those that counter it? How can I rhetorically engage the lived experiences of ostomies, GI diseases, and stigma? And what would such an approach add to the current research in these areas?

This chapter, accordingly, expands on the discussions begun in chapter 1 regarding praxiography as a productive approach for engaging lived experiences with ostomies, chronic GI conditions, and stigma. I begin by outlining contemporary critiques of stigma research, specifically, regarding how we treat the stories of people who experience stigma. These critiques, I argue, can be addressed by a rhetorically informed praxiographic approach. Therefore, I next describe how, throughout the research for this book, I relied on what Scott and Melonçon (2018) have characterized as RHM's "methodological mutability"—that is, RHM's "willingness and even obligation to pragmatically and ethically adjust aspects of methodology to changing exigencies, conditions, and relationships" (p. 5). Such methodological mutability enabled me to study stigma stories by building on previous RHM scholarship to adapt a praxiographic approach that foregrounds lived experiences with stigma in ways that honored people's stories and experiences, respected their privacy, attended to my own positionality, and approached stigma as a rhetorical, and experimental, phenomenon, not an innate quality. I then illustrate my praxiographic approach through engaging three stigma stories. Through these stories and the experiences shared within them, we can begin to see how stigma is enacted in diverse ways, which not only provides insight into the rhetorical processes of stigma but points to potential interventional spaces. Finally, I argue that the praxiographic approach I forward addresses not only practical but ethical methodological concerns.

Critiques of Stigma Research

In chapter 1, I established stigma as a rhetorical phenomenon emergent in practices and experiences in which particular entities (like ostomies or GI disease) are made to mean not only different but deviant. Such a definition extends previous rhetorical scholarship into stigma. This theorization departs in productive ways from a significant tenet of ongoing stigma research, much of which is happening outside rhetorical studies. In particular, much stigma research relies heavily on a simplified version of Goffman's original definition. As chapter 1 recalled, Goffman (1963) initially defined stigma as a "mark," "trait," "characteristic," or "attribute" that "is deeply discrediting"—a definition he later refined to focus on the management of information in interactions between so-called normals and the stigmatized (p. 12). Despite Goffman's richer theorization of stigma as a social process, a significant body of scholarship continues to cite and deploy Goffman's initial, simple, attribute-focused definition. In addition to the individualistic focus this definition circumscribes, perhaps what is most surprising about the continued use of Goffman's definition is that within the defining of stigma as an attribute is an implicit or sometimes explicit argument that particular objects, people, identities, or characteristics *inherently* carry stigma or are fundamentally stigma-worthy.

Sociological researchers Bruce Link and Jo Phelan point to this very problem within stigma research in their 2001 article "Conceptualizing Stigma." There, they argue that much stigma research has a "decidedly individualistic focus," which positions stigma as "something in the person" instead of something more relational (p. 366). They further argue:

> Even though Goffman (1963, p. 3) initially advised that we really needed a "language of relationships, not attributes," subsequent practice has often transformed stigmas or marks into attributes of persons (Fine and Asch, 1988). The stigma or mark is seen as something *in the person* rather than a designation or tag that others affix to the person. (p. 366; emphasis original)

With this individualistic focus comes an impulse to study only those who are targets of stigma, which neglects the sources and actions that perpetuate stigma in the first place, according to Link and Phelan. For example, if I were to apply an individualistic focus to stigma in the story that opens this chapter, I might argue that the narrator was stigmatized because GI diseases are inherently discrediting. I might also argue that stigma emerged because the narrator's GI practices conflicted with the accepted norms for alleviating oneself as well as the norms and accepted practices for public bathrooms. In either case, the narrator, her body, and her embodied practices violated norms, and this violation produces stigma. Little attention is given to the other characters in the story and their practices or to the larger cultural and historical context that enables the stigma in the first place.[3] I hope it is clear that this individu-

---

3. Disability scholars have criticized Goffman's work and the research that builds from it as failing to adequately account for historical and cultural factors that enable stigma. For a discussion of this criticism, see Brune et al. (2014).

alistic focus risks, if not encourages, a victim-blaming approach with stigmatized individuals as the central focus and stigma itself as some fixed variable that emerges within a predetermined social script. Although Link and Phelan do not use this language, readers familiar with disability studies will quickly recognize this "individualistic focus" in stigma literature as reinscribing the "individual tragedy model" (akin to the medical model) wherein the focus is on individuals with physical or mental impairments. Such models stand in contrast to social models that recognize how physical, social, and discursive conditions "impose limitations on certain groups or categories of people" (Oliver, 1996, p. 21). Despite decades of scholarship advocating alternatives, these individualistic models persist.

For example, within the ostomy-related stigma literature, several studies define stigma at the outset using Goffman's (1963) original definition, employ the "decidedly individual focus" that Link and Phelan (2001) critiqued, and consequently suggest that stigma is inherent in ostomies or ostomates (p. 365). For example, a 2018 study on ostomy stigma and selfies explained that "ostomates possess what Goffman (1963) describes as 'an attribute that is deeply discrediting' within a society" (Rademacher, 2018, p. 3860). Here "ostomy" and "an attribute that is deeply discrediting" are interchangeable. In other words, ostomates possess an ostomy; therefore, ostomates are automatically discredited. Similarly, as another recent study noted,

> Goffman (1963) defined stigma as "an attribute that is deeply discrediting" (p. 12) and an "undesired differentness from what we had anticipated" (p. 14). Goffman further stated that the general public believes the person with a stigma is not quite human, and *under this view, it is easy to see why people with ostomies might be stigmatized.* (Frohlich & Zmyslinski-Seelig, 2016, p. 221; emphasis added)

While Frohlich and Zmyslinski-Seelig (2016) do later draw on more recent stigma research, they do not trouble the idea that is implied in Goffman's definition: that ostomies, as an attribute, are somehow inherently discrediting. Again, the suggestion that it is "easy" to see why ostomies are stigmatized requires readers to see "ostomy" and "attribute that is deeply discrediting" as one and the same. Importantly, Frohlich and Zmyslinski-Seelig (2016) and Rademacher (2018) go on to examine how ostomy stigma is being challenged; they begin their arguments with these self-evident claims that stigma is within the essence of ostomies rather than within the social, rhetorical structures that shape understandings of ostomies. It is this use of Goffman's simplest definition of stigma that Link and Phelan also identify and take issue with.

Moreover, a significant thread of stigma research has extended Goffman's definition to examine stigma experiences as psychological or psychosocial. There are several such examples within research on ostomy and GI-related stigma. For instance, one study described the stigma surrounding cancer, GI disease, and ostomies as the "psychological area" of these conditions (Hurny & Holland, 1985, p. 171). Another, more recent, study that focused on stigma related to GI disease argued, "The nature of stigmatization lends itself well to targeted psychological intervention, especially cognitive-behavioral strategies that challenge patients' beliefs and assumptions" (Taft et al., 2012, p. 458). Often in research that takes this psychological or psychosocial approach, stigma is parsed into more fine-grained categories including (1) perceived, internalized, and enacted stigma (Van Brakel, 2006); (2) felt and enacted stigma (Jacoby 1994; Scambler, 1989); or (3) ascribed and achieved stigma (Falk, 2001).

Among these, perceived or felt stigma is arguably the most frequently studied (Taft & Keefer, 2016). In effect, perceived and felt stigma are used similarly if not interchangeably to describe an individual's "perception that others view them negatively due to their stigmatizing attribute(s)" (Rademacher, 2018, p. 3860). Perceived stigma, in other words, captures how people with discrediting attributes anticipate stigma—but stigma that is not necessarily considered real or "actual" (Taft et al., 2012, p. 452). Similarly, internalized stigma emerges when a person with a particular trait, identity, or quality embodies the stigma internally and stigmatizes themselves. This is also known as self-stigma and, like perceived stigma, tends to be studied and discussed as somehow fictional or "all in the head" of the stigmatized person. While individual attitudes, perspectives, opinions, no doubt, are part of stigma experience, this discrete focus on stigma as individualistic and psychological seems limited in methodological, ethical, and interventional scope. This approach further replicates the well-critiqued mind/body divides and, again, risks a victim-blaming approach.

In contrast, enacted stigma, as its name suggests, is explicitly enacted by an outsider toward someone or something else. For example, if one person said to another, "You are disgusting for having an ostomy," we would call that enacted stigma. Unsurprisingly, enacted stigma has been deemed a challenge for researchers because it requires them to observe stigmatization in the act, so to speak. However, framing enacted stigma as something that must be witnessed firsthand, rather than reported on, suggests that perceived stigma is somehow less valid or insufficient. Teasing out perceived and internalized stigma from enacted stigma not only positions stigmatized individuals as potentially questionable or unreliable but further assumes that perceived and internalized stigma can exist in the absence of enacted stigma. In other words, perceived and internalized stigma place the stigma as something "in the person" (Link & Phelan, 2001, p. 366), rather than a phenomenon emergent in social, historical, relational, and experiential contexts.

The story that opens this chapter highlights the very need for an approach that attends to Link and Phelan's (2001) concerns about stigma research. Specifically, the stigma emergent in the story is not "something in the person" crying behind the bathroom stall. Instead, stigma emerges among the activity and actors within that high school bathroom. Maybe stigma is even emerging now in the act of reading such a story and imagining the physical details implied but too embarrassing to be made explicit. The "decidedly individualistic focus" of much stigma research does not capture the relational nature of the stigma enacted in that story; nor does it capture the complexity of actors involved in stigmatization (Link & Phelan, 2001, p. 366). Indeed, the story demonstrates that stigma does not—cannot—live within particular individuals, identities, or objects. It requires multiple actors, human and nonhuman alike, as well as actions or practices that give meaning to entities, bodies, and people within particular moments and contexts. Commentary, digestive waste, laughter, bathroom stalls, intestines, pre-established cultural expectations regarding bowel movements, and the bowel movements themselves—all these and more participated in the emergence and meaning-making of stigma in the opening story. Studying and theorizing stigma, consequently, requires methods and methodologies that are attuned to the complexity of stigma itself.

In addition to illustrating the necessity for Link and Phelan's (2001) criticism of treating stigma as inherent in particular people, objects, or characteristics, the opening story also highlights the value in examining stigma "from the vantage point" of a researcher who belongs to a stigmatized group (p. 365). Though I surely do not enjoy sharing it, the story that opens this chapter is my own. I share it because it shows what my own experiences bring to this research, and it offers a window into the "vantage point" from which I conducted this research and wrote this book. Although my motivations for this work exist beyond my personal experiences (as detailed in chapter 1), there is no way for me to conduct this work outside of my own positionality as a person with Crohn's disease. So, when I ask "how can and should I study stigma?" I ask as a rhetorician of health and medicine, as a person with a chronic GI condition, as a person who very well may need an ostomy someday, and as a person who experiences stigma. Therefore, my desire to find a way out of individualistic approaches to stigma is grounded in the type of necessary positionality that Link and Phelan call for—my positionality as both researcher and stigmatized—because in both, my data and firsthand experience with stigma is neither inherent in some entities or people nor primarily psychological or individualistic.

According to the stigma experience detailed in my own story and in the experiences of the many other people with whom I engaged for this project, the rhetorical processes of stigma occur across a range of physical, social, textual, and embodied practices, often all at once. Therefore, I turn to praxiography and multiple ontologies theory as method/ology to capture the rhetorical process of stigmatization and the complex meaning-making practices that stage stigma. However, as I described in chapter 1, praxiography was initially designed to capture physical practices through traditional ethnographic observations. Therefore, I adapted praxiography to account for the diverse practices that staged stigma (as well as ostomies and chronic GI conditions) but that did not require me to follow people into both intimate and expansive spaces where stigma could occur. In the next section, I pick up the methodological discussions I introduced in chapter 1 to specifically detail how praxiography avoids contemporary concerns within stigma research regarding individualistic focus and vantage points.

Praxiographic Solutions

Praxiography, an ethnography of practices, as I alluded to in chapter 1, has been theorized considerably within RHM since Annemarie Mol first introduced it as a methodology in 2002 (Graham, 2015; Lawrence, 2020; Pender, 2018). Across this work, RHM scholars have mobilized praxiography to study how health and medical practices stage the realities of these various medical objects, bodies, and conditions. I aim to extend this work by demonstrating how praxiography provides solutions to concerns within stigma research regarding individualistic focus and vantage points of the researcher. Specifically, as part of multiple ontologies theory, praxiography moves away from perspectivalism—theories and approaches that encourage us to focus on the perspectives, perceptions, interpretations, even descriptions of a singular, stable reality.

One way that the individualistic focus critiqued by Link and Phelan (2001) has manifested in stigma research is in studies that suggest perceived stigma is somehow independent of what is called *enacted stigma*. When a divide is created between perceived and enacted stigma, research risks devaluing the stories and experiences of the stigmatized by demanding that those stories and experiences (perceived stigma) need be matched to "actual" reality (enacted stigma). Praxiography and multiple ontologies theory demonstrate that we can avoid such divisions. Indeed, Mol might describe this divide between perceived and enacted stigma as a manifestation of perspectivalism and the highly problematic divisions between reality and perspective, or the physical realities of disease and patient's feelings and stories (Mol, 2002; see also Pender, 2018). According to Mol, focusing on people's feelings, stories, and experiences as perspectives enables some perspectives to be pitted against others, like the perspectives of medical professionals being privileged over the perspectives of patients (as when disease and illness are dichotomized), or when enacted stigma observed by researchers is considered more real than perceived stigma reported by stigmatized people. Stigma research that takes an individualistic focus places stigma as an inherent, static entity within individuals; advances separations between perceived and enacted stigma; and risks subjugating patients' stories and experiences as less reliable than stigma observed firsthand by researchers.

In contrast, praxiography and multiple ontologies theory reject the idea that there are multiple points of view on a single object. Mol (2002) developed praxiography and multiple ontologies theory to resist the very idea that patients' stories and experiences needed to be calibrated to a supposedly external, stable reality. For example, a perspectival approach would explain how a researcher could say that stigmatization didn't occur even though a person with a chronic condition reports experiencing stigma. In this example, stigma itself remains a "single, passive object" about which the researcher and the patient had perspectives (Mol, 2002, p. 5). Praxiography, in a move away from perspectivalism, prioritizes practices and events through which objects and realities are *multiple*. Indeed, praxiography is ontologically focused on how practices stage realities and the entities that make up those realities. Accordingly, the focus is on practices, not perspectives. As Mol put it, "Ontology is not given in the order of things, but instead, ontologies are brought into being, sustained, and allowed to wither away in common, day-to-day sociometrical practices" (p. 6). That is, ontology is not an inherent property but a becoming: "objects come into being—and disappear—with the practices in which they are manipulated" (p. 5). Multiple ontologies theory thus avoids perspectivalism and subsequently divisions between perceptions/reality by contending that reality itself is multiple. Mol elaborated:

> If practices are foregrounded there is no longer a single passive object in the middle, waiting to be seen from the point of view of seemingly endless series of perspectives . . . And since the object of manipulation tends to differ from one practice to another, reality multiplies. The body, the patient, the disease,

the doctor, the technician, the technology: all of these are more than one. More than singular. (p. 5)

For instance, Mol conducted a praxiography of the disease atherosclerosis and found that it comes into being in the surgical ward as "something that can be pushed aside by a balloon" (p. 102) or as "the interaction between blood components and the vessel wall" in the hematology lab (p. 109). That is, different practices enact different entities—entities that may fall under a single name like *atherosclerosis*. There are not simply several perspectives about atherosclerosis; atherosclerosis is done differently in different (rhetorical) contexts.

Praxiography and multiple ontologies theory have been particularly useful in helping rhetoricians of health and medicine move toward analyses that study the practices that stage entities instead of focusing exclusively on the perspectives, language, and knowledge surrounding a particular stable object, idea, or reality. Consequently, a praxiographic approach has much to offer my research into stigma, as I work to avoid an individualistic focus and replicating divisions between perceptions of stigma and enacted stigma. Extending Mol's work for rhetorical studies, Kelly Pender (2018) argued that praxiography provides "a much-needed alternative to perspectivalism" because it enables scholars to "[follow] an artifact across time or space to investigate the spaces through which it emerged" (p. 77). Extending Pender's argument, I would add that the praxiographic approach guides scholars to investigate the range of entities (language, bodies, technologies, germs, cells, etc.) that come into being and become meaningful within health and medical situations, like ostomies, chronic GI conditions, and stigma. For example, rather than examine how different people perceive or discuss an ostomy, praxiography and multiple ontologies theory direct us to investigate what practices participate in the emergence and meaningfulness of that ostomy. Likewise, in a praxiographic approach, stigma is enacted in practices and experiences.

Ultimately, these praxiographic insights are helpful for my research into stigma practices, particularly in avoiding the pitfalls of stigma research identified by Link and Phelan (2001). Guided by praxiography, I attend to the ontological multiplicity of stigma, ostomies, and chronic GI conditions rather than the plurality of opinions or perspectives about these entities. I contend that stigma can be staged in multiple ways—through laughter in a bathroom, in comments made by a healthcare provider, or within something felt deeply by an ostomate—and therefore I listened to stigma stories for such enactments. Moreover, if entities like stigma, ostomies, or chronic GI conditions are done in practice, then they can be done differently in different contexts. As we'll see in the coming chapters, praxiography cogently maps how ostomies and chronic GI conditions are done differently across different stigma stories. Studying stigma as done in practice, I argue, provides a viable solution to the potential issues of separating perceived stigma from other forms. Relatedly, stigma as done in practice places stigma itself as an ontologically multiple entity that cannot live within individuals or be inherent in particular entities, bodies, or people. Praxiography, in other words, productively addresses concerns about individualistic focus within stigma research.

However, as I outlined earlier in this chapter, critiques of stigma research extend beyond the individualistic focus. Concerns over the "vantage point" of researchers have also been identified as a pressing problem. Praxiography, too, offers insight into how engaging practices through stories can privilege the voices and experiences of the stigmatized. Relatedly, even if I were committed to ethnographically studying the practices that stage stigma, where would I look? How and where do you study phenomena that could emerge at any time and in any place? How do you study an experience that is intimately personal and often painful or embarrassing? And even if the research is conducted from an ethical, self-reflexive vantage point, what about the vantage points of the stigmatized? In considering these questions, my own vantage point was actually quite useful. As someone who has faced stigma related to GI disease, I could not imagine letting someone (an observant stranger, no less) follow me around through my day, especially into the spaces where I have felt stigma most severely: the bathroom, the doctor's office, the bedroom. While I wanted a better understanding of the lived experience with ostomies and chronic GI conditions because I want to acknowledge and tackle stigma, I also know firsthand the deeply personal nature of these conditions and the weight that stigma can add.

Rather than exclusively privilege the vantage point of the researcher, Mol (2002) argued that praxiography enables researchers to engage with the practices and lived experiences of people with ostomies *on their own terms.* Therefore, I turned to stories to study stigma praxiographically. That is, I listened to stigma stories as "they tell about events [people] have lived through," about what it's like to live with an ostomy, chronic GI condition, and stigma (Mol, 2002, p. 20). Mol advocates that we operate in a "realist mode" in which we listen to each person (and their reports) as if they are their "own ethnographer. Not just an ethnographer of feelings, meanings, or perspectives. But someone who tells how living with an impaired body is done in practice" (p. 15; emphasis original). Understanding stigma shared through stories as entangled phenomena of bodies, diseases, and experiences "done in practice" has specific implications:

It is possible to listen to people's stories as if they tell about events. Through such listening an illness takes shape both as material and active . . . This illness is something being done to you, the patient. And that, as a patient you do. (Mol, 2002, p. 20)

Following Mol, instead of treating the language practices presented throughout this book (e.g., blog posts, tweets, and conversations with me as well as with others) as perspectives/representations of ostomies or stigma, or as metaphors used to connect to some underlying reality, I examine patients' language practices as praxiographic, as patients telling how living with an ostomy, disease, or other health conditions is done in practices or how experiencing stigma is done in practices.

In this approach, it is not necessary to follow people into bathroom stalls and hospitals to study the practices that stage stigma, ostomies, or GI conditions, when I could engage people's stories about their experiences. I could listen to people tell their stories in interviews and at events where ostomates came together to chat and support one another. "What people say in an interview," Mol (2002) explains, "doesn't only reveal their perspective, but also tells about events they have lived through" (p. 15). Further, I could listen to thousands of public stories from the people living and sharing these experiences online. After all, social media, blogs, and public advocacy groups have become primary avenues for people with all sorts of conditions and experiences to share, cope, advise, heal, and, often, fight stigmas. Whether through participant observations, interviews, or online stories, I listened in hopes of answering "What are the events people report on?" (Mol, 2002, pp. 25–26). What is it like to live with an ostomy or chronic GI condition? What is it like to face stigma?

Engaging stories praxiographically facilitated two important methodological cornerstones for my approach: (1) treating language not as a representation, perspective, or opinion about "the ostomy" or a singular "stigma" but instead as a practice itself through which I could study how living with an ostomy and dealing with ostomy stigma is done in practice; and (2) treating people as their own ethnographers, who could share their experiences on their own terms, including or excluding details per individual discretion. By listening to stigma stories as if they tell about events, I am able to respect and lift up the embodied experiences of people living with ostomies and chronic GI conditions from their own vantage points. Who, after all, can describe better what it is like to live with an ostomy, chronic GI condition, or stigma than those with firsthand, personal experience?

Importantly, however, not every story in this book is a firsthand account of life with an ostomy or chronic GI condition. While many stories are firsthand, some are mediated or even fictional. For example, Julia's story is a "real story," but it is mediated through a third party, the CDC. In addition, a few stories presented are entirely fictional, such as those shared through the TV medical drama *Grey's Anatomy*. Mol's (2002) original praxiography and its "realist" orientation were set up to focus on firsthand accounts collected through interviews or direct observation. This, in part, enabled Mol to treat stories and experiences as tellings of events, as praxiographic data outright. I conduct this same kind of work for many of the stories in this research; as explained earlier, I conducted observations and interviews with people living with ostomies and chronic GI conditions, where I listened to and collected firsthand stories. However, I also opted to include fictional and mediated stories because I am interested in the *public* meanings of ostomies and chronic GI conditions, which involve *all* stories that circulate in the public sphere. Thus, fictional stories have much to tell us about the kinds of lived experiences that become associated with and rhetorically involved in how ostomies and chronic GI conditions are made to mean. I work to treat fictional and mediated stories in the same way as firsthand accounts by focusing on lived experience and practices that stage ostomies, chronic GI conditions, and de/stigmatization.

This kind of mixed research—that is, examining a variety of stories—required multiple data-collection strategies, some of which I've mentioned (see chapter 1 for details on how I navigated collecting public stories online). To collect firsthand, mediated, and fictional stories, I fused textual, rhetorical, and cultural methods with rhetorical fieldwork (see Druschke & Rai, 2018; Middleton et al., 2011). This allowed my research to be mutable (Melonçon & Scott, 2018) and responsive to the different spaces in which stigma stories show up, like in conversations with other ostomates, in doctor's offices, on TV shows, and in public health commercials. While these data-collection strategies might seem disparate, they were productively calibrated within my praxiographic approach. Regardless of the kind of story or the space/form it took, I studied each story for two central rhetorical practices: (1) the lived experiences and practices shared, and (2) the meaning-making done through/with those lived experiences, particularly meaning-making that destabilized stigma. Praxiography provided a consistent focus across these stories and an intentional way to make sense of each and all of them. Using praxiography for RHM- and disability-studies-driven work allowed me to privilege lived experiences while critically attending to stigma's rhetorical processes.

Stigma in Practice

A praxiographic approach to stigma, as I argued in the previous sections, responds to the complex critiques of much stigma research. To illustrate the value of such an approach, I spend the remainder of the chapter exploring three stigma stories that demonstrate the diverse practices in which stigma is staged in the lived experiences of people with ostomies and chronic GI conditions.

Story 1: Disapprovals in the Bathroom

The first story was shared online by Sam Cleasby, a woman from the UK who has lived for years with GI conditions and an ostomy and who regularly chronicles her experiences on her website SoBadAss. In this post, which was circulated widely through various ostomy and GI communities online as well as by some news outlets in the UK, Cleasby (2015a) described an experience she had while out shopping with her children:

> Dear lady who loudly tutted at me using the disabled loos,
>
> I know you saw me running in, with my able-bodied legs and all. You saw me opening the door with my two working arms. You saw me without a wheelchair. Without any visible sign of disability.
>
> You tutted loudly as I rattled the handle with my hands that work perfectly and my able voice call to my kids that I'd be out in just a minute.
>
> My lack of wheelchair may have suggested to you that I was some lazy cow who didn't care. Some inconsiderate bitch who was using something I wasn't entitled to. (I actually carry a card to explain that I'm entitled to and have a disability key if you'd have cared to ask). You may have seen my face blushing as I caught your eye and assumed I was showing guilt at blagging the disabled loos.
>
> The fact is that I have no bowel. I have a pouch form from my small intestine which can't handle volume and so I have to go to the toilet and poo several times a day. My lack of large intestine means that my stool is totally liquid as I have no means of absorbing the fluids in food and so it's really hard to hold it when I need to go.
>
> I sometimes have accidents which means a large toilet that has a sink right by me means I can clean myself up when things go awry.
>
> I hate having to use the disabled loos as I have to deal with people like you starting, nudging, tutting . . .

Whilst I'm at it, I'd like to address the cleaner in the supermarket ladies toilets I used this week. As I ran in, knees together, bursting through the door and running into a cubicle, I'm sorry that the noise of my (lack of bowels) made you burst out laughing.

I can actually take the sniggering as since I had a pouch made from my small intestine because my disease ridden colon was removed during surgery, the noise I make when I defecate is hilariously loud. Seriously, I get it. It's comedic in its volume.

But before you ran outside the loos and called to your friend "OH MY GOD! You should hear the noise in there!!! I wouldn't go in if I was you !!!!!" Perhaps you could have noted my daughter who was waiting outside with our trolley because her mum had to leave her stranded to run to the toilet. Perhaps you could have stopped and heard me sobbing in pain because the acid in my stools has no way to be neutralized because I don't have a large intestine and so opening my bowels actually burns my skin.

Perhaps you both could have shown a little empathy, a little compassion, a little understanding. . . .

To everyone else reading this, the next time you see someone who doesn't "look disabled" using a toilet. Or someone busting through and crashing into the toilets noisily.

Take a moment. Remember that not all people who have the right to use disabled toilets are in a wheelchair. Some of us have a jpouch,[4] a lot of us have an ostomy bag that needs emptying and changing with the use of space, a skin, and a bin. And even more of us just don't want to shit our pants in public.

Think about the nearly 300,000 people in the country who have inflammatory bowel disease . . . who need to use the toilet urgently, noisily, smellily . . . It's an embarrassing enough thing to deal with before having to see disapproving looks.

In this story, Cleasby explained what her recent experience of using the public disabled bathroom must have looked like to another woman watching her. With Cleasby's "able-bodied legs," "two working arms," and without "a wheelchair" or "any visible sign of disability," the onlooking woman apparently had little reason to believe Cleasby was justified in using the disabled

4. A j-pouch is an internal pouch or reservoir created from the end of the small intestine. J-pouches are commonly created in patients whose colon has been removed, and usually require two or three surgeries. In between these surgeries, an ostomy is created and used; therefore, the creation of a j-pouch is one of the most common reasons people have temporary ostomies.

bathroom. The stark and honest language in this passage exposes the challenges of both living with an invisible disease and facing stigma. Through the onlooking woman's visual practices (staring) and verbal practices ("tutting," a British term for making a disapproving sound), Cleasby became a "lazy cow" and "inconsiderate bitch" who was using something she "wasn't entitled to." In the second scene, at the grocery story, Cleasby recalls another woman calling her disgusting and laughing at Cleasby's digestive sounds. That woman also abruptly leaves the bathroom upon sensing Cleasby's bodily noise and smell. The women's disapproving looks, sounds (laughter and tutting), and comments reported in Cleasby's story stage Cleasby, her body, and her chronic GI condition as undesirable and inappropriate. Cleasby's story also poignantly demonstrates that stigma operates at the intersection of disability and gender, an intersection magnified in the space of bathrooms. Cleasby was stigmatized through stares, comments, and sounds for neither looking disabled enough to use the disabled restroom nor behaving appropriately femininely in the women's restroom. In these ways, Cleasby's story aligns in important ways with my own story at the opening of this chapter.

Story 2: Eager Reversals

The second story comes from an interview with a young woman, Tonya,[5] who underwent ostomy surgery multiple times over the course of approximately a decade. As she and I chatted about what it's like to live with an ostomy and chronic GI condition, Tonya told me many positive stories about how her health had improved with her ostomy, how having these conditions enabled her to find a huge community of friends online, and how she was grateful overall for the freedom and health that her ostomy gave her. Over the course of our conversation, Tonya began describing that one of the difficulties of living with an ostomy is the lack of education and awareness of others about ostomies and related GI diseases. She explained how so few people know what an ostomy is, what purpose they serve, and how they can save lives. She said that her own parents, even after years of supporting her through her own disease and surgeries, seemed to lack the kind of awareness Tonya hoped for. According to one story she told me, her parents want her to pursue a reversal surgery as soon as possible because they don't understand why or how she would want to live with an ostomy:

---

5. Names of interview participants are pseudonymized to protect their identities. I use the real names of people who have written and published public stories online in order to credit their stories and to enable readers to find their stories, blogs, and websites for further reading.

Immediately post-op [my parents] were sort of already pushing me about when I was going to have my takedown.[6] And that's like their first concern with the doctor and the surgeon, and just like jumping over the fact that I'm healthy and just completely concerned with when I won't have the ostomy anymore . . . [I tell them] after my history, I am in absolutely no rush and with my history you guys should not be in a rush either . . . My mom I guess can't wrap her head around how her comments affect my body image . . . I just try to let it roll off.

Although she described her parents as overall supportive, I could feel the weight of these conversations on Tonya as she tried to reconcile her own positive experiences with her parents' negative comments and desires. Tonya specifically described these experiences with her parents as stigmatizing. She further explained to me that her parents' comments were especially painful and frustrating because she had been extremely sick with IBD prior to her ostomy surgery and her parents had witnessed the struggles that had led to the surgery. She personally approached surgery hopeful that the ostomy would enable her to regain her health, but it was clear that her parents did not see the surgery the same way. Instead, she reported, her parents' first thought was to find out how quickly she could have the ostomy reversed instead of focusing on how the ostomy might be able to help. According to her story, her parents just couldn't understand why she would want to have an ostomy. In these experiences, stigma was staged, according to Tonya, through her parents' conversations with her and with her healthcare providers. By asking her doctor and surgeon when she could reverse her ostomy "immediately" after she'd undergone surgery to *create* the ostomy, Tonya's parents made her feel that having an ostomy was undesirably different. In addition, they repeatedly questioned why she would want to have an ostomy and why she wasn't in more of a rush to have it reversed. For Tonya, stigma was done in her parents' discursive and attitudinal pressure to reverse her ostomy.

Story 3: Failed Bag Changes

In another interview, a woman named Hilary, like Tonya, told many ostomy-positive stories. However, as she began to tell me about various hospitalizations she'd experienced because of various complications with chronic GI conditions and her ostomy, she shared how some of her most negative experi-

---

6. Ostomy-reversal surgery is often referred to as *takedown surgery* or as a *takedown*.

ences with her ostomies have occurred in interactions with healthcare professionals (outside her GI care team) who struggled to change her ostomy bag when she was too ill to do it herself:

> You would think nurses would know how to change an ostomy bag. I can't tell you the number of nurses who have told me that it's "so sad" I have an ostomy or who have said things like "you're just too young to have a permanent ostomy." Like, these are the people who are supposed to be caring for us while we are hospitalized, making us feel better, and instead, they make these kinds of mean comments. On top of it, they have no idea how to change an ostomy bag! It took three nurses one time to change my bag. At that point, I might as well have done it myself, but I was too weak to move.

In Hilary's experiences, stigma emerged when healthcare providers failed to physically manage her ostomy properly. The nurses' lack of knowledge and skill regarding her ostomy, which resulted in a botched ostomy-bag change, made Hilary feel, as she said, "stigmatized." Hilary went on to summarize: "Medical professionals just really need sensitivity training." Hilary's story showcases, like the first two stories, the role discursive practices have in staging stigma. However, Hilary's story also highlights that material experiences enact stigma, too, such as mishandled bag changes by healthcare providers who Hilary felt should know better. Later in the interview, Hilary described such experiences with healthcare providers as one of the two most stigmatized contexts for ostomates (the other being "anytime you are around water . . . pools, water parks, beaches"). Stigma, in this story, was done in the inability to successfully remove, empty, and replace an ostomy bag combined with what Hilary described as "mean" comments about having an ostomy.

An Ethical Case for Engaging Stigma Praxiographically

These three stories demonstrate the diversity of practices in which stigma is and can be staged and how those practices enact stigma differently. Further, the stories shared showcase the value in treating people living with ostomies or chronic GI conditions as their own ethnographers. Ultimately, in exploring lived experiences with stigma, chronic GI conditions, and ostomies, my goal in this chapter is to articulate the value in examining stigma praxiographically, an approach that foregrounds practices, ontologies, and people's own stories to better understand lived experiences with chronic conditions and stigma. While this approach provides a way to make sense of how stigma comes into being and is made meaningful, what many rhetoricians might be wondering at this point is how this particular theory is distinctly rhetorical. And, since I looked at stories and language practices shared within them (e.g., stigmatizing comments), how a praxiographic approach is different from textual analyses of patient stories.

Understanding stories as reports of events, lived experiences, and practices instead of as representations, Mol (2002) argued for treating people as ethnographers of their own lives. That is, Mol advocated that we listen to each person (and their reports) as if the person is their "own ethnographer." Rather than evaluate the stories as perspectives/representations of stigma, chronic GI disease, or ostomies, praxiography can examines patients' language practices as ethnographic data, as tellings of how living with an ostomy, disease, or other health condition is done in practice. As a rhetorician, I, of course, recognize the power and influence of language. However, I propose praxiography as a way to understand the rhetorical work in peoples' lived experiences without subsuming all practices and activities into perspectives or representations. In his rhetorical-ontological inquiry, built on praxiography, Graham (2015) insisted, "Language is doing. It has impacts and consequences—social, political, material" (p. 84). Indeed, if language is doing, then a praxiographic study of stigma stories can account for the ways that language practices stage stigma within a "deeper ecology of practices" that make up people's lived experiences.

In following Mol (2002) and rhetoricians who have compellingly argued that ontologies emerge through practices, I argue that the enactments of stigma in the practices described throughout the exemplar stories are not simply different perspectives on stigma. Instead, they describe what it is like to live with an ostomy and how stigma manifests differently in practices. By treating Sam Cleasby, Tonya, and Hilary as ethnographers of their own lives, these stories serve as reports of events, of the practices that stage stigma. Moreover, they demonstrate stigma's ontological multiplicity. Stigma is done as stares in a public restroom, questions from parents, comments from healthcare providers, and failed bag changes. Each story and each of the practices that stage stigma illustrate that stigma is not something inside these individuals; instead, it emerges in actions and practices. My praxiographic approach considers each of these stories as an account of lived experiences with stigma, not as a perception of stigma that I needed to confirm through my own witnessing or triangulation with other, more objective data. The stories don't simply provide perspectives about potential stigma; by respecting Sam, Tonya, and Hilary as their own ethnographers reporting on events, it becomes "possible to understand" stigma as "manipulated in practices," which, as Mol argued, has the "far-reaching effect" of multiplying reality (p. 5). Stigma is not a "universal object" but is both emergent and manipulated in practices and experiences (p. 5).

My primary reason for studying stigma praxiographically is not theoretical, however. It is ethical. Praxiography, as this chapter has demonstrated, provides a robust solution to two key issues within stigma research; consequently, rhetorical adaptations of praxiography highlight the important insights that rhetoric can bring to understandings of stigma. Treating people with ostomies and chronic GI conditions as their own ethnographers enables exploration of what it is like to live with such conditions. It facilitates research into these lived experiences in a way that is not intrusive of people's lives and that takes people's own stories as useful data in its own right. Listening to people's stories praxiographically respects people's privacy, and it protects people's autonomy to tell their stories on their own terms. In their praxiographic study of diabetes, Mol and Law (2004) emphasized this very point:

> The quotes [provided through stories] . . . are not supposed to tell the reader about the specificities of the *people* uttering them. Instead, they are intended to inform us about *practices* of dealing with diabetes—practices that are so spread out that they are hard to study ethnographically for a limited number of researchers who have only limited time, and who would also prefer not to intrude for long periods into people's lives by spending days and days with them. So, we take professionals as well as people with diabetes as *(lay) ethnographers* in their own right, taking it upon ourselves to select, translate, combine, and contrast their stories. (p. 59; emphasis original)

Of course, as Mol (2002) and Pender (2018) pointed out, people are not necessarily the best ethnographers of their own lives. It very well may be that other people involved in these stories would report different experiences or that if I had observed those experiences directly I might have noticed different things. Those discrepancies, to me, do not signal an unreliable narrator or any reason to distrust the stories on the exact terms they were presented. In fact, reliving those experiences through the stories and memories of Cleasby and my interview participants is exactly what I set out to do, because it is their lives that are impacted by those stories, and it is their lives and experiences that I hope to understand and support through this research. When it comes to engaging highly personal conditions or experiences that are diffused across space and time, stories present a viable means to study lived experiences. It is an act of care for the participants of our research (Scott & Gouge, 2019), be they people with diabetes, ostomies, chronic GI conditions, or otherwise, *and* for ourselves as researchers to employ participants as lay ethnographers of their own lives.

My study of stigma encountered the same methodological challenges that Mol and Law (2004) describe. Stigma is neither easily isolatable or predictable. As the stories shared in this chapter testify, the instances in which stigma is staged are often inaccessible and inappropriate for an outside researcher. Public bathrooms, postoperative hospital rooms, and intensive care units: these are the spaces where stigma was staged in the experiences of Sam Cleasby, Tonya, and Hilary. And, like Mol and Law, I felt following participants into these spaces in search of stigma would unnecessarily "intrude" into people's lives (p. 59). While I could have asked for ethnographic access to such spaces, a praxiographic approach to stigma stories afforded flexibility and valued the space and autonomy of participants. Rhetorician of health and medicine Kristin Bivens (2018) has reminded, researchers in health and medicine need to "think about the needs and motivations of participants" and "prioritize the bodily experiences of both researcher and participants" (p. 147). Though Bivens made these suggestions specifically regarding consent for research studies, her suggestions for prioritizing research participants' needs, bodies, and experiences are highly important throughout the research process. Certainly, her argument resonates with my own work, especially as she extends Ratcliffe's (2005) concept of rhetorical listening as a research ethic for health and medical contexts. It is this ethic of listening and care that I work to extend as I build praxiography as a productive and ethical methodology for RHM and, more specifically, for studying stigma stories.

Additionally, praxiography mitigated a practical concern that I faced regarding my own ability to meaningfully study lived experiences with stigma. That is, it was and is a practical impossibility for me to follow several people with ostomies and chronic GI conditions around in order to capture stigma firsthand. Through interviews and participant observations, I listened to stories from people across the US, and through online stories, I listened to many more stories from around the globe. Had I privileged only my own ethnographic vantage point, I would have been restricted geographically, and, therefore, the people and lived experiences represented in my research, too, would have been limited by my location. Studying stigma through stories allowed me to listen to a broader community of people living with ostomies and chronic GI conditions. In this way, praxiography valued the vantage point of the very people living with chronic conditions and experiencing stigma. In other words, I believe that through praxiography I found one way to privilege and attend to what impacts those "with the most at stake" (Scott & Gouge, 2019, p. 191).

A praxiography of stories accommodates these practical and ethical challenges of researching lived experiences within health and medical contexts while attending to the specific challenges within stigma-related research. Through stigma stories, I am able to discern many rhetorical processes and practices that enact stigma, ostomies, and chronic GI conditions in meaningful and complex ways. It is through the experiences shared in these stories that we can begin to understand how stigma is done within rhetorical practices. This understanding, then, can inspire meaningful intervention. Kelly Pender (2018) aptly pointed out that the "turn to enactment" (a phrase credited to John Law), facilitated by praxiography, orients us toward practices that "participate in the making, and unmaking, and remaking of realities with the goal to intervene . . . rather than describe or tell" (p. 73). One problem with individualistic approaches to stigma, particularly those that focus on perceptions of stigma as separate from enacted or actual stigma, is that they have the potential to place the site of intervention *within* stigmatized individuals. If stigma is "something in the person," then treating and caring for the stigmatized might focus exclusively on attitudes, opinions, and perspectives about stigma or undesired differentness like ostomies or chronic GI conditions (Link & Phelan, 2001, p. 366). In other words, the primary interventional pathway is to tell patients to have a better attitude, to think, talk about, and perceive their ostomies differently. If stigma is done in practices, however, intervention sites become the practices themselves, which moves the locus of blame and agency toward a more diverse constellation of practices and away from stigmatized peoples' thoughts and attitudes. Toward this end, studying stigma stories as reports on lived experiences can equip rhetoricians of health and medicine to understand how people are engaged with entities like stigma, ostomies, and chronic conditions, and to use the insights of RHM to best contribute to the lives of the lay ethnographers to whom we are fortunate enough to listen.

However, finding practical points of intervention first requires rhetorical and praxiographic theorization of stigma through a range of stories. I began such work in this chapter but take it up over the course of the next several to show the different ways in which stigma is staged as well as the ways in which lived experiences and practices also work to counter stigma. As chapter 2 shows, stigma is not only staged through complex, visceral practices but is marshaled in the public ostomy stories to fuel stigma.

CHAPTER 3

Staging Stigma

Ostomies as Worst-Case Scenarios

OSTOMY SURGERIES have been performed for over 300 years to treat a range of gastrointestinal (GI) issues. Historically, ostomy-creating surgeries have been used to treat both acute and chronic GI problems, including hernias, battlefield wounds, and intestinal blockages.[1] In 1710, after the death of a six-day-old infant who was born without an anus, a French physician, Alexis Littre, hypothesized that creating an opening on the abdomen to reroute the digestive system might have saved the infant. Nearly 100 years later, Littre's ideas were proven viable. In 1793 Duret, another French physician, performed one of the first "deliberate" ostomy surgeries on a three-day-old infant (Anyanwu et al., 2013, p. 32). The baby died just one week later, but Duret's application of Littre's original idea fortified ostomy surgery as an option for previously untreatable bowel conditions. In the time between Littre's ideas and Duret's implementation, another revelatory ostomy procedure was performed, in 1743, that extended the life of an elderly woman by several years. This time, a seventy-three-year-old woman, Margaret White, began experiencing extreme pain and vomiting when a "rupture at her navel" that she had lived with for over twenty years unexpectedly "burst" (Cheselden, 1750;

---

1. An intestinal blockage or obstruction, as the names suggest, occurs when digested material is unable to move through the intestines and/or when the intestines are narrowed, often because of scar tissue or a tumor.

Wu, 2012). Her doctor, William Cheselden, reported finding White with what is known today as a hernia but he described as over twenty inches of "gut hanging out." According to his notes, Cheselden removed the exposed damaged intestine and deliberately left White with the end of her gut (presumably the end of her colon) exposed to prevent further internal damage and enable digestive evacuation, effectively creating what we would today call an ostomy. After recovering from this surgery, White went on to live for "many years," according to her doctor's account.

These surgeries serve as the origin story for ostomies, but it took hundreds more years before ostomy surgery developed into its modern form. In the meantime, ostomy surgery took its place as an option for treatment, but only as the *final* option to be pursued if and when all other treatments had failed. Until the early twentieth century, ostomy surgery itself was still very much developing in technique, which meant that it truly was a last resort or worst-case scenario for most patients. As these and other historical accounts reveal, ostomy surgery was only considered after attempting a range of other treatments including mercury, enemas, bed rest, sitz baths, or, in Margaret White's case, after living with a hernia for over twenty years (Cataldo, 1999; Doughty, 2008; Nichols, 2016).

Moreover, ostomy-pouch technology did not develop until hundreds of years after the first ostomy surgeries, making life with an ostomy between the 1700s and early 1900s rife with challenges. Historical accounts of ostomy surgery prior to the mid-1900s depict ostomates as "pioneers" who were "very much on their own" in terms of managing the stoma and handling stoma output (Doughty, 2008, p. 37). With surgical techniques still developing and ostomy-pouch technology virtually nonexistent, life after ostomy surgery was nothing if uncertain. The first mention of a collecting device was reported in 1795, but it wasn't until nearly two centuries later, in the 1970s, that the ostomy-appliance industry took off. Before manufactured ostomy appliances were available, ostomates innovated their own systems for handling output. These included moss, rags, tin boxes, leather pouches, metal cans, and rubber bags held over the stoma with belts, cement, adhesive tapes, and paste (Cataldo, 1999). For example, one historical account depicted a woman named Mabel who underwent ostomy surgery in the late 1930s at a time when ostomy-pouching technology had not yet developed (Riome, 2018). After surgery, Mabel returned home to use rags that she changed and cleaned in her family's outhouse. Mabel's husband, hoping to make her life easier, invented an at-home device made from a tin can and belt strap, and, while reportedly better than rags, this homemade device was described as "leaky and stinky"

(Riome, 2018). Even when "strapped tightly around her waist," Mabel's home-made device could only "reduce the leakage (not prevent leakage . . . just reduce)" (Riome, 2018).

Some historical accounts report that such homemade waste-collection systems were successful and often better than nothing, as Mabel's story show-cases. However, not every ostomate had the ability or resources to develop such at-home devices, so it's perhaps unsurprising that historically ostomates are described as "dread[ing]" life with an ostomy (Wu, 2012, p. 34). These early adversities, no doubt, led many ostomates to hide their surgeries and embodied differences. Without effective appliance technology, managing a stoma and stoma output were undoubtedly difficult since stomas are not con-trolled by muscular sphincters that enable deliberate opening and closing. That is, ostomies essentially render those living with them fecally inconti-nent[2] in that ostomies excrete waste whenever there is waste to be excreted, not when it is convenient or decided on by the ostomate. Given the historical lack of social, physical, and technological support for ostomates, it's ultimately unsurprising that leaks and other negative experiences have dominated public ostomy stories.

Since the first documented description of ostomy surgery at the start of the eighteenth century, the procedure itself has transformed substantially, as have the technologies used to protect stomas and collect waste. By most accounts, both ostomy surgery and technology have improved immensely. The mid-1900s, in particular, saw advancements in both ostomy surgery technique and pouching technology. Quality of life for ostomates has also "dramatically advanced" alongside these improved surgeries and technologies (Cataldo, 1999, p. 140). In the 1960s and 1970s, ostomy-supply companies began to focus on the needs and desires of ostomates themselves (Nichols, 2016), thereby enhancing ostomy-pouching technology and ostomates' lived experiences. In particular, many kinds of pouching systems now exist, which gives osto-mates options to find a pouch with the best fit for their individual bodies to most effectively mitigate leaks and other unwanted or potentially stigmatizing experiences.

---

2. This is not the case for every ostomate. Some people living with colostomies can "train" their stomas to excrete waste at predetermined times. The technical term for this process is *colostomy irrigation*. Many folks who choose and are able to practice irrigation use an ostomy plug rather than a pouching system. Plugs, as the name implies, are small devices inserted into the stoma that plug or block the opening to prevent fecal output from being excreted. To irri-gate, ostomates remove the plug and flush the ostomy with a water enema. Over time, repeating this process consistently (at the same time of day) regulates the GI tract to excrete waste on a schedule.

What has failed to advance alongside these technological, surgical, and embodied improvements, however, is the public ostomy story. Lived experiences with ostomies may have been riddled with leaks and social isolation in the 1700s, 1800s, and early 1900s, but advances in surgical technique, ostomy appliances, and the potential for increased social support through advocacy organizations and online communities have all significantly changed what life with an ostomy can be. Nevertheless, the public story about ostomies and ostomy experiences seems to have retained ostomy's historical reputation as a dreaded last resort. Indeed, public ostomy stories, as I explore in this chapter, have remained relatively consistent, focusing exclusively on negative experiences. Recall Julia, the participant in the Tips from Former Smokers campaign whose ostomy story focused on how she "hated" her ostomy because it leaked, smelled, and made her feel stuck at home (see chapter 1). Even though Julia's story may have been consistent with her lived experiences, her story angered thousands of people living with ostomies and chronic GI conditions because, according to their responses, Julia's story engendered stigma and unfairly suggested that life with an ostomy was unquestionably negative and, worse yet, a punishment for poor health choices. Julia's participation in the Tips campaign, in addition to other stories I review in this chapter, suggests that negative ostomy experiences persist as the primary, if not only, story about ostomies circulating widely in the public sphere. Accordingly, the stories presented in this chapter point to the public's continued familiarity with and acceptance of this negative, stigmatizing ostomy story.

This chapter picks up Julia's story again to examine how public ostomy stories both feed and feed on stigma. I argue that the public stories that rhetors like Julia (and the CDC) tell about ostomies emphasize negative lived experiences with leaks, uncontrollability, and social outcasting. In doing so, these stories (aim to) evoke emotional and embodied responses in their audiences, particularly fear, which rhetorically fuels the stories as they enter and circulate in the public sphere. These stories thus tap into what Johnson (2016) has called "visceral publics"—publics united by intense, embodied feelings—by forwarding a familiar metanarrative about ostomies (ostomies are leaky, smelly, and disabling) and enacting the ostomy as unilaterally negative. As a result, these stories and the experiences featured in them simultaneously rely on and calcify ostomy stigma.

In the remainder of this chapter, I review previous scholarship that has demonstrated the interconnectedness of stigma, leaks, disability, and visceral publics. In doing so, I build on the histories of ostomies outlined in the introduction of this chapter and detail the social relationship between leakiness / bodily leaks and fear and disgust directed at disabled bodies, a connection that subsequently activates stigma. I then examine four key public ostomy stories: Julia's story in the Tips from Former Smokers campaign; a story told by the Cincinnati, Ohio, Police Department to teenagers at risk of gun violence; and two stories told in the popular medical drama *Grey's Anatomy*. Examining these stories together reveals consistency in terms of the kinds of practices shared and the kinds of rhetorical moves used to effect change or evoke response in the stories' listeners. I specifically demonstrate that highly public ostomy stories consistently omit important details, which helps maintain a negative meaning of ostomies; frequently rely on discussions of bodily leakiness and on disability stereotypes; and, ultimately, rhetorically leverage fear of ostomies to accomplish often unrelated goals. Further, I illustrate the immense rhetorical importance of these public ostomy stories, especially given their broad audiences. In many cases, these stories may very well be the only ostomy story viewers have access to, thus compounding their rhetorical impacts and risks.

Together, these highly public ostomy stories evidence that the public ostomy story rhetorically serves as what Adichie (2009) might describe as a *single* story that shows ostomates "as one thing, as only one thing, over and over again." This single ostomy story, in turn, communicates that ostomy experience is singularly negative and undesirable. As Adichie (2009) explained, "The single story creates stereotypes, and the problem with stereotypes is not that they are untrue, but that they are incomplete. They make *one* story become the *only* story" (emphasis added). Critically, Adichie was referring to the dangers of a single story about a culture or race; nevertheless, her sentiment illuminates the stigmatizing danger of telling a single ostomy story. Indeed, "the danger of a single story" is that single stories breed misunderstanding; they prey on fear, stereotypes, and incomplete, flattened experiences. With Adichie's insights in mind, the analysis of the public ostomy story presented in this chapter provides insight into why ostomy stigma is so pervasive and difficult to counter.

Finally, these ostomy stories, and the single public story they collectively create, complicate a commonly held notion about the rhetorical effects of stigma, which I discuss in the final sections of this chapter. Much of the work on stigma in rhetorical studies focuses on stigmas' rhetorically disabling effect—reducing credibility or replacing it with anticredibility (*kakoethos*) altogether (Johnson, 2010; Molloy, 2015; Prendergast, 2001). This is not always the case, however, when it comes to the stigmatization of ostomies. Instead of removing ostomate rhetors from the polis, these public ostomy stories and the experiences within them have proved highly persuasive in the public domain. So persuasive and credible, for instance, that the CDC selected Julia, an ostomate, to tell her story as part of a national antismoking health campaign that would be viewed by millions of Americans. These public enactments of ostomies become especially credible because they use (potential) ostomates and their lived experiences as evidence to support negative understandings of ostomies that are, in turn, often used to motivate audiences to action. What is more persuasive, after all, than an ostomate herself, trusted sources like the CDC and police officers, or even a favorite TV show, arguing that ostomies are terrible?

Leaks, Stigma, and Visceral Publics

Ostomies' historical reputation (as leaky, uncontrollable last resorts) is deeply rooted in powerful, oppressive systems and ideologies that cast particular kinds of bodies as threatening, frightening, disgusting, and unruly. This reputation, as the stories explored in this chapter highlight, remains insidiously powerful in our present moment. First, however, an overview of the interconnectedness of leakiness, stigma, and disability helps contextualize the stories and analysis in this chapter.

I outlined in chapter 1 that disability scholars and rhetoricians have theorized the deep entanglement of disability and stigma. Specifically, disabilities and embodied differences are stigmatized as a measure of exacting control through demarcation and oppression (Garland-Thomson, 1997; Johnson, 2010). Being disabled has historically "been read as a sign of evil, and associated with weakness, criminality, asexuality, vagrancy, dangerousness, and worthlessness" (Johnson, 2010, p. 465). The "disabled figure," as Garland-Thomson (1997) so poignantly demonstrated in *Extraordinary Bodies*, "operates as the *vividly embodied, stigmatized* other whose social role is to symbolically free the privileged, idealized figure of the American self from the vagaries and vulnerabilities of embodiment" (p. 7; emphasis added). In other words, disability and embodied differences have been positioned as antithetical to normality, creating a "perverse taxonomy of 'normals' and the 'stigmatized'" (Garland-Thomson, 2014).

This opposition between so-called normals and stigmatized is generated, at least in part, by social structures that stage particular bodies "as less bounded and more porous" (Johnson, 2016, p. 5) and thus "dangerous because they are perceived as out of control" (Garland-Thomson, 1997, p. 37). Indeed, scholars across rhetorical, feminist, disability, and cultural studies have demonstrated that fear and stigma regarding embodied differences are commonly tied to fear and stigma regarding leaks and leaky bodies, including physical leaks (leaky urine, saliva, feces, blood) but also leaks that blur the separation of mind and body and subsequently challenge the idea that the mind controls the body. Most systems of power in Western society, particularly able-ism and sexism, are predicated on the idea that "normal" bodies are stable, bounded, and neatly controlled by the rational mind. To be normal is to be male, young, White, cisgender, heterosexual, athletic, and stereotypically able (Goffman, 1963, p. 128). Anybody that defies these "normal" characteristics is deemed abnormal and is thus vulnerable to stigmatization. For example, dis-abled, female, trans, queer, and non-White bodies are often figured as leaky, uncontrollable, and erratic, and thus problematic, threatening, and inferior.

Leakiness and uncontrollability—whether physical or cognitive, actual or anticipated—challenge a "sense of order" in which bodies are tightly bounded, rigidly able, and tidily controlled by the rational mind (Turner, 2003, p. 4). Leaks, such as menstrual blood, breast milk, and stoma output, "breach the boundaries of the proper" (Shildrick, 1997, p. 12) and "remind us that total control of the body is an unachievable goal" (MacDonald, 2007, p. 329). Leak-ing excrement, in particular, Elizabeth Grosz (1994) argued, "poses a threat . . . to life, to the proper, the clean," and compels people to "establish as great a separation as possible from the excremental" (p. 207). In fact, some of the very first social training we receive as humans (potty training) teaches us to manage our bodies such that bodily fluids are contained, controlled, and invis-ible (Gunn, 2006; Turner, 2003). This social training responds to the cultural expectation that perceived or actual leaky bodies are dangerous threats to self-certainty, autonomy, and social norms, and are consequently stigmatized (Grosz, 1994; MacDonald, 2007; Shildrick, 1997; Turner, 2003).

Centralizing bodily leaks, particularly leaking fecal matter, is rhetorically powerful in ostomy stories given the historical and continuing stigmatiza-tion of leaks. As I mentioned in the introduction to this chapter, ostomy stories and the experiences shared within them are marked by leakiness, particularly before ostomy-pouching technology was developed, when ostomates were forced to create their own pouching systems. Despite sig-nificant advances in such technology, public stories of ostomies and thus public understandings of ostomies remain characterized by leakiness. Con-sequently, public fear regarding ostomies and their leaks rhetorically fuels public stigmatization of ostomies. The public stories retold in this chapter indicate how immensely persuasive and entrenched fears regarding leaks and uncontrollable bodies are.

In particular, public ostomy stories not only target but rely on audiences' fear of leaky, disabled bodies and, relatedly, the stigmatization of ostomies. In this way, the audiences of the public ostomy stories I analyze in this chapter constitute what Johnson (2016) has called a "visceral public" or publics united by shared, intense feelings. Johnson theorized, "Visceral publics have two defining qualities: they emerge from discourse about boundaries, and they cohere by means of intense feeling" (p. 2). Unlike other notions of publics that focus on discursive and ideological affinities that bring together individuals into publics, Johnson's concept of visceral publics focuses squarely on the emotional and embodied responses that unite people in the public sphere (Johnson, 2016; Winderman et al., 2019).

As Johnson and others have further pointed out, these unifying emotional and embodied responses often include fear, disgust, and hate (Johnson, 2016; Winderman et al., 2019). These feelings are felt so deeply and so viscerally that they "present as self-evident forms of truth" (Johnson, 2016, p. 4; see also Ahmed, 2003, 2015). For instance, fear and disgust as responses to human waste or blood are often experienced and positioned as natural, even primordial. In other words, feeling disgusted at the site of blood is seen as a natural response. In the contexts of public ostomy stories, such seemingly self-evident visceral feelings, particularly those that emerge in response to stories about leaky, disabling ostomies, make the stigmatization of ostomies also appear self-evident. That is, fear and disgust are presumed to be unquestionable, obvious, and natural reactions to public ostomy stories and the visceral publics these stories evoke and sustain.

In addition to sharing these intense, embodied feelings, visceral publics are often united by the shared desire to do something about those feelings, to prevent or mitigate them in the future. Johnson (2016) argued, "Collective visceral feelings of vulnerability and fear often serve as inarguable, self-evident rationales" for policies like government-mandated fluoridation of water and public health responses more broadly (p. 5). Similarly, fear, Michael William Pfau (2007) has argued, "is an influential emotion whose history reveals its impacts not only on individuals, but on entire communities, economies, and political systems" (p. 216). Shared feelings of fear mobilize visceral publics to take action, to respond not only individually but also communally, to assuage that fear and neutralize threats. As we'll see with ostomies, intense, visceral reactions often emerge in response to particular and embodied practices that rely upon and concretize stigma.

Worst-Case Scenarios: Ostomies in Public Health Campaigns

Three years after launching the Tips campaign, the CDC continued to roll out additional stories, and in March 2015 Julia's story was released both online and on national television. In step with the other Tips participants, Julia shared the negative consequences of her smoking, which include colorectal cancer, chemotherapy treatments, surgery, and a colostomy bag. According to her profile on the Tips campaign website, Julia—a smoker for over twenty years—began noticing a variety of GI symptoms including cramps, bloating, diarrhea, and vomiting, which she originally tried to manage "on her own" (CDC, 2015a). However, when these symptoms escalated, she underwent a colonoscopy that found that not only were her intestines blocked but, worse, this blockage was due to a cancerous tumor. Immediate surgery successfully removed the tumor but left Julia in need of a temporary colostomy bag as she underwent treatment for cancer and while her GI tract healed from surgery.

Years later, after she both recovered and quit smoking, Julia joined Tips to share her experiences in "hopes that people who hear her story about smoking and colon cancer will quit as soon as possible" (CDC, 2015a). Like other former smokers in the campaign, Julia shares these experiences through a series of online materials and videos, as well as national TV ads. Julia's first video aired in March 2015. This thirty-second video featured Julia in what appeared to be her home as she narrated her smoking-related experiences and concluded with a tip for viewers. The video opened with Julia looking squarely into the camera, as she explained:

> I smoked and I got colon cancer. I had chemo and two surgeries, but *what I hated the most was the colostomy bag.* That's where they re-route your intestines, so you have bowel movements that go into a bag through a hole in your stomach. (CDC, 2015a; emphasis added)

Julia's smoking experience, as depicted in her video, centered on living with her colostomy bag. In the video's next scene, she continued, "You go wherever it goes. You have no control. If it comes loose, it smells. I had no control." Here and throughout the video, Julia referred to her ostomy as *It* as she narrated her experiences and held her colostomy bag away from her body and toward the camera.

Elaborating on the impact of this lack of control and potential leakiness on her life, Julia told viewers that she "had to wear it for a whole year," which meant that she "was at home the majority of the time because [she] was scared it would come loose and it would smell." Julia explains that the risk of the ostomy coming loose and smelling meant that she "didn't want to be around anyone" and was, therefore, "stuck at home." Finally, Julia summarized her experiences and sentiment in her tip for viewers. As she sat on the edge of her bed and held her colostomy bag, the video closed with the following message:

"My tip is to get over being squeamish. You're going to be emptying your bag six times a day."

Julia's experiences with an unexpected cancer diagnosis, surgery, and chemotherapy, undoubtedly "communicate the real-life health consequences of smoking" (CDC, 2020b). However, Julia stressed that "what she hated most" was her colostomy. The risk of her ostomy leaking, and the leak's potential smell, left her feeling trapped in her home and completely isolated from others. Julia's story positions herself and her body as physically and socially abject through the bodily breaches and potential leakiness caused by her ostomy. Julia's focus on leaks and feces throughout her story serves the larger rhetorical purpose of her story—to convince viewers to stop smoking —by assuming that they will be disgusted by her story, body, and ostomy. The goal of the Tips ads is to promote smoking cessation; thus, it seems the CDC assumed that their national audience would be persuaded by Julia's story and agree that ostomies are abject and undesirable. Julia's focus on the embodied leakiness and smell of her ostomy (and its contents) assumed an audience that agrees with Julia's own disgust with her ostomy.

Some of Julia's additional campaign materials further shared this ostomy-negative message. For example, a print ad featured Julia looking directly at the camera with the caption "Jokes about gas are funny, until they find a tumor in your colon." Additionally, in a podcast released alongside her original video, Julia admitted:

> I certainly don't want to tell you about having a colostomy bag . . . I don't want to talk about emptying or changing that thing . . . There's so much I don't want to tell you, but I did because my tip is tell what you know about smoking because someone might listen. Then there'd be a lot less stories to tell like mine. (CDC, 2017)

Julia's reference to her ostomy as *that thing* is notable. This discursive practice, like her use of the word *it* in her video, creates rhetorical distance between Julia and the ostomy and, in turn, communicates to audiences that the ostomy is something to stay away from, to avoid if at all possible. The distance created through this language as well as the physical distance staged in her video by holding the ostomy bag away from her body materially reflects Julia's stated aversion to engaging with her ostomy and telling about such experiences. These material-discursive practices, alongside Julia's overall story about her lived experiences with fear, leaks, and being stuck at home, rhetorically enact her ostomy as dehumanizing and undesirable. Embedded within the

Tips campaign, Julia's negative ostomy story forecasts for viewers a bleak but potentially avoidable future so long as viewers take action and quit smoking.

Julia's message within the Tips campaign isn't an anomaly as far as its public staging of ostomies goes. In fact, the negative ostomy experience shared in Julia's campaign materials relies on a familiar ostomy narrative—one that positions the ostomy as a worst-case scenario, something that can be prevented or avoided, and something to fear. For example, just two years before Julia's materials were released, the police department (PD) in Cincinnati, Ohio, told a similar ostomy story as part of an anti-gun-violence campaign for teens. Specifically, the Cincinnati PD was visiting local high schools across the city to speak to at-risk teenage boys about the harms of gun violence. In preparing for these presentations, the police officers contacted a local trauma center to learn more about the health consequences of gun violence directly from victims themselves. Through this local trauma center, the officers learned of one gunshot victim whose abdominal bullet wound led to surgery and the need for a colostomy bag. With this example in mind, the police officers delivered their presentations at local high schools, using colostomies as a key illustration of gun violence's risks and consequences. A lieutenant shared photos of colostomies while describing the following scene during the presentation: "You're not killed, but you're walking around with a colostomy bag and that's just not the way to get a girl's attention, by limping down Warsaw Avenue with a colostomy bag" (Warren, 2013).

Taken in context, the lieutenant's fictional story seems to be an attempt to appeal directly to his audience. As a local news outlet described at the time, this "first of its kind" initiative "will appeal to the vanity of teenage boys living a life of drugs and crime" (Warren, 2013). It appears the lieutenant assumed that his teenage audience was highly invested in being attractive and would therefore be motivated to avoid gun violence if it risked appealing to "girls." Drawing on hypermasculine, heteronormative messaging and stereotypical teenage pressure to fit in by being perceived as good-looking, the lieutenant's comments feature ostomies as an antithesis of attractive, able, masculinity. In other words, limping and having an ostomy conflicts with being attractive and "getting a girl's attention." To support his audience in drawing this conclusion, the lieutenant rhetorically strung together a series of events and consequences that enthymematically communicated two potential outcomes of participating in gun-violence and gang-related activities. In the worst case, as he explicitly described, the teens participate in gun violence, end up shot, wounded, and with an ostomy that disables, stigmatizes, and renders them socially, sexually, aesthetically ruined. As the lieutenant projected these all but certain negative consequences of participating in gun violence, the lieutenant also implicitly painted a contrasting and ideal or at least much more optimistic future for the at-risk teen audience: the only way to stay normal, attractive, and physically able is to avoid gun violence and avoid an ostomy. These oppositional and hypothetical stories stage the ostomy as one, if not the scariest, outcome of participating in gun violence, second only to death itself.

The binary futures depicted and implied by the lieutenant also disturbingly weaponize disability as a scare tactic. The lieutenant, like Julia's video, asked audiences to envision themselves with an ostomy through the use of second-person language. This imagined future self not only has an ostomy but is limping down the street, debilitated and unable to attract a romantic partner. In other words, according to the lieutenant's prediction, an ostomy will both physically and socially disable anyone who needs one, and that disability will automatically and irreparably stigmatize them. Through this brief but nonetheless significant story, the lieutenant played on a highly entrenched trope connecting disability and stigma (see, e.g., Brune et al., 2014). In claiming that an ostomy will make you "limp down Warsaw Avenue," the lieutenant warned his audience: having an ostomy will disable you and make you worthless and weak.

When enacted as part of these public campaigns, whether Tips or Cincinnati PD gun-violence prevention, the ostomy becomes not just a terrible outcome but, worse, the result of bad choices. So, the story goes like this: Lifelong smoker? Quit so you don't need an ostomy and get stuck at home all the time. Considering joining a gang? Don't, because you could get shot, need an ostomy, and become an outcast. Julia lost her freedom and, in its place, found herself isolated in fear that her ostomy would leak and smell. Similarly, in the Cincinnati PD story, a life full of opportunity and confidence is replaced by a crippling ostomy. These are stories of undesirable experiences gained and desirable experiences lost. Particular rhetorical practices including use of the second person, discursive distancing (e.g., use of *thing* or *it* to refer to the ostomy), and physical distancing (e.g., visuals of the ostomy being held away from the body) propel these negative ostomy stories. Moreover, the experiences highlighted in these campaigns' stories focus exclusively on the limitations of an ostomy, specifically physical, embodied limitations like limping and leaks, as well as social limitations including social isolation or loss of sexual attractiveness. These stories leverage lived and embodied experiences to stigmatize ostomies and advance additional rhetorical goals such as smoking cessation and gun-violence prevention. In highly public contexts like these public health campaigns, the ostomy is enrolled exclusively as a scare tactic in a cautionary tale.

Ostomies on TV:
Fear and Disgust in Popular Media

In addition to campaigns like Tips from Former Smokers and the Cincinnati PD's gun-violence prevention, negative ostomy narratives permeate other
public contexts, including random celebrity references, like those mentioned
in chapter 1, as well as popular media like TV shows. For example, in 2009,
season 6 of *Grey's Anatomy*, the longest-running medical drama on American television, premiered complete with a two-episode ostomy storyline. With
millions of viewers' eyes peeled, the first episode of season 6 begins as a young
woman, Clara, arrives at the hospital via ambulance after an accident involv-
ing a boat propeller that severed both legs and one arm, leaving her near death
(Vernoff & Ornelas, 2009).

Clara remains hospitalized for several days to recover, during which her
health deteriorates when an abscess (a pocket of infection) develops in her
small bowel, probably from "something she picked up in the water" during
the boating accident that took her limbs. Clara's doctors urgently recommend
immediate surgery to address the abscess, but Clara quickly refuses, repeating several times, "No. Not another surgery." Wanting to give Clara space and
time to process this news, Clara's primary doctor, Dr. Bailey, steps out of the
room, but not before quietly instructing the two residents in the room to
order preoperative antibiotics and book an operating room, a move suggesting
that Dr. Bailey assumes Clara will come around to the idea of this necessary
GI surgery.

However, as soon as Dr. Bailey is gone, Clara turns to the residents,
clearly panicking over the thought of another surgery, and asks, "What are the
options? Can you give me drugs?" The residents reassure Clara that the surgery would be simple and straightforward, but she pushes them for a "worst-
case" prognosis. After a hesitant pause and exchange of glances between the
residents, one warily replies, "Well, worst case is that we'd have to take out a
part of our colon and give you a colostomy bag."

Without hesitation, Clara begins to plead with the residents, seeming both
repulsed and confused by the idea that she could wake up from surgery with
an ostomy. "Colostomy bag? A poo bag outside of your body?" Clara's initial
panic and rejection of the surgery seem only solidified by the mere thought of
an ostomy. Thinking aloud about this distressing news and implying to viewers that ostomies are only for older people, Clara then shares that her "granddad" had an ostomy and questions how someone so young, like herself, could
possibly be at risk of needing one. Both residents attempt to emphasize that
a colostomy is really only a small possibility, but neither attempts to reframe

Clara's response by offering that an ostomy might actually *save* Clara's life, nor do they mention that worldwide, thousands of people, young and old, live happy, successful lives with ostomies. Instead, the residents remind her that the infection will kill her if she does not have the surgery. The scene ends as Clara firmly refuses the necessary, but potentially ostomy-creating, surgery.

Viewers are brought back to Clara's story when the attending physician, Dr. Bailey, angrily confronts one of the residents in a hospital hallway, demanding to know why the resident is "trying to kill" Clara. A short, heated exchange reveals Dr. Bailey felt that, in effect, the resident has served Clara a death sentence by merely mentioning the risk of an ostomy because it has led her to refuse surgery. Dr. Bailey further explains that she certainly would not have told Clara about the risk of a colostomy. Even more, Dr. Bailey laments that she would not have shared details about a potential ostomy with any patient without careful consideration, which implies that an ostomy is something so feared by patients that it requires unique rhetorical planning or complete obfuscation. The impression to viewers: obviously a more experienced physician would know better than to mention so bluntly or haphazardly the terrifying possibility of an ostomy.

The conflation in Clara's storyline between ostomies and death, specifically that death is perceived by patients as preferable to living with an ostomy, is both significant and familiar. Indeed, disability studies scholars have dubbed this way of thinking about disability "the personal tragedy model," in which life with a disability is inherently and always tragic. According to the tragedy model, living with a disability is considered antithetical to a positive, happy, full life. In other words, better to be dead than disabled (see Reynolds, 2017; Swain & French, 2000).

This tragedy framing is so pervasive that its appearance in this *Grey's Anatomy* episode is nearly unremarkable. As disability studies scholars John Swain and Sally French (2000) explained, "the idea that disabled people cannot be happy, or enjoy an adequate quality of life" (p. 572), is not only "dominant" and "prevalent" in Western public culture; it is "infused throughout media representations, language, cultural beliefs, research, policy and professional practice" (p. 573). Indeed, this *better dead than disabled* narrative is the core of Clara's storyline. Embedded within the exchange between Dr. Bailey and the resident physicians who mention an ostomy to Clara is this worn tragedy model: either the potential of needing an ostomy is itself a death sentence *or* being dead would be better than having an ostomy.

It's not until Clara has nearly succumbed to the infection that she not so much consents to the potentially ostomy-inducing surgery but passively allows the nursing staff to take her to the operating room. The infection has escalated such that Clara needs to have part of her small bowel resected, but the small possibility of receiving an ostomy is actually avoided. When viewers next see Clara, she has recovered from the GI surgery and is preparing to take her first steps with her new prosthetic leg. An ostomy isn't mentioned again.

Just weeks later in season 6, ostomies make yet another appearance in *Grey's* (Cragg & Rimes, 2010). This time, a character named Mary arrives at the hospital to undergo surgery to have her ostomy reversed. Like Clara, Mary is being cared for by Dr. Bailey, and viewers meet Mary for the first time as the two of them, along with another physician, Dr. Percy, discuss Mary's surgery. In the scene, Dr. Bailey and Dr. Percy deliver "bad" news to Mary; she is ineligible for her reversal surgery that day because her red-blood-cell counts are low. Mary, clearly frustrated, protests:

> Do you know how long I've been living with a colostomy bag? A bag of poop is attached to me. Do you know what that's like? It's gross. It's truly the grossest thing I've ever had to deal with.

In response, Dr. Bailey calmly offers that Dr. Percy will give Mary a blood transfusion to hopefully improve her cell counts and enable the surgery to take place. Dr. Bailey ends their conversation by promising they'll soon revisit the timing of Mary's surgery: "tomorrow, we'll see if we can help lose the poop bag." Viewers don't hear about Mary, her "poop bag," or her surgery again for several episodes until she returns for takedown surgery and unexpectedly dies from unrelated organ failure caused by the anesthesia.

Like the ostomy enacted in the Tips and the Cincinnati PD's campaigns, the ostomy and ostomy experience staged in Clara and Mary's storylines is highly negative, even abhorrent. Similarly, too, both stories stage the ostomy as a worst-case scenario. Clara's potential ostomy is literally described as the worst-case scenario, and Mary's actual ostomy is staged as a gross nightmare she'd like to end as soon as possible. The stories in these episodes fixate on fearing and resisting ostomies through avoidance (Clara's surgery refusal) and reversal (Mary's desire for reversal surgery). Through these stories, either the lived experiences with ostomies are predicted to be deeply undesirable or the lived experiences are stated as such.

Additionally, Clara's and Mary's storylines highlight one of stigma's most significant dimensions. Stigma is not just enacted by what is explicitly said or visibly done; stigma is perhaps most insidious when it is enacted through what is *not* said or done. In Clara's and Mary's stories, stigma is explicitly manifested through comments about poop bags and stereotypes about the elderly, but it is also emerges through what is left unsaid, unclarified, unseen by the character's lines and actions. For instance, there are several opportunities throughout Clara's story in which characters could have complicated the idea of ostomies as the worst case. In the dialogue between Clara and the residents who first mention ostomies, a line could have been included that clarified the idea that any ostomy would be Clara's worst-case outcome. For instance, one of the residents might have explained that while an ostomy may actually be considered the "worst case," only because ostomy surgery is invasive and significant. Or the show might have incorporated an additional scene in which Dr. Bailey visits Clara to follow up on the conversation with the residents and explain that an ostomy is a lifesaving procedure that could enable Clara to live a meaningful and positive life. Similarly, the show's writers might have included a small rebuttal to Mary's comments about poop bags and the ostomy being the "grossest thing" she's ever experienced. A simple line from one of the physicians like "I'm sorry you've had such negative experiences; I wish we'd done more to help you live more successfully with your ostomy" could have encouraged viewers to think in more complex ways about ostomies and to see life with an ostomy as multidimensional and something that can evolve beyond tragedy. These proposed suggestions would have been relatively small and simple additions that would not have otherwise altered the storylines; however, the show didn't complicate the ostomy narrative running through Clara's and Mary's stories, which demonstrates just how rhetorically invasive a single ostomy story is within mainstream public culture. Too, these stories, in context with their millions of viewers, further cement that single story in public culture. Stigmatization of ostomies is ultimately reinforced through Mary and Clara and their connection to this single story repeatedly told about ostomies, disabilities, or other embodied experiences.

Staging Stigma through Fear

Although both Mary's and Clara's stories are of course fictional, they align with Julia's and the Cincinnati PD's stories. The similarity across these stories illustrates how pervasive negative ostomy stories are in American public life and how individual ostomy stories, like the four described in this chapter, sediment into a single ostomy story. All four stories enact the ostomy as a worst-case scenario through negative experiences focused on leaks, fear, isolation, unattractiveness, and disgust. These public ostomy stories cohere to create a single, consistent ostomy story that figures all ostomy experiences as negative. Additionally, they consistently draw on negative experiences as the primary rhetorical strategy to connect with audiences, whether for enter-tainment (*Grey's Anatomy*) or for public health purposes (Tips from Former Smokers and the Cincinnati PD).

Importantly, I do not mean to suggest that any of the experiences for-warded in these stories are invalid or not based in real experiences, including even the fictionalized stories on *Grey's Anatomy*. My goal in tracking these stories is not to debunk them[3] but, instead, to listen to the practices within the stories that shape how ostomies are made to mean. In an interview about her participation in Tips, Julia explained, "I shared my story with the Tips from Former Smokers campaign because now I know firsthand how danger-ous smoking can be. My hope is that my message will get smokers to quit, for themselves and their families" (Fight Colorectal Cancer, 2015). It seems that Julia shared her story authentically in the sincere hope that it would help oth-ers avoid life-threatening experiences with cancer. My analysis suggests that Julia's story had more complex outcomes than convincing viewers to avoid smoking; however, it's unfair and harmful to villainize Julia and her lived experiences. Additionally, it would be inappropriate and inaccurate for me to suggest that Julia's negative ostomy experiences were entirely unique; I've spoken with many ostomates who deal with leaks, embarrassment, and other challenges. The point here is that Julia's experiences need not be invalidated by an analysis that identifies the practices within these stories that, when cir-culated in the public sphere, stage stigma.

Furthermore, research has demonstrated that leaks are a primary con-cern for many ostomates and that the fear of leaks does indeed push many to stay home, where they can more comfortably navigate issues, like leaks, that could occur with their ostomies (Davis et al., 2011). I discussed Julia's case with many of my interview participants, most of whom critiqued her story and the Tips campaign (which I discuss at length in chapter 4). However, in response to excerpts from Julia's video, one participant, Cade, emphatically said, "Yes. She's exactly right." Cade further explained that though his overall outlook and long-term experiences with his ostomy differed from Julia's, his experiences immediately after his ostomy surgery were very similar to hers.

Julia and Cade remind us, much like the historical stories that open this chapter, that life with an ostomy does come with challenges and often undesirable experiences. My goal, therefore, in examining these stories is to not to prove them wrong but to understand the potential motivations

---

3. Here I am echoing Kelly Pender's (2018) work in *Being at Genetic Risk*, in which she discusses the consequences of debunking and how praxiographic approaches can address the issues that emerge from rhetorical debunking (pp. 72–75).

and rhetorical consequences of the single, negative ostomy story. It is these challenges and undesirable experiences that public ostomy stories have perpetually highlighted as inherent and central to life with an ostomy. Moreover, negative experiences are featured as the *only* experiences enabled by an ostomy. Across the public stories presented in this chapter, the overarching message communicated is that undergoing ostomy surgery and living with an ostomy is definitively a worst-case scenario that is entirely undesirable and that should be prevented by avoiding risky behaviors, if possible. In other words, the takeaway repeatedly stressed to audiences is that life with an ostomy is the worst.

This message tells us something important about the kinds of assumptions that went into creating and telling these stories. Public ostomy stories, like those we've seen in this chapter, both assume and establish a visceral public—that is, a public defined "by intense, shared feeling over a perceived threat of boundary violations" (Winderman et al., 2019, p. 115). In these cases, the perceived threat is an ostomy. If the public does not already fear the ostomy or if the public is not moved to share in the fear promoted by these stories, the stories lose much of their persuasiveness. In other words, the rhetorical gravitas of these negative ostomy stories individually and collectively is supported by the "configuration" of visceral public(s) (Winderman et al., 2019). For instance, Julia's story rhetorically heightens the (perceived) intense threat created by ostomies to convince people to give up smoking. Fear is central to the success of this strategy. That is, Julia's video banks on a public that either intensely fears ostomies already or will fear them readily after listening to Julia's story.

This rhetorical use of fear directly catalyzes stigma. As Coleman (1986) suggested, fear is central to stigmatization. This certainly seems to be the case in these public ostomy stories. Stigma tied to fear of ostomies circulates within the rhetorical ecology that enables these stories to be impactful. In turn, these stories individually and collectively assume listeners will share in the negative feelings enacted toward ostomies while heightening those negative feelings through exclusively negative ostomy stories. Specifically, fear functions to sustain visceral publics and consequently enact stigma in four key ways: (1) rhetorical omissions that obscure richer understandings of ostomies and isolate ostomies as inherently negative, (2) discussions of leaks and leakiness, (3) disability stereotypes, and (4) fear as a motivator for action. In the sections that follow, I trace each of these strategies within the public ostomy stories, identifying how they rhetorically stage the ostomy as a worst-case scenario and, in doing so, elicit visceral publics and enact stigma.

Rhetorical Omissions

Perhaps as rhetorically significant as what each of these public stories says is what each story doesn't say. Such omissions have profound rhetorical purpose in that they reinforce the pre-existing negative single ostomy story. That is, these stories assume that people listen to or view them with the preconceived notion that ostomies are tragic, gross, and terrible, or, at the very least, that public(s) will be easily persuaded to see ostomies in those ways. Therefore, the public ostomy story shared, whether by the CDC, the Cincinnati PD, or *Grey's Anatomy*, is designed to sync with the well-worn tread of a single ostomy story, like a record needle finding the groove in a vinyl. Each story depends on visceral public united by a single ostomy story and negative, visceral emotions evoked by that single story.

One illustration of the assumption of both a single story and an attendant visceral public across these stories is the rhetorical decision to not define *ostomy*. Not defining an ostomy suggests one of two things. Either these public rhetors, whether writers of *Grey's Anatomy* scripts or a local police officer, expected their listeners to have some working knowledge of ostomies, *or* writers of these stories assumed that an actual definition of an ostomy was not needed and that listeners could infer all they need to know about ostomies through these stories.

To be fair, Julia's story does provide a definition, though it is somewhat suspect. In the video's opening moments, Julia explains that having a colostomy means that your bowel movements "go into a bag through a hole in your stomach." Of course, this definition very well may be how Julia describes the experience of having an ostomy, and I do not mean to discredit her lived experiences. However, medically speaking, Julia's definition is misleading. A colostomy is not a hole in the stomach; it is an opening in the colon. Regardless, Julia's simplified characterization of ostomies supposes that this colloquial definition is sufficient for the context and purpose of the video. The goal of the video, after all, is not to educate viewers about ostomies so much as it is to encourage viewers to be so repulsed by ostomies that they quit smoking. The characterization of ostomies as a "hole in your stomach" through which excrements "go into a bag," in combination with Julia's seemingly bitter tone, impactfully simplifies (perhaps even stereotypes) ostomies and promotes negative connotations of their purpose.

This misstep in definition might seem insignificant to those outside the ostomy and chronic GI disease communities; however, it was and is highly important to many ostomates. When I asked interview participants generally about Julia's story, many took issue specifically with the ostomy definition provided in it. As one participant, Shalane, stated, "Clearly, [Julia] doesn't know what she even had. It's not a hole in your stomach." Shalane went on to say, in what I understood as an empathetic tone, that Julia appeared to be either not educated at all about her ostomy or misinformed. For Shalane, this was especially significant because she felt that much of the stigma around ostomies stems from such misinformation and lack of awareness.

In addition to definitional issues, these stories largely overlook or de-emphasize the conditions that lead to the need for an ostomy. This omission subsequently works to rhetorically spotlight the ostomy itself. Although two of the stories rhetorically operationalize ostomies in service of broader public health goals—decrease smoking and prevent gun violence—the ostomy and negative ostomy experiences become the focal point. Rather than emphasize that one in twenty-three men and one in twenty-four women will develop colorectal cancer (American Cancer Society, 2020) or stress that over 100 people die in the US each day from firearms (CDC, 2020c), these stories target ostomies. "What I *hated the most* was the colostomy bag," as Julia puts it. Similarly, in the *Grey's Anatomy* episodes, Clara is brutally injured by a boat propeller, but the climax of her story is her close call with getting an ostomy, and when Mary's bloodwork requires that her ostomy-takedown surgery be postponed, her story tells viewers that just one more day with an ostomy is too long. Each and all of these stories neglect to offer viewers richer context about ostomies that would enable and even encourage viewers to understand the complex, often life-threatening experiences that can lead to an ostomy. In doing so, they fail to communicate that ostomies, though challenging at times, can be lifesaving. The rhetorical gaps that audiences are expected to fill and the matter-of-fact way in which each of these public stories expects negative feelings about ostomies to be self-evident illustrate the presumption of a visceral public.

Leaks

Centralizing bodily leaks, particularly leaking fecal matter, is immensely rhetorically powerful in ostomy stories, as illustrated in the four stories presented in this chapter. The connection between ostomies and feces is perhaps the most rhetorically significant dimension of ostomies. Fear and stigma regarding ostomies, leaks, and uncontrolled feces profoundly animate the "intense, shared feelings" that unite a visceral public (Johnson, 2016). Evidence of the invocation of a visceral public is most easily seen in the ways these public ostomy stories overlook specificity and assume audience familiarity. For example, Julia's Tips video is a mere thirty seconds, and her podcast clip is just over a minute, which suggests that Julia and the CDC were counting heavily on audiences' previous knowledge, assumptions, and feelings about ostomies and ostomy experiences. When Julia says "I certainly don't want to tell you about having a colostomy bag . . . I don't want to talk about emptying or changing that thing," she doesn't (have to) explain why she wouldn't want to open this discussion. Viewers, it is presumed, would be able to fill in these gaps; they would understand why Julia wouldn't want to openly talk about "that thing." Ideally, viewers would even empathize with Julia, seeing themselves in her story and using that identification to quit smoking. Similarly, the Cincinnati PD didn't feel the need to explain why an ostomy would prevent "get[tting] a girl's attention" (Warren, 2013). Their teen audience would recognize the implied message: an ostomy is inherently gross and undesirable, and ostomates don't get the girl. The negative comments and experiences showcased in these stories succeed rhetorically because they are circulated in a culture of ostomy stigma.

Ostomy stigma, as well as these public ostomy stories, is rhetorically fueled by this social fear regarding leaks and leaking feces. Julia's narrative, for instance, taps into rampant "social unease" or "collective disturbance" (Turner, 2003, p. 4) regarding bodily fluids and leaks when she reports being unable to leave the house for fear of her ostomy "coming loose" and "smelling" (CDC, 2015a). Further, both characters on *Grey's Anatomy*, Clara and Mary, refer, with a tinge of repulsion, to ostomies as "poop" or "poo" bags. Mary also emphasizes disgust at having to wear the "grossest thing ever," a "poop bag"—a rhetorical move that signals to the audience that ostomies require a disturbing and unnatural proximity to misplaced feces (Cragg & Rimes, 2010). As Mary Douglas (1966) might describe, poop worn in a bag is "matter out of place." In both Julia's and Mary's stories case, emphasis is made on the leaky, out-of-place nature of ostomies, be it the leaky potential of the ostomy bag itself or the leaky nature of a stoma that involuntarily expels human waste into a "poop bag" worn on a person.

Moreover, "that which oozes or secrets from the human body," Turner (2003) argued, causes "public embarrassment" and is "regarded as dangerous" because of fear of "infection, disease, destruction" (pp. 3–4). These public ostomy stories exemplify this by showcasing experiences with "bodily betrayals" of uncontrolled ostomy-bag leaks and rerouted digestive systems that force people "to shun public spaces" to avoid the threat of embarrassment (Turner, 2003, p. 4). Leaks thus precipitate stigmatization and social isolation. It is not surprising, then, that as Julia and the CDC collaborated to script Julia's Tips materials, her fears about and experiences with leaks became a focal point of her story. This makes sense given that her story, alongside the other stories in the campaign, was designed, after all, to show the long-term health risks of smoking as imminent threats that can be mitigated by giving up tobacco. Similarly, the other public ostomy stories in this chapter rhetorically exploit stigma surrounding ostomies vis-à-vis leaks to advance other goals.

Disability Stereotypes

Additionally, experiences with disfigurement and disability appear frequently in these public ostomy stories, particularly in Clara's story and the Cincinnati PD comments. Just as leakiness incites concerns over bodily boundaries and autonomy, disability is an "attribution of corporeal deviance" that is perceived as dangerous and perverse (Garland-Thomson, 1997, p. 6). Consequently, stigmatizing ostomy stories commonly draw on disability stereotypes and the personal tragedy model. For instance, the Cincinnati PD visualizes the fictional ostomate "limping down Warsaw Avenue." To be sure, undergoing ostomy surgery does not typically impact the long-term ability to walk, yet the ostomy experience imagined by the Cincinnati PD threatens the abilities of the entire body. Put another way, the ostomy's disabling effect is diffuse. According to the Cincinnati police, an ostomy doesn't just refigure your GI tract; it refigures your entire embodiment and all its capabilities. Such rhetoric stigmatizes by "cast[ing] disability as [a] burden" that is not easily accommodated individually or socially (Wilson, 2002, p. 73). In addition to the physical disability portrayed via limping, the ostomate in the Cincinnati PD's story is socially disabled because, as was argued, limping down the street with an ostomy is no way to gain attention or attraction. This connection established between disability, stigma, and attractiveness aligns with Coleman's (1986) contention that "stigmatized people are not expected to be intelligent, attractive, or upper class" (p. 220). Ostomates, as disabled and stigmatized, are not expected to be, nor perhaps even capable of being, attractive, according to the Cincinnati PD's story.

Moreover, Clara's storyline in *Grey's Anatomy* also taps into disability stereotypes when Clara assumes that ostomies are only for older people and thus deploys that assumption as a reason to reject a surgery that could result in an ostomy. Specifically, Clara expresses confusion about how an ostomy, or what she repeatedly calls "a poo bag," could be her worst-case scenario because her "granddad had one of those" (Vernoff & D'Elia, 2009). This dialogue indicates a disconnect in logic for Clara—how could an ostomy be a possibility for her as a young person? Although she also indicates concern about undergoing another surgery (remember, her character had previously endured several surgeries related to a boating accident), a primary reason Clara rejects the surgery is her understanding that ostomies are poo bags, only necessary for older people. For Clara, the stereotype that ostomies are only for elderly people echoes the "common stereotypes about old age," including beliefs that "older people" are "sick" and "disabled" (Sheets, 2005, p. 38). "Aging is disabling" because it is marked by a decrease in control, namely a decrease in the ability to prevent embodied decline that inevitably comes with age (Wendell, 1989, p. 108. Clara's story underscores this connection between age and disability. Not only does Clara express fear and confusion; her refusal to undergo the surgery suggests that she fully rejects the possibility that she could become like her granddad, disabled prematurely by an ostomy.

These disability stereotypes are rhetorically dependent on enthymematic arguments that position life with a disability as, without exception, negative and automatically tragic. In Clara's story, in particular, death is suggested to be better than the disabled life that is assumed to certainly accompany an ostomy. The rhetorical conflation of ostomy, disability, and death is highly effective with a visceral public audience that is (problematically) incited and motivated by negative feelings toward all three.

Fear as a Motivator

While fear ripples through all these public ostomy stories, its rhetorical work as a motivator is particularly significant and helps explain why the single public ostomy story is especially powerful in seemingly unrelated rhetorical contexts like antismoking or anti-gun-violence campaigns. As I outlined in earlier sections of this chapter, Johnson (2016) has demonstrated that fear as a visceral feeling can be used to rationalize action. Similarly, Sara Ahmed (2013) has argued that fear motivates action, specifically as it is directed at other bodies to help us establish and reinforce separation from what we fear. In this way, fear is rooted in a primal response in which a fight-or-flight reaction kicks in to create literal distance from a perceived threat. In the case of ostomies and public stories (and potentially other stigmatized entities), fear is manifested through portrayals of both perceived physical (i.e., becoming physically disabled) and social threats (i.e., being rendered an unattractive social outcast who is stuck at home). These perceived threats and their potential to invoke fear and motivate action are perhaps precisely why the CDC and the Cincinnati PD selected ostomies as part of their campaigns. The stories presented in this chapter demonstrate that collective visceral feelings, particularly fear, can be rhetorically used to motivate behavioral change and intensify dramatic effect.

Importantly, it is not my intention to suggest that the rhetorical use of fear is inherently negative or unethical. Millions of people in the US smoke despite the well-documented and serious health consequences, and a 200 percent increase in juvenile shooting victims motivated the Cincinnati PD's campaign (Warren, 2013). These campaigns attempted to use fear to motivate audiences to quit smoking and to avoid gun violence. Goals that, decontextualized, are worthwhile, no doubt. However, as Guttman and Salmon (2004) have posed:

> How does one reconcile the use of persuasive appeals that on the one hand scare people regarding potential hazards, and thus raise motivation to avoid it, but may, on the other hand, present a negative image of those who have the disease? (p. 547)

Although I endorse efforts to reduce smoking and gun violence, given the public retaliation each of these public stories received,[4] primarily from the ostomy and IBD communities, it seems critical to question the motivation and decision to rhetorically leverage ostomies in these stories and to examine the (unintended) consequences of sharing these particular ostomy stories as part of these campaigns.

Upon its release, Julia's story joined the ranks of the highly successful Tips campaign. That is, by the time Julia joined the campaign, nearly three years after its original launch, Tips had been deemed a massive success. Between 2012 and 2015 the campaign reportedly resulted in "approximately 522,000 sustained quits" among US adult smokers (Murphy-Hoefer et al., 2018). This success, as the CDC itself points out, can largely be attributed to the (rhetorical) use of fear within the campaign. In the CDC's (2020a) words:

> Hard-hitting media campaigns have been proven to raise awareness about the dangers of smoking and to motivate smokers to quit. Many studies have shown that ads carrying strong graphic and emotional messages about health consequences are more effective than other forms of advertising, such as humorous or emotionally neutral advertisements. Given the large scientific evidence base supporting this approach, CDC uses graphic and emotional advertisements in its Tips from Former Smokers (Tips) campaign.

---

4. Chapter 4 addresses these public criticisms and protests at length. See also Hafner (2009), Rund (2015), and Warren (2013).

The CDC certainly did its homework in designing this campaign. Research across disciplines including marketing, health communication, and public health has demonstrated the effectiveness of scare-tactic strategies in health-related messaging. Since the 1950s fear has been considered a successful strategy for warranting changes in health behavior (Janis & Feshbach, 1953). As one public health researcher wrote, "a large number of health promotion campaigns are based on a simple strategy: get behind people with a big stick (lots of threat and fear) in the hope that this will drive them in the desired direction" (Soames Job, 1988, p. 163). Grounded in the idea that fear is highly persuasive, scare tactics have become a staple in decades of health campaigns. Fear- and disgust-inducing messages are not only more likely to capture the attention of audiences but also more likely to be remembered and, most importantly, to elicit action or to change behavior (Cho & Witte, 2005; Janis & Feshbach, 1953; Leshner et al., 2009). If the goal is to show people why they should stop engaging in a particular behavior—be it smoking, eating processed foods, drinking alcohol, or texting and driving—then highlighting the "terrifying" consequences of such actions appears to be a productive (though not necessarily ethical) way to do it (Leshner et al., 2009). Rhetoricians will easily recognize this as pathos in its prime.

Fear-based health messaging typically looks something like this: a threat or fear appeal is presented to the audience through graphic imagery and/or disgust-inducing messages. These "persuasive" messages are "designed to scare people by describing the terrible things that will happen to them if they do not do what the message recommends" (Witte, 1992, p. 329). Such appeals need to be more than well-crafted marketing messages, though. They must elicit embodied reactions in viewers, making the risk or threat feel real and imminent (Cho & Witte, 2005, p, 483). In other words, for fear appeals to stage a threat or enact risk, the viewer must identify with the threat itself or with another person who has already been affected—that is, the viewer must be able to envision a future version of themselves that is affected by the threat. As Burke (1969) might summarize: "Here is perhaps the simplest case of persuasion. You persuade a man insofar as you can talk his language by speech, gesture, tonality, order, image, attitude, idea, identifying your ways with his" (p. 158). This identification enables the fear appeal to work. The Tips campaign encourages viewers to identify with a variety of threats: COPD, premature birth and pregnancy complications, death—and, in Julia's case, a colostomy bag. Emery et al. (2014) explained, "The Tips campaign contained high levels of fear appeals, represented by graphic descriptions of health effects such as cancer, facial damage, amputation, and hair loss" (p. 282). By presenting these health effects to viewers, the Tips campaign strategically stages the smoking body as at risk of such threats and encourages viewers to feel themselves as potentially at risk of such threats too.

No doubt, the CDC wanted to ensure that Tips would successfully produce the desired results (decrease in smoking) and understood that identifying the right strategy was key in actually affecting health-related behavioral change, especially when it comes to a behavior as addicting as smoking. Because fear messaging has been empirically proved to work, the CDC curated a series of "real stories" that would effectively scare viewers to give up smoking and each of these stories, including Julia's (2020a). And, as a result, the Tips campaign was associated with "a 12% relative increase in quit attempts" in its first year alone (McAfee et al., 2013, p. 2003) and these success rates have been sustained in the years since (Murphy-Hoefer et al., 2018). As the CDC (2020b) summarizes on the "Impacts & Results" page of the Tips campaign website:

> Scientific studies have shown that hard-hitting media campaigns are effective in helping people quit smoking. Study results suggest that emotionally evocative tobacco education media campaigns featuring graphic images of the health effects of smoking can increase quitline calls and website visits and that these campaigns' effects decrease rapidly once they are discontinued.

Indeed, the CDC's deployment of "emotionally evocative" messages and "graphic images" worked toward a worthwhile goal, considering that smoking takes nearly 480,000 American lives each year and is the leading preventable cause of death and disease in the US. Julia's message certainly aligned with the overall Tips campaign mission to share the "hard-hitting" realities of smoking.

It seems less likely that the other public stories in this chapter deliberately used fear messaging as a rhetorical strategy in the same way the CDC's did. However, that isn't to say that fear wasn't evoked toward a specific end. In the other stories, the use of fear appears to be more intuitive and intended for heightened emotional and rhetorical impact. The *Grey's Anatomy* storylines and the Cincinnati PD's campaign attempted to rhetorically conjure fear within these ostomy stories when they, like Julia's story, foreground embodied experiences with leaks, disability, isolation, and social outcasting. Across these stories, viewers are encouraged to see a frightening future—stuck at home, worrying about a leaky, smelly hole in their stomach[5] covered with an ostomy bag. The ostomy life staged in these stories is grim, which makes sense given their motivations and goals. This is not to say that public health messages of

---

5. I am deliberately invoking the language used in Julia's video here, which incorrectly describes ostomy as a "hole in the stomach."

the Tips campaign and the Cincinnati PD's efforts, nor the supposedly low-stakes entertainment content of the *Grey's* episode, warrant the staging of stigma and fear regarding ostomies. Nonetheless, it is helpful to contextualize these negative public ostomy stories within their broader contexts, intentions, and rationales. This fear messaging ultimately engenders the visceral public audiences that these stories rely on.

Credibility Enhanced through Stigma

These four rhetorical elements—omissions, leaks, disability stereotypes, and fear—whether used in isolation or in combination throughout these stories, work to effect particular outcomes (i.e., don't smoke; don't mess with guns) and responses (i.e., be afraid of ostomies, smoking, guns, disabilities). Importantly, too, each rhetorical move is tied to specific practices or experiences, whether it be what an ostomy is (definitions of ostomies), what an ostomy does (leaks, isolates), or what kinds of emotional or embodied responses ostomies invoke for those who have them (fear, disgust, disability). Together, these rhetorical moves and their intended goals both engage and configure visceral public audiences, which sheds light on the rhetoricity of stigma. Specifically, stigmatization is enacted in and through the consistently negative practices that are invoked in each of these stories, which build on the single ostomy-story template that figures ostomies as negative, undesirable surgeries, technologies, and ways to live. Praxiographic analysis of these stories that focuses on these practices tells us important things not only about the rhetoricity of ostomies within the public sphere but also about the larger rhetorical implications of stigma itself. In particular, stigma has been theorized as a rhetorical black mark. To be stigmatized is to be deemed arhetorical[6] at worst, untrustworthy and uncredible at best. However, these individual ostomies stories and the broader single ostomy story complicate stigma's relationship to credibility in a few key ways.

First, the staging of ostomies as worst-case scenarios through these stories is made powerful by the credibility of the sources advancing their negative ostomy messages. The Centers for Disease Control and Prevention. A police department. A highly revered TV show. These are the rhetors that promoted negative ostomy stories. Overall, these are credible, reliable authorities. Each source was advantaged by pre-established credibility. The CDC, after all, is one of the US's top health agencies. It's no surprise that viewers would trust

---

6. For a complete discussion on arhetoricity, see Yergeau (2018).

information branded under its umbrella. With stigma as part of the rhetorical context, the visceral public audiences of each of these stories were prepared to believe and agree with the negative ostomy stories presented. Making these cases all the more powerful is their public and, in two of the cases, mass media, impact.

For example, by 2010 and long before the end of its sixth season, *Grey's Anatomy* had solidified its place in American popular culture. *Grey's* has boasted a steady average of over fifteen million viewers per episode since its start in 2005. Known for its dramatic storylines and love triangles, the show provides a fictional window into the world of medicine. Though the show is based in real Western medicine, *Grey's* is not intended to teach audiences the intricacies of neonatal surgery or the diagnostic criteria for fungal infections. Regardless of its intended entertainment purposes, research has found that viewers often consume the show as a form of "infotainment"—information + entertainment—rather than as purely fictional content. In fact, research has demonstrated that viewers tend to trust the show as realistic, perceive the doctors as credible, and absorb what they believe to be factual medical information presented in the show (Chung, 2014; Quick, 2009; Quick et al., 2014). "The more people watched the show," one study found, "the more realistic they perceived" it to be (Quick, 2009, p. 50).

For these reasons, when the show included Clara's and Mary's stories, there was a lot on the line. Millions of viewers saw Clara's episode, many of whom probably had little prior exposure to ostomies. If, as research has suggested, these viewers took Clara's storyline seriously and trusted the credibility of the doctors who treated her, what would they have learned? For starters, they would have heard an ostomy described as a "poo bag" several times, and as something elderly people need. They might have learned that doctors, or at least the ones they trust on *Grey's*, think that ostomies are a "worst-case scenario." And, based on the exchange between Dr. Bailey and the resident, they might have walked away thinking that just talking about an ostomy with a patient is an attempt "to kill" the patient (Dr. Bailey's words) because an ostomy is so horrifying that the mere thought would dissuade a patient from lifesaving surgery. These takeaways, of course, require some logical leaps, though leaps that *Grey's* audiences have been shown likely to make.

Similarly, the Tips and Cincinnati PD campaigns were designed to reach broader public audiences. Obviously, the Cincinnati police case did not reach nearly the national scale of the Tips campaign or *Grey's Anatomy* episodes, but it was part of a citywide effort. The PD's efforts were thwarted by public backlash that occurred too early to show whether the campaign itself was successful. However, the choice to use a negative ostomy story in a citywide public health campaign suggests that the Cincinnati PD believed in its potential to be highly effective. The Tips campaign, on the other hand, has reached millions, if not billions, of viewers. Its success rates alone demonstrate this. According to the CDC's (2020b) own research, between 2012 and 2018 "more than 16.4 million people who smoke have attempted to quit and approximately one million have successfully quit because of the Tips campaign." These success rates point to the campaign's wide-reaching effect.

It wasn't just the CDC that was able to stage the ostomy as a worst-case scenario. Nor did the Cincinnati PD simply make up their ostomy story at random. In both cases these larger, trusted, public sources relied on actual people living with ostomies and their experiences to advance these negative ostomy stories and affiliated campaigns. The CDC strongly emphasize that Tips campaign participants are real people sharing their actual stories and experiences, just as the Cincinnati PD tied their ostomy story to the gunshot-wound victim they met while researching for their antigun campaign. The fact that ostomates—who are at risk themselves of being stigmatized—were perceived as credible sources in these examples is especially important to note.

In fact, Julia's credibility complicates previous understandings of the rhetorical impact of stigma. Rhetoricians, particularly in RHM, have theorized stigma's "rhetorically disabling effect" on rhetors (Johnson, 2010; Miller, 2019; Molloy, 2019; Prendergast, 2001). Such work has primarily focused on people with mental illnesses, whose actions and discursive practices are perceived as unintentional or uncontrollable, and therefore as nonrhetorical or arhetorical (Johnson, 2010; Molloy, 2019; Prendergast, 2001; Pryal, 2010). Specifically, this work has demonstrated how stigma surrounding mental illnesses leads to "rhetorical foreclosure . . . that permanently arrest[s] one's rhetorical ethos at the moment of imprint" (Johnson, 2010, p. 464). Put another way, stigma engenders "ethos deficit, damage, or loss" (Molloy, 2015, p. 160). For example, Molloy's 2019 book *Rhetorical Ethos in Health and Medicine: Patient Credibility, Stigma, and Misdiagnosis* richly explores how people living with mental illness are stripped of credibility and rhetorical ability in clinical encounters, as they are repeatedly told that their symptoms are "all in their head." As I argued in chapter 1, one of stigma's most profound rhetorical effects is its silencing power that demands stigmatized individuals or groups conform to cultural *nomos* (Johnson, 2010) or otherwise make themselves invisible.

In contrast, it seems that ostomy stigma actually enables the public stories of some rhetors like Julia. Whereas participants in Molloy's (2019) research needed to "recuperate" their credibility and agency, Julia, despite having a stigmatized condition, is deemed highly credible from the start. She expends little rhetorical effort to establish her credibility other than to self-identify as an insider of the smoking community. Notably, she does not self-identify as a part of the ostomy community, which not only helps separate her from her ostomy and ostomy experiences but encourages further aversion to ostomies. Mostly, Julia establishes her ethos by telling a familiar ostomy story, one that, as I've already pointed out, audiences are prepared to accept through previous cultural knowledge, assumptions, and stereotypes. Similar moves are made in the Cincinnati PD example, though on a much smaller scale.

Rather than be rhetorically foreclosed, Julia is granted credibility because she does not stray from the negative ostomy story that audiences and the CDC presumed to be the only ostomy story. If alternative ostomy experiences were considered, even momentarily, it seems they were deemed so rare that Julia's experience could speak universally of the ostomy experience. The ostomy as a worst-case scenario aligns readily with the stories, beliefs, and cultural conditions that enable ostomy stigma in the first place. Exploring public ostomy stories like Julia's suggests that, in some cases, stigma can rhetorically enable stigmatized rhetors, so long as the rhetor plays into the stigma. In this way, public ostomy stories like Julia's or the Cincinnati PD's not only depend on but reinforce ostomy stigma as they lean into ostomy stereotypes and present ostomy experience as categorically negative.

Perhaps the most compelling manifestation of the credibility of these public ostomy stories is the responses they received. For each story explored in this chapter, hundreds if not thousands of tweets, Facebook posts, signatures on petitions, blogs, and articles passionately reject it. As I mentioned in chapter 1, Julia's commercial alone generated a 10,000-plus-signature petition. As one petition against Julia's commercial put it, "The situation is especially serious precisely because the CDC, a trusted source of important medical information, has spread the message" (Burns et al., 2015). Similarly, the Cincinnati PD story was protested in articles published by HuffPost and Uncover Ostomy, and through a petition garnering over 2,600 signatures. Angered members of the ostomy and chronic GI communities also targeted Grey's Anatomy for Mary's and Clara's episodes. Individual branches of the United Ostomy Association of America support groups wrote letters to Grey's producers, and a 400-plus-member Facebook group called "Shame on Grey's Anatomy for Their Negative Views of an Ostomy" was established to monitor the show's ostomy stories and post educational ostomy information in response.

These various responses, which I explore in more detail in chapter 4, underscore the presumed rhetorical power of these negative public ostomy stories. If these communities felt that the negative public ostomy stories were going to be discredited, then the exigency for protesting dwindles. However, these communities anticipated the high-impact credibility of these public stories and therefore publicly worked to combat the stigma perpetuated by sharing their own stories that spotlight different experiences, practices, and events with their ostomies and chronic GI conditions.

Conclusion

The stories presented in this chapter not only have high impact in the broader public sphere through their credibility and successful rhetorical strategies; they also have high impact on individual lives and stories, particularly of people living with ostomies, considering elective surgery, or waking up with a new or unexpected ostomy. As I listened to comments about smelly, leaky poop bags in each of these stories, I couldn't help but be reminded of Seven Charles's story. Where do ten-year-olds learn to bully a classmate for having an ostomy? Through TV shows or commercials? In language picked up from parents, bus drivers, local police officers, or doctors? From watching their grandparents struggle with an ostomy? It's hard to trace the specific tendrils, but it's not hard to see how our larger public discourse impacts our cultural understandings as well as our individual lived experiences and practices.

In following these public ostomy stories, or, better, these variations on a single ostomy story that has created not necessarily "untrue" but certainly "incomplete" stereotypes[7] about life with an ostomy, I've worked to understand stigma's rhetoricity in more complex and concrete ways. Namely, I've argued that stigma is rhetorically enacted through repeated discussion of particular practices, lived experiences, and stereotypes—in the case of ostomies: fear, leaks, social isolation, and concerns about becoming disabled. Additionally, it has been my intention to illuminate the reciprocal connections between stigmatization and visceral publics as these two feed off and on each other within complex rhetorical ecologies and histories. These findings help enrich our currently understanding of stigma's rhetoricity by complicating stigma's relationship to credibility and by arguing for the ways in which stigma, visceral feelings, and visceral publics do work in the world on people's lives, bodies, and experiences.

Importantly, I have not intended to suggest that the rhetorical use of fear and the invocation of a visceral public audience is inherently negative, unethical, or stigmatizing. No doubt, the configuration of a visceral public can be essential to advancing necessary public health goals. For example, collec-

---

7. Here I am invoking Adichie (2009).

tive public fear experienced throughout the COVID-19 pandemic has helped ensure social distancing, masking, and other necessary measures to mitigate the spread of disease. And in the ostomy cases presented in this chapter, fear was similarly provoked to meet important public health goals. These campaigns attempted to use fear to motivate audiences to quit smoking and to avoid gun violence. Goals that, decontextualized, are worthwhile, no doubt. But at what cost?

Threading the needle between appropriate use of fear and stigmatizing use of fear seems like an impossible task. So impossible that, in many ways, it's hard for me to not vilify the CDC, Cincinnati PD, or *Grey's Anatomy*, and honestly, I'm not sure that I haven't done that at times in this chapter. I've done my best to fairly consider the potential intentions alongside the implications as I rhetorically assess each of these stories. However, I acknowledge that my personal identities as a patient muddy these waters significantly.

I'll admit my personal feelings about Julia's story have evolved significantly since I first met Julia, heard her story, and began to think through the rhetorical work and implications of the Tips campaign and Julia's story. Too, with each additional public story I found in researching and writing this chapter, my researcher perspective approached with interest and curiosity, only to be overruled by my personal patient identity, who felt anger, defensiveness, and erasure in each of these stories. I couldn't help but feel betrayed by the publicity of these stories, but not because I didn't relate to the challenges presented in each story. Surely, I have felt the fear and dread about the possibility that I might need an ostomy someday myself for the very same reasons that Julia outlines (though I'm not proud to admit it). However, as many in the IBD and ostomy communities historically and continually advocate, we must make space for the diverse, complex, contradictory, expected, and unexpected stories and experiences of those who live with ostomies, because no single story can possibly tell the whole story.

CHAPTER 4

Protesting Stigma

*Disruptive Stories, Temporality,
and Ostomies as Lifesavers*

DURING INTERVIEWS, I asked people living with ostomies and chronic gastrointestinal (GI) conditions what they thought of mainstream stories about these conditions and, specifically, Julia's story in the Tips campaign. Often, participants knew about Julia's story just by mere mention of her name; only a few[1] had never heard of Julia or the campaign. Regardless of their familiarity, I read Julia's story to each participant, and asked each to share reactions. While I'll share the responses of several participants in this chapter, I'd like to begin with just one.

During this interview, like I did during all of them, I finished reading Julia's story, waited a brief moment, and asked, "Hearing Julia's story, what is your reaction? Can you describe how her story makes you feel?" Usually, participants had a lot to say about Julia's story and were eager to say it. This time, though, there was a long, disquieting pause. At first I thought we might have been disconnected, but then, very softly, I heard what sounded like sniffles coming from the other end of the line. Eventually, Stella—my interview participant, who had been living with an ileostomy for about six months—replied:

---

1. Of my twenty interviews, two people admitted to having never heard of Julia's story or the Tips from Former Smokers campaign.

It makes me really sad because I don't feel that way at all. I really feel like my ostomy—sorry I'm getting really emotional—my ostomy did the exact opposite for me. It let me have my life back and it gave me freedom to like go about the world, like I don't have to always worry about where the bathroom is anymore . . . and it just feels like her statements were out of fear . . . but I guess it was cancer and she probably didn't have it for as long as somebody with [inflammatory bowel disease] IBD has . . . It just makes me really sad and wonder what kind of support she had from like her family and even from like medical staff if she felt like her ostomy wouldn't stay on or wasn't secured. It makes me sad that that's what was shared with the public about what an ostomy is or what it's like to have an ostomy.

Stella's response poignantly illustrates that although the most widely circulated ostomy stories may be stigmatizing through an exclusive focus on negative experiences, they do not speak for all ostomy experiences. Further, listening to the experiences within Stella's response is instructive. As she tries to understand Julia's story, Stella compares her own experiences—not having "to worry about where the bathroom is anymore" and the "freedom" enabled by her ostomy—with Julia's. Julia's ostomy became a worst-case scenario, as it constrained her life, leaked, and left her isolated. Stella's ostomy, on the other hand, improved her life, giving her the freedom to go out into the world and not always worry about being close to a bathroom. Put another way, Julia's and Stella's experiences with their respective ostomies are dramatically different, and, subsequently, so are their ostomies.

In this chapter, I explore alternative stories that both shed light on the diversity of ostomy experiences and trouble the dominant, public metanarrative that positions all ostomies and ostomy experiences as negative. In doing so, I follow Judy Segal's (2012) call to identify diverse illness stories as a means to resist the "ubiquity" or "hegemony" of particular illness story (p. 307). Specifically, Segal argues:

Each of us, when we face a diagnosis of serious illness—heart disease, neurodegenerative disease, *any* cancer—need to get oriented to the new place in which we find ourselves. The stories we might tell of the experience, if we wish to tell a story at all, do need to be honored, even if they are—especially if they are—the ones no one really expected to hear. (p. 313; emphasis original)

Indeed, stories about illness, whether or not they align with cultural expectations, "need to be honored" and listened to carefully. I take up this task in this chapter as I aim to listen to the ostomy stories that perhaps no one expects to hear—that is, stories in which ostomies and chronic GI conditions are staged through diverse practices that extend beyond leaking, smelling, and worst-case scenarios. In doing so, I work to disrupt the single, negative, and often stigmatizing ostomy story discussed in the previous chapter that circulates in the public sphere.

Listening to a range of stories and experiences is central to understanding how illnesses, conditions, and disabilities are made meaningful on individual, community, and cultural levels. Whether about cancer, addiction, bionic limbs, blindness, ostomies, or otherwise, stories are "prescriptive, or at least, advisory" as they "help the rest of us answer the question, 'How shall I be ill?'" and, consequently, shape our cultural and experiential expectations about what it means to be ill or disabled (Segal, 2012, p. 295). As sociologist Arthur Frank (2013) has argued, "Published stories . . . have a particular influence: they affect how others tell their stories, creating the social rhetoric of illness" (p. 21). For these reasons, stories, such as those told about ostomies, need be "varied, complex, honest, and true" (Segal, 2012, p. 295). But of course this is not always the case, particularly when one narrative dominates and becomes the single story of an illness. For instance, many have argued that *the* cancer story is one of resilience and triumph that stages cancer as a didactic gift (Brenner, 2016; Ehrenreich, 2001, 2009; King, 2006; Nielsen, 2019; Segal, 2012). Or, as chapter 3 discussed, *the* ostomy story is negative, disabling, and tragic.

Dominant narratives may seem harmless at first, especially when they are positive and bring awareness of a particular condition. However, as I alluded to in chapter 3, rhetorical and lived tensions emerge when one kind of story dominates the "social rhetoric of illness" (Frank, 2013, p. 21). For people living with a variety of conditions, failure to adhere to the culturally prescribed expectations for illness or disability[2] often results in disbelief, skepticism, alienation, and stigmatization (Nielsen, 2019; Segal, 2012). In the case of cancer, although bright-sided stories reflect the resilience and strength of many cancer patients, they can also encourage a bootstrap culture, telling people with cancer that the way to live with it is to prepare for a battle, dig deep, find strength, and pick themselves up to overcome an often debilitating and incurable disease. For many people experiencing cancer, living this bright-sided story is impossible and painfully conflicts with "the actual experience

---

2. For example, when people with cancer do not or cannot find the bright side of cancer, or, alternatively, when ostomates have positive experiences with their ostomies.

of disease" (Segal, 2012, p. 307).[3] It is critical, then, to "expand the possibilities for what people with serious illness can say about their experience" (p. 307) for a range of reasons: to broaden cultural understandings of what it means to live with embodied difference, to allow people to share their authentic experiences, and to resist the idea that there is a universal illness or disability experience and thereby resist minoritizing and stigmatizing anyone whose experiences may buck the status quo.

Importantly, too, lived experiences and stories of health, medicine, and disability are entangled with live experiences of race, gender, sexuality, and class. Therefore, in addition to Segal's call to expand the possibilities of illness stories, this chapter is motivated and guided by Aja Martinez's (2014, 2020) advocacy of counterstory, which both aligns with and differs from Segal in important ways.[4] Drawing on critical race theory, counterstory is a "method of telling stories by people whose experiences are not often told" (Martinez, 2014, p. 70). Counterstory is invested in untold stories, importantly, as it aims to "expose, analyze, and challenge stock stories of *racial privilege* to help strength traditions of social political and cultural survival and resistance" (p. 70; emphasis added). Counterstory also centers "the experiential and embodied knowledge of people of color" as a means of "understanding racism that is often well disguised in the rhetoric of normalized structural values and practices" (p. 69). In this way, counterstory aims to empower the minoritized through the "formation of stories that [. . .] disrupt erasures" (Martinez, 2020, p. 3). Thus, both Segal and Martinez insist on the importance of alternative stories that resist the hegemony of single or stock stories.

However, Segal (2012) argued for unexpected stories that complicate or altogether conflict with dominating stories of life with a particular illness, while Martinez's (2014) counterstory is committed specifically to the stories of racially marginalized people whose voices and experiences are often otherwise silenced or invalidated by "ignorance," "assumptions," and "stock stories" (pp. 53). Counterstory further insists on an intersectional approach to stories that illuminates marginalization and privilege, particularly related to race, which are always at work in stories and lived experiences, especially those about illness, disability, or disease. Together, the work of Segal and Martinez facilitates a critical attunement that I bring to both identifying and analyzing the untold stories about chronic GI conditions as ostomies.

---

3. To read more about the complexities of bright-sided cancer narratives, see Moeller (2014).

4. In doing so, I also draw on Krista Ratcliffe's (2005) rhetorical listening. For more discussion of rhetorical listening, see the preface to this book.

In particular, Segal (2012) argued that cancer narratives in the public sphere are overwhelmingly bright-sided and aimed to resist the hegemony of positive cancer stories; however, the familiar public ostomy story is "doom-filled"[5] that insists on entirely negative ostomy experiences and consequently (re-)enforces ostomy stigma. As I searched for and traced a more expansive set of ostomy stories, it quickly became clear that doom-filled ostomy stories are certainly not the only, and perhaps not even the most common, ostomy stories, as Stella's interview comments demonstrate. Responses to Julia's video and the CDC, as well as to the Cincinnati PD and the Grey's Anatomy episodes, show that several other ostomy stories also need to be told and honored. At the same time, dominant public ostomy stories, regardless of their doom-filled or bright-sided focus, effectively erase racialized experiences with ostomies and chronic GI conditions. That isn't to say that Black, Indigenous, and people of color (BIPOC) with ostomies or chronic GI conditions aren't represented, but their stories are often circulated as if their racial experiences don't impact their health-related experiences.

Therefore, this chapter aims to disrupt simplified, stock stories about ostomies or GI conditions by taking into account the intersectional embodiments and identities that influence how ostomies and GI conditions are made to mean. At the same time, the chapter aims to "expand the possibilities" about ostomy stories and to trace the rhetoricity of different ostomy experiences by examining (and simultaneously amplifying) a broader set of ostomy stories, including what might be categorized as "bright-sided" ostomy stories as well as stories that grapple with experiences that fit less neatly into a binary of positive or negative experience.

In searching for ostomy stories that ostomates tell themselves, rather than stories told through an institution or secondhand source like the CDC or a TV show, I further advance Mol's (2002) praxiographic call for allowing people to serve as their own ethnographers and to tell of the events and experiences of their own lives. The stories in this chapter are those shared in protests against mainstream doom-filled ostomy stories, as well as stories told through personal blogs, podcasts, and interviews with me. As we'll see, these stories diverge from the negative ostomy metanarrative by resisting the idea that life *before* an ostomy is universally better than life after. On the contrary, the ostomy stories presented in this chapter—what I refer to as *disruptive ostomy stories*[6] because they aim to disrupt the negative ostomy meta-

---

5. Emilia Nielsen (2019) develops a similar term, "down-beat stories," for breast cancer narratives that "resist the normative aspects of breast cancer culture" (p. 7).

6. As I explain more later in this chapter, I use the term *disruptive*, following the work of Emilia Nielsen (2019), who, like Segal, studied disruptive breast cancer stories.

narrative—illustrate that experiences *after/with* an ostomy are actually better for many people. In following such stories, I argue that disruptive ostomy stories resist the rhetorical system in which ostomies are staged as unequivocally disabling, negative, isolating, and always leaking.

Engaging disruptive ostomy stories, particularly as a means of complicating doom-filled ostomy stories, raises several questions: How are disruptive ostomy stories and the ostomy experiences shared within them different from stories like Julia's? Is the ostomy staged differently, and if so, how? How are these stories used to complicate, challenge, or confirm stigma? Using these questions to guide my analysis of disruptive ostomy stories, I theorize that doom-filled ostomy stories have become the ubiquitous ostomy story because they enact what Alison Kafer (2013) has called "compulsory nostalgia," or the presumed longing for the predisabled self and, in this case, preostomy self. At its core, compulsory nostalgia is marked by the acquisition or emergence of a condition, which creates before and after selves and experiences.

Tracing compulsory nostalgia in disruptive ostomy stories, then, becomes a temporal analysis that seeks both to explore differences in these before and after selves and experiences and to track the de/stabilization of stigma. In other words, I analyze disruptive ostomy stories to examine how the sequence of experiences meaningfully influences how ostomies are staged within the lives and stories of ostomates. Whether a story is bright-sided, doom-filled, or somewhere in between is shaped, at least in part, by the progression of experiences: specifically, those experiences that change over time as a person acquires and lives with a condition. As Kafer (2013) notes, people "are described (and often describe themselves) as if they were multiple, as if there were two of them existing in different but parallel planes, the 'before disability' and the 'after disability' self (as if the distinction were always so clear, always so binary)" (p. 42). For instance, notice how the ostomy marked a shift in Stella's self and lived experiences (opening of this chapter) as well as Julia's. Undergoing ostomy surgery represents a rupture in time for both Stella and Julia that shapes how these two women move forward in time and experience. In both stories, before-ostomy experiences are compared directly with after-ostomy experiences. Stella's after-ostomy life is seemingly much improved, as Stella notes how her ostomy "let [her] have her life back." Julia's experiences through time, however, moved from normal to negative as she experienced her after-ostomy life, filled with leaks, isolation, and being stuck at home as much worse than her life before her ostomy.

Specifically, this chapter shows how compulsory nostalgia helps reveal stigma's rhetorical viability and how the meaning of ostomies/ostomy experience relies at least partially on temporality and order of experience. Thus,

I forward the argument that stigma is contextual both culturally (Johnson, 2010) and temporally (Kafer, 2013). In what follows, I begin by exploring the relationship between temporality, disability, and lived experiences. Then, I examine disruptive ostomy stories and the role of compulsory nostalgia in staging or resisting stigma and argue that before-ostomy and after-ostomy experiences significantly shape the meaning-making of ostomies and the de/stabilizing of stigma.

Temporality, Disability, and Progressions of Experience

Scholars across disability, queer, and feminist studies have demonstrated the role of temporality in understanding embodiment, normality, and difference (see Edelman, 2004; Freeman, 2007, 2010, 2019; Halberstam, 2005; Kafer, 2013). Time and progressions of time, Halberstam (2005) argued, "form the basis of nearly every definition" of what it means to be human and normal (p. 152). That is, normalcy is deeply entangled with temporal expectations and milestones. A quick internet search for *childhood development timeline* will provide the age, down to the very month, at which "normal" children should be able to smile, lift their own head, respond to their name, be potty trained, express social desires, and much more.

At the same time, time and progressions of time also shape nearly every definition of what it means to be disabled or ill.[7] In *Feminist, Queer, Crip*, Kafer (2013) theorizes temporality, particularly futurity, as central to defining and de/stigmatizing disability. She contends:

> Familiar categories of illness and disability—congenital and acquired, diagnosis and prognosis, remission and relapse, temporarily able-bodied, and "illness, age, or accident"—are temporal; they are orientation in and to time, even though we rarely recognize or discuss them as such. (p. 33)

Time is so deeply ingrained in our understanding of normalcy, and consequently disability, that it goes almost undetectable. When bodies or minds fall out of sync with "normal" temporal expectations, especially when they fall behind in time, they are typically deemed abnormal or disabled. In other words, when embodied practices operate out of, especially behind, time, they are frequently stigmatized as defective.

---

7. See Jain (2007) as one example of theorizations of temporality and disease, what she calls "living in prognosis."

Tracing temporality's entanglement with disability, Kafer (2013) further argues that disability and living with illness "push time 'out of joint'" (p. 36, citing Freeman, 2007). Disability and illness disrupt time—by accelerating bodily or cognitive breakdown, halting expected development,[8] or challenging the progress of an individual or society[9]—and are, consequently, often devalued and stigmatized. These embodied disruptions in time evidence human fragility; they expose and remind us that able-bodiedness/mindedness is temporary, which, in turn, rocks the stability of able-bodied/mindedness, creating discomfort and often stigma for those who disturb temporal normality. "Failure to adhere to norms of bodies as unchanging, impermeable, long-lasting, and stable," Kafer argues, leads to "the devaluation of disabled bodies" (p. 41). Disability and illness thus push people out of joint with cultural expectations of time and bodily progression. For a quick example of such out-of-jointed-ness, recall the *Grey's Anatomy* episode in which the character Clara resists ostomy surgery because ostomies are for "old" people (see chapter 3). A young ostomized body is a body temporally out of joint, and a body thus worth rejecting. Disability and illness are resisted, devalued, and stigmatized because they serve as reminders that normality and able-bodiedness are temporary at best.

Kafer (2013) calls this temporal tension between normal and disabled a discrepancy between "curative time" and "crip time." Curative time orients us toward the absolution of disability and illness. It is the temporal progression toward cure and the timeline on which ableist systems of power and stigma require disabled people to live. *How long until you are cured? When is the cure coming? How long have you been this way and when will it end? What is your prognosis?* These curative time questions are the often impossible bar against which disabled and chronically ill lives are measured. Undoubtedly, such questions are familiar to those living with ostomies, chronic GI conditions, and chronic conditions more generally. Crip time,[10] as an alternative to

---

8. Kafer (2013) theorizes the role of temporality through the case of Ashley X, whose case became famous when her parents, along with her healthcare providers, decided to stop her sexual and physical development (through hormonal and surgical intervention) to make Ashley easier to care for as she aged. Through Ashley's case, Kafer theorizes that her parents and providers justified her treatment by arguing that it would restore temporal alignment between her mind (which, because of static encephalopathy, remained that of an infant) and her physically maturing body.

9. Drawing on queer theorists including Lee Edelman (2004), Lauren Berlant (1997), and Patrick McCreery (2008), Kafer (2013) argues that disability and queerness are framed within a "politics based in futurity" in which humanity's progress is dependent on "able-bodied/able-minded heteronormativity" (p. 29). One obvious example of a politics of futurity is pro-eugenics arguments.

10. See also Zola (1993).

curative time, is "flex time not just expanded but exploded," and it "requires reimagining our notions of what can and should happen in time" (p. 27). In crip time, there is no universal timeline, no milestones broadly marked on the chronology of human lives, bodies, or minds. Our timelines, instead, are our own, not constrained or evaluated by medical, historical, or cultural templates. Crip time, unlike curative time, has no predetermined destination or outcome (e.g., a cure, treatment, or timeline for embodied improvement).

Crip time and curative time are especially important to disability, Kafer (2013) argues, when placed on a continuum of past, present, and futures of disability. Engaging the past and present, Kafer articulates "compulsory nostalgia" to describe the experiential trajectory on which many people with acquired disabilities find themselves. Compulsory nostalgia creates two selves—a "before disability" self and an "after disability" self—in which the before-disability self is preferred and longed for. As Kafer explained:

> Compulsory nostalgia is at work . . . with a cultural expectation that the relation between these two selves is always one of loss and of loss that moves in only one direction . . . The "after" self longs for the time "before" but not the other way around; we cannot imagine someone regaining the ability to walk, for example, only to miss the sensation of pushing a wheelchair. (p. 43)

This expectation of loss and nostalgia for a pre-disability time assumes that life with a disability is inherently worse than life without one.[11] Such thinking is deeply entangled with the tragedy model discussed in chapter 3—that is, a disabled-self/after-disability life is compulsorily assumed to be accompanied by decreased quality of life, or perhaps no quality of life at all.

Compulsory nostalgia and curative time animate stigma, and we can see evidence in the rhetorical implications of ostomy stories. When audiences listen to stories about ostomies (or illness or disability), they come with expectations about order of events and progressions through time. That is, they are primed to listen "to normative narratives of time" (Halberstam, 2005, p. 152) in which the progression of events through time results in (a return to) normalcy through cure. Thus, experiences after undergoing ostomy surgery, acquiring a disability, or becoming ill are expected to be less positive than those prior, and ostomies, disabilities, and illnesses are expected to progress toward a cure so that the disabled and ill can return to the preferred,

---

11. Importantly, compulsory nostalgia is most evident in cases of acquired disability. Those with congenital disabilities, however, are often treated with the same compulsory nostalgic thinking; however, it usually assumes that those born with disabilities should want to be cured, treated, or otherwise fixed to rid themselves of their disability.

before-disability self. If and when these temporal expectations are not met, people with illness and disabilities are rendered less than human, and particular experiences and conditions are deemed undesirable and sometimes abject. When bodies and minds deviate from expected timelines—that is, the "natural, common-sense course of human development" (Kafer, 2013, p. 35)—stigma often emerges.

Kafer's claims productively map onto mainstream understandings of ostomies and ostomy experience timelines. Stories, like those explored in chapter 3, in which compulsory nostalgia is evident and the after-ostomy self is undesirable, are rhetorically effective because they affirm cultural expectations about ostomies and ostomy experiences. Put another way, ostomy stigma emerges when (and demands that) after-ostomy selves are worse than before-ostomy selves, so ostomy stories that confirm this expectation are rhetorically successful. In contrast, stories in which after-ostomy selves are more desirable than preostomy selves are rhetorically untenable in an ableist culture (i.e., who could possibly prefer living with an ostomy? a disability?).[12] Negative ostomy stories, like Julia's, in which compulsory nostalgia is validated, are unsurprisingly the most persuasive and widely circulated.

Indeed, each of the negative ostomy stories presented in chapter 3 demonstrates compulsory nostalgia in action[13] and provides a basis for which disruptive ostomy stories might be compared. Julia' story and the Cincinnati PD story rely on a preostomy self as a silent referent within the stories. Rereading Julia's story through the lens of temporality and compulsory nostalgia illuminates the rhetorical power of the "before disability self." Through her story, Julia highlights the negativity, isolation, and leaking that can accompany an ostomy. These experiences and Julia's story, positioned within the Tips campaign, tell the audience that Julia's before-ostomy self (or the before-disability self, as Kafer might name it) is far better than her after-ostomy self. Put simply, Julia's message is "change your habits now to prevent an after-ostomy self ever becoming possible." Julia's story is rhetorically contingent on her own compulsory nostalgia. Moreover, her story, positioned within the Tips campaign, assumes that viewers will also be motivated by a temporary, imagined experience with compulsory nostalgia and invites viewers to participate in that nostalgia by using second-person language, which helps viewers imagine their after-ostomy lives. Similarly, the Cincinnati PD story anticipates the audience's ability to envision a future self filled with compulsory nostalgia. In

---

12. I hope my sarcastic criticism and rejection of such thinking comes through clearly, but here's clarity in case it doesn't.

13. Though, in some cases, it is anticipated or imagined. For example, Clara fears what life will be like with an ostomy and pleads to prevent that life. This implies to viewers that no matter the risk, she prefers her current life and embodiment.

this case, the lieutenant directly calls on his audience to imagine themselves as the after-ostomy self, "limping down Warsaw Avenue with a colostomy bag." By forecasting this future for the audience, the lieutenant's story leverages compulsory nostalgia for a life without an ostomy in his audience and thereby hopes to persuade them to prevent that very nostalgia from coming to fruition by avoiding gun violence in the present. The manipulation of temporal experience in these stories relies on compulsory nostalgia and ableist envisioning of ostomy experience. As Kafer (2013) might describe, a future with an ostomy in these stories is a "future of no futures"—that is, a future with an ostomy is not a future worth living (p. 33).

The order of experiential events in these stigmatizing ostomy stories enables compulsory nostalgia. In many stories and experiences, when life before the ostomy is considered "normal" and desirable and life after the ostomy worse, the overall experience of ostomy is negative, and the preostomy self is longed for. However, many responded to the public circulation of compulsory nostalgia and the stigma it strengthens with anger, frustration, and protest. To complicate and disrupt this compulsory nostalgia, many people living with ostomies and related chronic GI conditions publicly told their own stories. In the following sections, I analyze these disruptive ostomy stories that were shared in protest as well as ostomy stories that were shared with me during interviews and publicly online that diverge from the ostomy stock story showcased in chapter 3. Specifically, I examine how experiences unfold temporally in these stories to engage compulsory nostalgia and attend to the meaningfulness of the before- and after-ostomy selves. In doing so, I consider the different ways in which ostomies are staged and made to mean through(out) these disruptive stories.

Rejecting Compulsory Nostalgia: Disruptive Ostomy Stories as Protest

Not long after the Cincinnati PD's comments about ostomies during their antigun initiative, nor long after the airing of the *Grey's Anatomy* episodes, people living with GI conditions and ostomies signed petitions, started social media campaigns, and wrote letters challenging the negative ostomy stories that were perpetuated in these highly public contexts. In response to the Cincinnati PD, a Cincinnati citizen with IBD told a local news station:

> When this went out publicly it presented an image of a colostomy bag as unattractive, disgusting, and related to gangs. [The lieutenant's depiction of

ostomies] created a negative image for those who have never heard about a colostomy. That image would be very difficult to change to a positive one. (Warren, 2013)

For this person with IBD, the lieutenant's remarks were particularly persuasive and concerning because they reached an audience of "those who have never heard about a colostomy" (Warren, 2013). People with previous experience or knowledge of ostomies may have been able to be more critical of the lieutenant's comments or, at the very least, may have had broader medicocultural contexts in which to situate the lieutenant's story as *one* potential ostomy story, not the only one.

Similarly, a state chapter of the UOAA petitioned against the *Grey's Anatomy* episodes, arguing, "We, as ostomates, are trying so hard to erase the stigma that goes with [having an ostomy] and that episode certainly didn't help. I'm sure you are aware, in real life, that ostomies have saved 1000s of people's lives who are now leading productive, healthy, and successful lives" (Hafner, 2009). Like the response to Julia's story, this petition against the *Grey's Anatomy* episodes called out the show writers for "obviously [giving] no thought whatsoever to the thousands of people who have colostomies." Such criticisms oppose the ubiquity of doom-filled ostomy stories by suggesting that these stigmatizing stories do not represent the experiences of many living with ostomies. Further, this petition explicitly rejected compulsory nostalgia, temporal expectations, and stereotypes regarding ostomies, contending that

> we [ostomates] are not all "old Grandpas" like depicted in the patient's comments. We are mothers, spouses, children, young, old, sisters, brothers, coworkers, and employers . . . What about all the viewers out there that may be scheduled for an ostomy . . . and then to hear it "is the worst thing that could happen?" (n.p.)

This petition, in addition to other responses, specifically refuted the "stigmatizing" message put forward in the stories of the Cincinnati PD and *Grey's Anatomy* episodes. Importantly, too, these responses, as we'll see is also in the case in responses to Julia's story, advocate for the ostomy as "lifesaving" rather than as a worst-case scenario. These responses, consequently, disrupt the dominant doom-filled ostomy narrative and outright reject compulsory nostalgia by arguing that life after receiving an ostomy is not only positive but *only possible* because of ostomies. Responses to Julia's video not only expressed similar concerns but were significantly louder and broader in scale.

Almost immediately after Julia's message aired nationally, a significant backlash emerged in the form of social media posts, petitions, phone calls, and letters aimed at the CDC. Together, thousands of people living with ostomies and GI conditions, especially those with IBD, and their allies rallied to demand that the CDC remove Julia's materials. It wasn't just individual people responding to the CDC and Julia, either. Major national organizations, including the United Ostomy Association of America (UOAA), the Crohn's & Colitis Foundation of America (CCFA), and Fight Colorectal Cancer joined in the outcry against the CDC's message about ostomies. So overwhelming was this response that within just a few days of Julia's story release, the CDC's Facebook page actually crashed from the number of posts that flooded it. Consistent across these calls and posts was a clear message: Julia's materials should be removed from public circulation because the CDC, by including Julia's video in the Tips from Former Smokers campaign, was perpetuating stigma by broadcasting Julia's story as representative of all ostomy experiences.

The anger, distress, and disappointment at the core of these responses was palpable. At best, it seemed that people felt caught in some rhetorical crossfire. Many protesters of Julia's video acknowledged that the Tips goal of encouraging people to quit smoking was well intentioned but still questioned whether accomplishing the goal needed to be at the expense of millions of people who are alive because of ostomies. At worst, it seemed that folks were outraged that the CDC (2019a), a premiere public health and medical organization, dedicated to "saving and protecting lives," had either incidentally overlooked a significant portion of the ostomy community or simply didn't care about them. A petition to remove the video argued that the video "sends the wrong message to the general public, at a time when those of us who have permanent ostomies are trying to educate others about this condition" (Rund, 2015). The petition further explained that the "fear of being stigmatized, including the extreme negative body image that our society has placed on those with ostomies, sometimes leads people to forego [sic] those lifesaving surgeries" (Rund, 2015).

Many who spoke out against the video did not reject Julia's experience outright, suggest life with an ostomy is easy nor did they dispute the challenges of living with and wearing an ostomy pouch. Instead, much of the resistance to Julia rejected the idea that life with an ostomy is universally or inherently negative and argued that Julia's story pictured life with an ostomy as *exclusively* negative, gross, constraining, which ignored that many find that an ostomy enables a life that would otherwise be impossible because of the disease or condition that preceded it. Even more, insofar as it reached a nationwide audience, the CDC's depiction of ostomies undercut the efforts of campaigns and advocacy work by organizations like CCFA and UOAA to dismantle the stigma surrounding ostomies. A joint letter to the CDC from the UOAA and the CCFA explained, "The situation is especially serious precisely because the CDC, a trusted source of important medical information, has spread the message. . . . [W]e know that your ads are undermining what we have done to empower, educate, and reduce the stigma of ostomy surgery" (Burns et al., 2015). The UOAA and CCFA emphasize the rhetorical importance of the CDC here. The CDC, as a leading health organization, validated the story, granting it credibility in the public sphere. Had Julia posted this video on her personal YouTube channel, other ostomates might have left educational materials, resources, invitations to Facebook groups, or perhaps criticisms and angry comments, but it seems less likely that full-fledged petitions and public outcry would have ensued. The expansiveness of a public nationwide audience, the media through which this ad was made available—both TV and online—and the fact that this campaign emerged amid several ongoing ostomy-positive social media campaigns aligned to create the rhetorical opportunity for Julia's ad and the response it received. Importantly, these activist responses are not the only discourse in which compulsory nostalgia is contradicted. Many other stories celebrate ostomies as lifesaving and champion after-ostomy life.

In addition to the petitions and letters rejecting these mainstream negative ostomy stories, many individual ostomates have shared their own stories to disrupt the hegemony of doom-filled ostomy stories. Jessica Grossman, a well-known ostomate and blogger, is one such individual. In a fiercely written blog post, entitled "Dear CDC" (2015), which she posted on her ostomy-positive site Uncover Ostomy, Jessica wrote:

Dear CDC,
    My name is Jessica Grossman.
    In my 25 years of life, I've tried to live as healthy as possible.
    I watch my diet.
    I exercise.
    I take vitamins.
    I don't really drink.
    And I certainly do not smoke.
    BUT I HAVE AN OSTOMY.
    I get it. You want people to quit smoking . . . But you're doing it wrong. So. Very. Wrong. And I'm here to call you out. I'm here to enlighten you on something you really should already know. You are a major health organiza-

tion after all. Center for Disease Control, this video that you put out, featuring a woman named Julia, is what you think is the perfect way to scare people out of smoking.

From the outset, Grossman positioned her experience as at odds with Julia's, specifically by highlighting her before-ostomy practices *and* with-ostomy practices as categorically healthy (e.g., exercising, taking vitamins, avoiding tobacco). In framing her experiences both before and with an ostomy as healthful, Grossman rhetorically resisted the idea implied in many publicized ostomy stories: that her ostomy was somehow a self-inflicted tragedy or the result of unhealthy choices. In other words, her story argued that many of her experiences, particularly those she can control (e.g., diet, exercise, drinking, and notably, smoking), remained unchanged (and healthy) as she transitioned from her before-ostomy self to her after-ostomy self.

In the next sections of her story, Grossman (2015) questioned how having an ostomy could be worse than chemotherapy and cancer, and addressed Julia directly:

> I'm not entirely sure, but I assume that you, Julia, are a real person with this story. But, Julia, if this is your real story. I am saddened for you. You had colon cancer due to smoking and you needed an ostomy. But what you said in this video, Julia, to be honest, shocked me . . . Julia, the only time I've ever been stuck at home was during the time I was sick with my disease. My bag rarely ever comes loose, and thanks to my healthy diet, it doesn't even smell. . . . Julia maybe you didn't know we were out there—others with ostomies who could help you. Others who live meaningful and enjoyable lives. Lives that, without an ostomy bag, would not exist. I can't blame you though, Julia. It's hard to find us. It's hard to find the positive light hidden within our ostomy bags. *You know why, Julia? Because of organizations like the CDC. Yes, CDC, because of you.* (emphasis original)

Obvious in Grossman's response is a significant conflict between her own ostomy experience (and seemingly what she feels is representative of others' experiences) and the ostomy experience shared by Julia and the CDC. Grossman also countered compulsory nostalgia for her before-ostomy self when she explained that the "only time" she felt stuck at home like Julia was when she was sick with disease prior to her ostomy surgery. Grossman further rejected a longing for her before-ostomy self and simultaneously championed her after-ostomy self when she emphasized her "meaningful and enjoyable" life that "would not exist" without an ostomy.

Additionally, Grossman's post complicated the idea that experiences with leaks, isolation, and smells define life with an ostomy, as she argued that such experiences are "rare" for her. Such negative experiences, in contrast, are central to the doom-filled stories challenged for perpetuating stigma. Echoing Grossman, a change.org petition that garnered nearly 11,000 signatures and received a public endorsement from the UOAA, argued that people with ostomies "are not necessarily 'smelly' nor do we hide in our homes to avoid leaks." Similarly, Active Guts, another ostomy-positive site, wrote in a letter (2015) to the CDC that Julia's video "vilifies ostomies" and "contributes to misunderstandings and fears about having an ostomy." The Active Guts letter ended by calling for the media to "present ostomies realistically," which suggested that the ostomy presented in the Tips campaign failed to do so. Collectively, the stories, petitions, tweets, and letters shared in response can be interpreted as an effort to expand the possibilities for what can be said about living with an ostomy and, thus, as an effort to resist compulsory nostalgia and the hegemony of doom-filled, stigmatizing ostomy stories. These responses forcefully insisted that public, doom-filled ostomy stories are both distressingly narrow and problematically ubiquitous.

Overall, responses to doom-filled ostomy stories (Julia's and otherwise) hinge on the idea that despite the realities of some people living with ostomies, many other ostomates experience an after-ostomy life that is not *always* or *only* centered around leaks, uncontrollability, isolation, and fear. Instead, these responses emphasize repeatedly how the after-ostomy self and life is improved and desirable, and how the ostomy itself is lifesaving. These responses reveal significant differences across the lived experiences with ostomies. At the same time, they demonstrate how these different lived experiences can and do function as a way to resist stigma by highlighting alternative and more positive ostomy experiences. Further, compulsory nostalgia for preostomy life is countered across these stories as the after-ostomy self is framed as better, more desirable, than the before-ostomy self.

In addition to arguing that doom-filled stories are not representative of many ostomates' experiences, responses repeatedly made two points: (1) doom-filled stories, especially those advanced by institutions (e.g., the CDC), not individuals, rely on stigma and perpetuate it; and (2) perpetuation of stigma is itself a pressing health threat insofar as ostomy stigma may prevent people from undergoing potentially lifesaving ostomy surgery, much in the way that the fictional Dr. Bailey from *Grey's Anatomy* feared that Clara was refusing lifesaving surgery out of ostomy fear. For instance, the change. org petition pointed out that stigma was at the core of the CDC's message in Julia's video:

The negative stigma that is spread by this ad is itself a health threat. Fear of being stigmatized, including the extreme negative body image that our society has placed on those with ostomies, sometimes leads people to forego [*sic*] these life-saving surgeries, or to postpone them for so long that their health is irretrievably damaged.

Other responses made a similar argument, including a joint letter from the UOAA and CCFA[14]:

We write because the ads may lead individuals who need life-saving surgeries to delay or refuse those surgeries because of the stigma being reinforced through the campaign. While we understand that the CDC is promoting the benefits of not smoking in order to reduce the risk of cancer (thus saving lives), your message—funded by taxpayer dollars and splayed across national media—that having ostomy surgery is miserable and should be avoided/delayed at all costs is both offensive and dangerous. The ads may result in increased expense to the health systems as individuals needing those life-saving surgeries delay or refuse them due to misconceptions and the *stigma the ads are reinforcing.* (emphasis added)

Understanding the sentiment offered in the above quotes requires some additional understanding of ostomies themselves. For many, undergoing ostomy surgery is a lifesaving effort for people who have exhausted many other options and/or whose disease or condition has irreparably damaged their GI tract. After months, sometimes years, of dealing with uncontrollable symptoms, hospital visits, and side-effect-riddled treatments, patients often consider ostomy surgery as a viable (and sometimes the only) treatment option. As Grossman explained in her post to the CDC, "For reasons completely out of my control, due to Crohn's disease, at the age of 13 years-old, I was told that my disease was going to kill me unless I had life-saving ostomy surgery. 12 years later, I'm alive." Similarly, in reflecting back on Julia's video, one interview participant pointed out that "the life-saving piece [of ostomies] is what [the CDC & Julia] weren't showing."

What becomes clear in comparing doom-filled stories with these responses is that lived experiences before and after receiving an ostomy are drastically different, and consequently the ostomies themselves are drastically different. For example, in their letters to the CDC, both Grossman and Active Guts

---

14. This joint letter has since been removed from the UOAA and CCFA websites. The analysis presented here is based on copies of the letters I downloaded before their removal from public circulation.

describe their ostomy and ostomy experience as lifesaving. Similarly, as the change.org petition explained, "There are thousands and thousands of people living active lives with colostomies, urostomies and ileostomies every day." The ostomy as lifesaving and ostomy experience as positive described in these responses to Julia's video advance ostomy empowerment both within and beyond the context of the Julia controversy. Indeed, in their letter to the CDC, the UOAA and CCFA contend that "the misconception that one cannot lead a normal life with an ostomy pouch" is a "myth" that leads people to believe that "death is a better choice than having these *life-saving* surgical procedures" (Burns et al., 2015; emphasis added). With these words, this letter affronted the rhetorical leveraging of the *better dead than disabled* tragedy model of disability, calling that very story of ostomy life a life-threatening myth. Collectively, these activist responses refute ostomy stigma by emphasizing that ostomies are lifesaving and detailing how the lived experiences that lead up to ostomy surgery, for many, are relentless and life-threatening. The responses draw an explicit contrast between the negative before-ostomy experiences and the after-ostomy experiences and highlight that ostomies save lives and help to normalize.

Importantly, disruptive ostomy stories are not unique to protests against stigmatizing ostomy stories. In fact, as I spoke with ostomates in interviews and read additional stories online, I found that ostomy stories often focus on the empowering experiences enabled by having an ostomy. In these stories, the experiential progression is similar to what was present in the responses to Julia, the Cincinnati PD, and *Grey's Anatomy* episodes. Specifically, the stories point to the experiences and events that are *enabled* by the ostomy, thus arguing that the after-ostomy self is improved and often preferred.

Nearly every person I interviewed said that "freedom" was the best thing about their ostomy—freedom from bathrooms; freedom to eat whatever sounded good; freedom to go to the gym, pool, or work; freedom to have sex or begin dating again; freedom from hospitals. In many ways, these stories reject compulsory nostalgia and demonstrate that after-ostomy experiences facilitate gratitude, optimism, and empowerment. An interview participant, Nora, explained to me that her own experiences with her ostomy were "very different" from Julia's. Nora continued, "When I used to have a rectum [i.e., *before* ostomy surgery], I was going [to the bathroom] thirty to forty times a day. Carrying extra underwear everywhere." In contrast, Nora told me earlier in our interview that the best thing about having an ostomy is "the freedom it's given [her]." For Nora, her before-ostomy life was overwhelmed by urgency, trips to the bathroom, and dealing with the uncontrollability of her bowels. In contrast, she found "freedom" in her after-ostomy life specifically *because* her ostomy enabled it. Similarly, Toni, who had been living with a temporary ostomy for about eight months, told me that the best thing about her ostomy was the food freedom it gave her:

> Honestly, because of my ostomy, I can eat whatever I want . . . [before my ostomy surgery] I just felt like I was walking on eggshells all the time, worrying about what's going to jump out and be painful or be bad and just having food freedom is amazing and also really not being on medications feels great too. It's a huge relief.

Additionally, Morgan, who had been living with a permanent ostomy for several years, explained that life after ostomy surgery is much more "controlled" because he is "not running to the bathroom all the time. I'm not having panic moments and worrying about always having to be close to a facility . . . but not being totally controlled by a bathroom and its closeness to me . . . my life is much simpler, much more controlled." Morgan's repeated emphasis on the control his ostomy facilitates stands in stark contrast to Julia's experiences with leaks, smells, and fear of her ostomy coming loose.

When I interviewed Stacy, who was not only severely sick for most of her childhood and teenage years but who had actively avoided ostomy surgery, I also heard about freedom and control. However, as I listened to Stacy tell stories about her life before and after her ostomy surgery, I was struck by how her experiences changed over time. She shared that her before-ostomy life was bedridden and, most of the time, spent in a hospital because her GI disease and related complications were so severe. According to Stacy, when she wasn't "stuck in the hospital," she was "stuck in the bathroom." Despite the restrictions her disease imposed on her life, she was afraid of pursuing an ostomy and avoided it for several years because, as she explained,

> I was thinking that I was going to be miserable and also have an ostomy. I didn't think that I'd be able to travel and do more stuff outside. I wasn't thinking that I'd have a more normal life. I was just thinking "oh good, now I'm going to have additional misery."

Eventually, Stacy decided to meet with a surgeon to discuss the ostomy surgery and was surprised when he told her "that he thought he could help [her] feel much better" and that "ostomy surgery could be a life-changer." With the support of this surgeon, and "once people [with ostomies] explained that [she] wouldn't have to spend hours in the bathroom anymore," Stacy decided to pursue ostomy surgery. When I asked her to tell me how her life has been with her ostomy, Stacy said:

> My view of my life now, my life post-ostomy is so positive because I have extra hours in the day because before I was spending so many extra hours just stuck in the bathroom and so now, I have this extra time every day, after surgery that I did not have before. I used to fantasize about what I would do with the extra time outside the bathroom and now I have that so it's very special.

The change Stacy experienced between her before-ostomy and after-ostomy lives enabled her to live more fully. In addition, her own lived experiences and positive outcomes with her ostomy empowered her to become a patient advocate in the IBD and ostomy communities, with the goal of supporting others as they consider ostomy surgery and navigate after-ostomy life. For Nora, Toni, Morgan, and Stacy, life after ostomy surgery and with an ostomy was characterized not by debilitating experiences with chronic GI conditions but by many activities that were otherwise not possible before their ostomy surgeries.

As I cataloged disruptive ostomy stories, I also found many ostomy stories shared publicly in which the ostomy enabled desirable experiences and a sense of normality for ostomates. One such example is Stomalicious—an online blog by a woman named Laura who lives with Crohn's disease and an ostomy who aims to "spread awareness of IBD and inspire others living life and traveling the world with an ostomy" (Stomalicious, 2015a). To explain the purpose of Stomalicious, Laura offered her story to readers:

> As anyone with an understanding of [IBD] knows, it can be a daily battle to get out of bed, leave the house, and live a normal life. The symptoms can take over and be debilitating. After 4 years of far more downs than ups (including trying lots of different medications, nightly enemas, side effects, diets, psychologists, fistulas, abscesses, flare after flare, and several stints in hospital), I eventually decided to go down the path of surgery. On the 24th of September 2013 I had a pan proctocolectomy and end ileostomy. It wasn't an easy decision knowing I would have a permanent stoma. Within weeks after recovering from surgery, I knew I had made the right decision. For the first time in a long time, I felt well. I felt like a new person! Not long after surgery, we made another big decision. . . . to travel the world!. I was inspired by other IBD campaigners, and I hope my story helps, encourages and inspires oth-

ers too! Traveling and living with a stoma can be daunting, and whilst there certainly may be a few hiccups along the way, having a stoma has really given me my life back, and enabled me to fulfill some lifelong dreams that a for a long time I feared may never be possible. (Stomalicious, 2015a; emphasis added)

The Stomalicious website is filled with blog posts about Laura's travels, many of which feature her revealing her ostomy at various destinations such as the Leaning Tower of Pisa, the Eiffel Tower, and Times Square. Like the stories of my interview participants, Laura at Stomalicious focused explicitly on what her stoma and ostomy "enabled" her to do, including international travel and a life that she "feared" impossible. Further, like other disruptive ostomy stories, Laura's story emphasized a positive shift between her before-ostomy and after-ostomy lives. Her ostomy liberated her from debilitating symptoms, ineffective treatments, and repeated hospitalizations, freeing her to pursue her dreams.

Importantly, too, like many of the disruptive ostomy stories I read online and heard during interviews, Stomalicious didn't just paint life with an ostomy as universally positive. Laura clarified that Stomalicious is "a place to learn more about, spread awareness of and embrace our lives with IBD" and a space where people are encouraged to "share their stories, emotions, and feelings about living with IBD," including "personal experiences of struggle" (Stomalicious, 2015b). In most cases, disruptive ostomy stories are shared in order to destigmatize ostomies by showing that life with an ostomy is not only worth living but can be desirable, while also acknowledging that it can be challenging. As Stomalicious put it, the goal is to share "the good, the bad, and the ugly," which includes "living with Crohn's and a stoma . . . traveling the world, food, friends, family, relationships, sex, pooping [her] pants, medication and side effects, coping and management techniques, hospitals and surgery, stoma stories, toilet trivia," and more. The point is that those sharing disruptive ostomy stories and battling stigma aren't working to make the ubiquitous ostomy story exclusively positive. Instead, the goal seems to be to create a rhetorical space for all ostomy stories to be valued without (the risk of) stigmatization. In each story, the ostomates trace their experiences through time, from before ostomy to after ostomy, showing that life with an ostomy has much to offer, even if there are some challenges.

Disruptive Stories, Disruptive Timelines

Disruptive ostomy stories work to destigmatize, at least in part, by defying compulsory nostalgia. Though compulsory nostalgia anticipates life after disability or after ostomy to be worse than life before, the ostomates and their stories shared in this chapter dispute just how compulsory nostalgia for before-ostomy life really is. The embodied experiences of people like Nora, Toni, Morgan, Stacy, Jessica Grossman, and Stomalicious changed through time from experiences of constraint and suffering with chronic GI disease to enabling, empowered experiences made possible through ostomies. Specifically, these ostomates are able to pursue experiences and activities like eating, traveling, and living normal (as they individually define it) lives *because* their ostomies became integrated into their embodied realities. In sharing their stories, these ostomates work to transform the dominating public narrative about ostomies, and rewrite what it means to live with an ostomy.

However, because disruptive ostomy stories resist compulsory nostalgia, they also frequently fly under the public radar. That is, these stories often struggle rhetorically and consequently struggle to become more mainstream because compulsory nostalgia is *compulsory*. The presumed desire to rid life of disability is so embedded and normalized that it is difficult, even impossible, to believe stories that value an after-disability life. Further, disruptive ostomy stories and their resistance to compulsory nostalgia are also caught up in curative logics and time expectations. As I outlined earlier in this chapter, compulsory nostalgia operates within curative time—that is, a sense of time in which we are expected to move toward cure and the eradication of disability. Kafer (2013) explained:

> In our disabled state, we are not part of the dominant narratives of progress, but once rehabilitated, normalized, and hopefully cured, we play a starring role: the sign of progress, the proof of development, the triumph over the mind or body. Within this frame of curative time, then, the only appropriate disabled body/mind is one cured or moving toward cure. Cure, in this context, most obviously signals the elimination of impairment but can also mean normalizing treatments that work to assimilate the disabled mind/body as much as possible. (p. 28)

Usually, a cure enables the sick or disabled to normalize and regain as much ability as possible. For example, prosthetic limbs enable people with limb differences to move toward normalization (Kafer, 2013, p. 107; see also Siebers, 2008). People with disability and chronic conditions are expected to long for normality through desire for before-disability life or a cure. Amputees are expected to desire prosthetics; deaf people should want to use cochlear implants; people who have been paralyzed should dream of walking again. Therefore, happiness with a disability or incurable disabilities creates a rupture in curative time. When disabilities are preferred or incurable, progress toward a disability-less future is stunted and the ever-desired march toward eradicating disease and disability is stalled (Kafer, 2013; see also Titchkosky & Michalko, 2012, p. 135; Baynton, 2017). Ostomies disrupt curative time in both ways; they are considered inherently disabling and consequently cannot be curative or ever fully normalize. Therefore, stories in which ostomies are curative and *enable* desirable lived experiences typically have been less rhetorically viable than doom-filled ostomy stories.

Ostomies' relationships with cures, the unequivocal desirability of cures, and curative timelines are highly complicated. For certain conditions, ostomies do hold curative potential. Familial adenomatous polyposis (FAP), a serious genetic GI condition that often results in an ostomy, causes precancerous polyps to develop in the colon and rectum. Untreated, FAP will eventually cause colon cancer in nearly 100 percent of cases (Cleveland Clinic, 2020). In many cases, those with FAP undergo surgery to remove the colon[15] and/or rectum[16] and live with an ostomy either temporarily or permanently to prevent the cancer polyps from developing. In other words, an ostomy offers curative-like treatment for FAP.[17] Additionally, ostomies are often discussed as a curative option for ulcerative colitis[18] (UC), a form of IBD that affects the colon and rectum only. Surgery to remove the colon is often discussed as "curative" (see, e.g., Cima & Pemberton, 2004) but often requires a temporary or permanent ostomy.

Despite the curative[19] potential of ostomies for conditions like FAP and UC, ostomies are caught in the false binary between disability and cure.

---

15. Surgical removal of the colon is referred to as a *colectomy.*

16. Surgical removal of the colon and rectum is referred to as a *proctocolectomy.*

17. Importantly, ostomies do not definitively cure FAP. People with FAP, even if they have had their colon and/or rectum surgically removed, can still develop polyps in other areas of their GI tract.

18. While the medical establishment discusses ostomies as a curative option for UC, many people with UC who have ostomies (either from elective or emergency surgery) report that ostomies do not completely resolve all the issues caused by UC. For example, one interview participant explicitly and repeatedly told me that colectomies and ostomies do not cure UC because, even though she underwent colectomy surgery, she continued to struggle with bowel obstructions, extra-GI issues (such as dehydration and fatigue), and challenges with the ostomy itself. Also, she ultimately said that her ostomy was lifesaving and agreed that, although technically speaking, removal of the colon and rectum does cure UC, such a cure does not mean that challenges with chronic GI issues are over.

19. The distinction here between curative and cure is important. While ostomies offer curative potential for some conditions like UC or FAP, they do not *fully* cure in those cases. Removing the colon and receiving an ostomy in the case of UC, for example, can effectively alleviate UC in an individual since UC is specific to the colon. However, it is not uncommon for people with UC and permanent ostomies to develop systems or complications elsewhere (e.g., stomal collapse or an abscess higher in the GI tract). Therefore, I use *curative* as a signal

Though ostomies are positioned as cures or at least as curative by ostomates and the medical establishment in certain cases, they are not socially granted the positive valence associated with cures because they do not normalize; specifically, they do not normalize appearance, bathroom practices, or human waste (by making it invisible). Ostomies do enable normalization, however, when it comes to leaving the hospital, establishing a healthy weight, or participating in so-called normal activities like traveling, finding a partner, eating preferred foods, or going to school. As many ostomates have told me, having an ostomy just means that you go to the bathroom differently. Implied in that statement is the idea that life with an ostomy is otherwise normal. Ostomies' curative potential requires that cures encompass embodied difference. In an ableist culture, though, disability cannot be made synonymous with cure; therefore, ostomies cannot be fully curative and normalizing as long as they are perceived as disabling. "Disability," as Tanya Titchkosky and Rod Michalko (2012) argue, "may participate in normalcy, but it can never be normal, let alone be valuable, enjoyable, or necessary" (p. 128). Ostomies cannot be curative because they are not positioned as a replacement for a faulty organ or body part. Instead, they are staged as an abject device that brings us closer to otherwise invisible/concealable bodily functions and accelerate the feared breakdown of our bodies through time. In other words, rather than slow progress toward disability, ostomies accelerate that timeline, and rather than tip the scales toward normality, they render bodies more abnormal.

One of my interview participants, Jo, and her ostomy story demonstrate the presumed incompatibility between "ostomy" and "cure." Jo chose to have a permanent ostomy after being diagnosed with FAP. In telling me her story, Jo explained that she "opted to have the permanent ileostomy surgery because [she] just wanted to have one surgery and be done" because otherwise "by the age of thirty-five" she had a 100 percent chance of developing colon cancer. Later in the interview, Jo said that among the biggest challenges of living with a permanent ostomy are "the arguments that transpire" when people ask 'why would you want that [a permanent ostomy]? Are you sure you made the right decision? Because that's gross.'" When I asked how she responds to such questions, Jo laughed and said, "I always say I'd rather be alive and here than have cancer. Even if I would have waited, I would have gotten cancer and would have ended up with an ileostomy." Jo's frustration with "arguments" regarding her choice to live with a permanent ostomy and avoid "multiple surgeries" and all but sure development of cancer demonstrates the conflict between ostomies and cures. Undergoing surgery to remove her colon and rectum and

---

that ostomies can, in some cases, move an individual *toward* a cure, but not fully to the destination of complete cure and disease eradication.

receive a permanent ostomy is a treatment, potentially curative, for her FAP, which alleviated Jo's worry of developing cancer. Even though her ostomy prevented the development of cancer, Jo's ostomy is still questioned by others and is presumed undesirable. Jo's story illustrates that the rhetorical power of ableism and its by-product, stigma, stage ostomies as inherently disabling and life with an ostomy as universally unwelcome and abject.

Additionally, while ostomies themselves serve as a visible sign of disability and difference, their curative potential is culturally negated because of the invisibility of most GI conditions. The disruptive ostomy stories in this chapter repeatedly emphasize that life before an ostomy was filled with unbearable difficulties such as long hospital stays, restricted eating, isolation, and exhaustion. Many such experiences, however, go unseen by the general public. Unless a person has a chronic GI condition or personally knows someone who does, the debilitating symptoms and experiences of such conditions are usually hidden and privatized by those suffering, at least in part because of the sometimes severe social penalties for allowing these conditions to become visible. The often invisible nature of chronic GI conditions contributes to the stigmatization of ostomies, the ubiquity of doom-filled ostomy stories, and compulsory nostalgia. In other words, before-ostomy life is falsely considered better than after-ostomy life because the severity and difficulty of before-ostomy life is invisible. This helps explain differences between the experiences of someone like Julia and those of people like Jessica Grossman or Laura at Stomalicious. Until Julia's cancer was found, her life was seemingly free of GI issues. Julia's ostomy therefore marked a difference in time between her "normal" life and her less-than-normal life with an ostomy. The immediate and unexpected circumstances that led to Julia's ostomy likely contributed to her negative ostomy experiences. In contrast, for people like Jessica Grossman and Laura at Stomalicious, whose lives were chronically plagued with debilitating GI issues, ostomy surgery serves as a juncture between before-ostomy life that was disabling and after-ostomy life that returned to their versions of normal. The sequence of experiences and whether people moved toward normalization or away from it as they received their ostomies seems to play a powerful role in the kinds of experiences disabled or enabled by the ostomy, the meaning-making of the ostomy, and the kind of story these ostomates are able to tell.

Complicating a Two-Sided Story

While the analysis I've presented so far is productive for tracking the significance of temporality within stigma stories and the de/stabilization of stigma, it's essential that I pause here to complicate a picture that I am otherwise painting as two-sided and straightforward, with negative public ostomy stories on one side (doom-filled) and responses insist that ostomies are actually positive and lifesaving (bright-sided) on the other. While this suggestion very generally reflects the stories and experiences I've outlined in this chapter and in chapter 3, it also problematically oversimplifies the rhetorical forces involved in these stories. Thus far I have focused on the lived experiences and practices shared within both the dominant public and disruptive ostomy stories, in an effort to track the rhetorical emergence and resistance of ostomy-specific stigma. In doing so, I've attempted to stay with the discourse of each of these cases. That is, I've tried to represent the stories and the ways they were shared and received publicly, which focused most heavily on some aspects within them (e.g., ostomy-specific practices like leaking, wearing an ostomy pouch, and ostomy-specific ideological and symbolic elements like stereotypes and ableist assumptions). This has been productive for unearthing some dimensions of ostomy stigma's rhetoricity, but it has also encouraged dichotomous thinking, pitting negative ostomy stories and the people who lived them against those with disruptive, alternative experiences. It also assumes that the two sides are monolithic, filled with people living with ostomies and chronic GI conditions who are otherwise comparable in their identities and lived experiences. Comparing apples to apples, if you will.

However, obviously not every person with an ostomy shares the same identities and experiences beyond having an ostomy. For instance, it is obviously ridiculous to compare the experiences of two ostomates' stories based *only* on their shared ostomy identity: for example, to suggest that it is possible to compare the ostomy experiences of White, upper-class, cis, straight men with an ostomy, who are otherwise the epitome of normality, with the ostomy experiences of a BIPOC, lower-class, and/or queer person living with an ostomy is not only problematic but also suggests that other life experiences and identities can be parsed from ostomy-related experiences. This presumption reduces the identities of ostomates to a single identity politic—the ostomy—and neglects other co-constitutive identities and experiences that intersectionally impact lived experiences. As Nirmala Erevelles and Andrea Minear (2010) argued, citing Antonio Pastrana's intersectional work, "part of the problem 'of relying on a static or singular notion of being or of identity' (Pastrana, 75) is that the single characteristic that is foregrounded (e.g., female or Black) is expected to explain all of the other life experiences of the individual or the group" (p. 129). This false truncation to a single or static being or identity is especially problematic when we know that "gender, race, ethnicity, sexuality, class, and ability systems exert tremendous social pressures to shape, regulate, and normalize subjugated bodies" (Garland-Thomson, 2017, p. 367). It's imperative to address the composite effects of being multiply marginalized. While I've so far prioritized ostomy experiences and practices, as those have been the primary focus of both dominant and disruptive stories, rereading these stories through an intersectional lens, motivated by Martinez's (2014; 2020) counterstory, "mediat[es] multiple differences" (Erevelles & Minear, 2010, p. 130) present within these stories and provides an alternative and possibly less polarizing understanding of negative ostomy stories, particularly Julia's.

Though most of the backlash against Julia's Tips video was directed at the CDC specifically, it is hard to separate a critique of Julia and her real lived experiences from a critique of the CDC's negligence in sharing her story as part of the Tips campaign. The CDC's insistence that the videos are "real people" telling "real stories" makes the line between Julia's truth and the CDC's antismoking efforts particularly blurry. Consequently, it is tempting to impulsively or uncritically villainize Julia with or instead of the CDC for widely promoting a negative story of ostomies. Julia, after all, did choose to participate in the Tips campaign, and she did share experiences with her ostomy that stigmatized ostomies and those who require them to live. And it is easy to oversimplify Julia's story and reduce her lived experiences to those explicitly shared within her Tips video. I can imagine many ostomates listening to or seeing Julia's story for the first time while watching television on the couch after work or between streams of YouTube videos online and being stunned by the blunt depiction of ostomies. To be honest, seeing Julia's video for the first time took my breath away as a person living with a chronic GI condition. The sharp sting of shame I felt as I identified with Julia's fear and disgust was matched only by my frustration that the CDC, with one thirty-second commercial, could undo years of hard work to quell GI-related stigmas. However, the initial, even hasty, reactions by me and others in the ostomy and IBD communities obscure a more critical engagement with Julia's story, which I'm attempting to foreground now. Such emotional and visceral responses to Julia's video perhaps enabled many upset viewers, including myself, to overlook the intersecting rhetorical forces, particularly racism and sexism, that may have impacted Julia's lived experiences with her ostomy and the ways in which her story was received in the public sphere.

As I've mentioned, many of the responses to and criticisms of Julia's story were careful to not discredit Julia as a person, invalidate lived experiences with ostomies, or suggest that life with an ostomy is always easy. I haven't seen any responses that explicitly addressed Julia's racial or gendered identities as Black woman. However, some responses did target Julia as an individual

(Grossman's blog, discussed earlier in this section, serves as one particularly harsh example). In general, Julia's multiply marginalized identities as a Black woman were erased both in her Tips video[20] and in the circulating responses, petitions, and public outcry. This is a highly problematic move that elides the compounding stigmatization that often accompanies being Black and being a woman. As Garland-Thomson (2017) has argued, "Female, disabled, and dark bodies are supposed to be dependent, incomplete, vulnerable, and incompetent bodies" (p. 365). Most individual responses to Julia and her experiences explicitly defined her solely by her ostomy identity and experiences, which signals the potential of implicit assumptions and bias toward Julia and/or suggests that responses to Julia overlooked how her racialized and gendered identities may have impacted her ostomy experience.

Even more, the letters from national organizations like CCFA and UOAA are telling of the ways in which Julia's multiple identity politics were left unaccounted for. Neither letter addresses the unique experiences of BIPOC in the context of chronic GI conditions and ostomies. Again, Julia's race, and gender, were ignored altogether or deemed irrelevant to her ostomy experiences; or, perhaps worse, those identities laid the groundwork for stereotypes and biases that went unchecked. The lack of intersectional awareness shown by these organizations at the time illustrates broader racial and gender inequities in the chronic GI communities, in both the expert and the public spheres. Rather than attune to the "violent interstices of multiple differences" at which disabled people of color are positioned (Erevelles & Minear, 2010, p. 383), CCFA and UOAA, and the vast majority of individual responses to Julia, focused exclusively on her ostomy identity to evaluate her story and its rhetorical role. No explicit effort was made to contextualize her experience within knowledge of the disparities that are now well known to exist across race when it comes to chronic GI conditions and ostomies (see Afzali & Cross, 2016; Montgomery et al., 2018; Sewell et al., 2010; Sharp et al., 2020). Nor did the responses from such organizations account for the broader history of mistreatment and stigmatization of BIPOC folks within medicine and the healthcare system (see, e.g., Bailey et al., 2017; Bhopal, 2001; Ford & Airhihenbuwa, 2010; see

---

20. The CDC does list Julia's story under the Tips website's "African American" category. Many Tips participants are tagged under various marginalized identities, including race, sexuality, and disability. Visitors to the website can search for participants by condition (e.g., ostomy, lung cancer, pregnancy) or by "specific groups." In addition to all the Tips stories from Black participants, the "African American" page includes only two statistics about smoking and Black adults: "Smoking cigarettes puts you at risk for heart disease, cancer, and stroke, which are among the leading causes of death for African Americans in the United States. About 1 in 7 (14.9%) non-Hispanic Black adults in the U.S. smoke cigarettes." No other information is provided. See CDC (2021a).

also Washington, 2006). Instead, Julia's race and gender as well as the role of those identities (and their accompanying politics and oppression) are unacknowledged as impactful in Julia's negative ostomy experiences. Her experiences with leaks and feeling stuck at home were tied to her personally rather than to interlocking webs of social, structural, and personal factors that likely influenced her experiences with her ostomy directly and indirectly.

In terms of the other public responses to Julia's story, especially those from individuals in the ostomy and IBD communities, it seems that some, especially White, folks may have also engaged with Julia and her story from implicit biases rooted in privilege, Whiteness, and patriarchy, even if those biases did not explicitly manifest in their specific comments and criticism of Julia's story. These unchecked ideologies and assumptions may have led to defensiveness toward and alienation of Julia and her right to her own lived experiences. Admittedly, this was the case for me initially, as a young White woman with IBD. I was quick to judge and criticize Julia's willingness to participate in the Tips campaign and to stigmatize herself, ostomies, and GI conditions through her Tips story. My initial reactions to Julia, perhaps like those of others in the IBD and ostomy community, measured her story one-for-one against mine, assuming that she had equal access to healthcare, familial and social support, and the same social and political privilege that I have as a White, highly educated, fully insured, middle-class woman with the time, resources, and support to seek whatever care is necessary to navigate the complexities of living with a chronic GI condition and (the possibility of) an ostomy. My own problematic perspective offers an example of how privileged it is to see ostomy stories as *only* ostomy stories rather than as complex stories embedded with structures that evaluate bodies and lives differently, marginalizing some while privileging others. Re-examining Julia's story in this more robust context helps disperse more fairly the rhetorical agency afforded to her individual story and the rhetorical blame directed at her for presenting the public with a doom-filled ostomy story.

Research has shown repeatedly that Black people, especially Black women, are less likely to receive adequate care because of racial biases that lead healthcare providers to take seriously minoritized people's experiences and reported symptoms. When it comes to cancer specifically, Black women, on average, are diagnosed later and have a worse prognosis than their White counterparts (see, for one example, Penner et al., 2012). Taking this research into account is essential in separating a critique of Julia from a critique of the CDC. What if we see Julia's negative ostomy experiences as a reflection not of poor healthcare choices but of poor healthcare and a racist and misogynistic society? As Stella asked in her interview with me, did Julia have support with her ostomy? Did Julia get the kind of care and support she need as she learned to live with an ostomy? I would add, was she listened to and taken seriously when she reported GI issues, or was she dismissed and stereotyped as hysterical or angry? Did she suffer with symptoms, leaks, and ostomy-related issues because she reasonably mistrusted the medical system and its ability to care for her? I don't have the answers to these questions, but raising them is essential to justly complicating the stories we tell and accept about lived experiences with ostomy and chronic GI conditions. These questions are further necessary to resist vilifying Julia and other individual storytellers and to remind us that it was the CDC's responsibility to resist ostomy stigma, not Julia's.

Criticizing Julia and her experiences suggests that there is one "right" way to live with an ostomy, which, for the most part, the responses to Julia and other doom-filled ostomy stories resist doing. I don't know the identities or experiences of every single person who responded to Julia's story. Nor am I necessarily arguing that the criticisms directed specifically at the CDC were unwarranted. However, we must also see that the loudest and most power-ful voices speaking out against Julia's story did not acknowledge the systemic and structural oppression and stigma that undoubtedly compounded in her lived experiences. Just as the CDC or *Grey's Anatomy* writers or Cincinnati PD could have done more to nuance their stories, to resist a single nega-tive ostomy story, so, too, could the responses have been more careful, more empathetic, more aware that patients cannot isolate ostomy experiences from racial, temporal, socioeconomic, medical, or gendered power dynamics and rhetorical expectations. What I mean to say here is that identifying a right and wrong side of ostomy stories and, consequently, the stories that stigmatize and those that destigmatize, is not straightforward. It is tempting to divide the stories in chapter 3 from those in this chapter, but rather than provide a nuanced understanding of lived experiences with ostomies and the diverse ways in which ostomies are staged and made meaningful, such dichotomiz-ing results in two single stories, polarized by the idea that ostomy experience is *either* bright-sided or doom-filled. Rainbows and butterflies or a complete tragedy. In sync with our assumptions regarding aging, disability, embodied and temporal experience or out of sync. Curative or crip.

Praxiographic and disruptive approaches to the rhetoricity of stigma and the lived experiences with ostomies and chronic GI conditions requires us to recognize that stigma, lived experience, and ostomies are all multiplicitous. All these entities involved in lived experiences with ostomies are intra-actively emergent (see Barad, 2007; Kessler, 2020) within specific rhetorical ecologies where many diverse forces are at work. Thus, what I'm arguing for here is a nuanced, careful, and critical attunement to these complex forces (racism, ableism, feces, access to healthcare, leaks, temporal unfoldings, food freedom, social support, hospital stays and discharges, visceral emotions, ostomy technology, education, etc.). Such an approach not only helps us honor the disruptive stories but also allows us to see how those stories rhetorically stage the meaning of lived experiences with ostomies and chronic GI conditions to be stigmatized or not. Attending to these forces importantly shows how Julia's story was disruptive in its own right. A counterstory (Martinez, 2020) that worked to make visible an otherwise invisible story of what it is like for her as Black woman with an ostomy. Though Julia's story doesn't disrupt the hegemony of doom-filled ostomy stories, it does disrupt White ostomy stories from being the only ostomy stories.

Conclusion

Disruptive stories work against ableist assumptions by sharing positive experiences with ostomies, in which disability does not unequivocally decrease quality of life, sense of self-worth, or the ability to engage in desired activities. By highlighting experiences in which a future with an ostomy is positive, empowered, able, and even enticing, disruptive ostomy stories dispel fear and dismantle ostomy stigma. These stories reject the idea that a future with an ostomy is "a future of no futures" (Kafer, 2013) and, instead, show that for many, a future with an ostomy is the *only* future possible. These stories repudiate ableist, normalizing timelines in two key ways. First, as we saw in the activist responses to the *Grey's Anatomy* episodes and Julia's story, disruptive stories dismiss the idea that ostomies are exclusively for the elderly or the result of unhealthy choices (e.g., smoking). Second, disruptive ostomy stories belie compulsory nostalgia and curative timeline.

The disruptive ostomy stories in this chapter present a radical (re-)envisioning for ostomy futures—that is, an after-ostomy future that is enabling. These stories both directly and indirectly protest stigma and the stigmatizing idea that all lived experiences with ostomies are defined by leaks, isolation, debilitation, and loss. Stories both disruptive and dominant not only create a social rhetoric of illness (Frank, 2013); they provide a platform for updating and revising that social rhetoric. In the case of ostomies, the stories explored in this chapter highlight that ostomies' normalizing potential requires the idea of "normal" itself to be more diverse, complex, and inclusive, a point that disability studies scholars and disability activists have long advocated. Although many similarities emerged across the stories in this chapter, it's clear that "normal" and "normal with an ostomy" are different for every ostomate, and that all ostomates need space to live, share, and navigate their own experiences and stories. Certainly, many people who receive ostomies yearn for their before-ostomy lives. However, this is not always, or perhaps even often, the case. Listening to disruptive ostomy stories alongside more ubiquitous ostomy stories showcases that no ostomy single ostomy story can or should speak for all ostomy experiences.

It was my goal in this chapter to follow Segal's call to honor and listen to as many ostomy stories as possible, especially those that are unexpected, different, resistant, or disruptive, and to enact Martinez's call to listen to and make space for counterstories by acknowledging the always-present intersectional dynamics in storytelling. In doing so, I heard stories about lifesaving surgeries, being discharged from the hospital, eating favorite foods, traveling the world, and choosing life with an ostomy. Placing these stories in conversation with dominant public stories like Julia's helps demonstrate the significance of listening to people as their own ethnographers and the importance of temporality within ostomy, illness, and disability experience. Julia's and Jessica Grossman's stories, while dramatically different, paint an incomplete picture of the embodied practices and possibilities of ostomies. Together, however, they begin to materialize a more nuanced understanding of lived experiences with ostomies and chronic GI conditions. To paint an ostomy as universally anything, doom-filled or bright-sided, is to set up a rhetorical dynamic prime for the emergence of stigma. Where the ostomy is a static object on which different perspectives are projected, social and structural forces will continue to (de)value ostomies in ways that are familiar (see Mol, 2002). In a praxiographic approach to ostomy stories, the ostomy is not a "universal object" across these stories—not something that either Julia or Jessica Grossman got right or wrong—instead, it is both emergent and made meaningful within the lives, realities (political, material, social, rhetorical), and unique timelines of individuals.

Even more, listening to this range of stories showcased the role of temporality within lived experiences and reiterated the role of ableism, racism, sexism, and normalization in stigmatization. The relationship between before-ostomy life and after-ostomy life, unsurprisingly, plays a profound role in how the ostomy is made to mean for individuals, and we can map these shifts over time by praxiographically listening to ostomy stories. When ostomy stories, like other stories of disability and illness, are shared publicly, audiences are primed to listen for a particular unfolding of experiences. Stories of embodied and temporal difference are stigmatized when ableism holds cultural power, and it is incumbent that single stories, whatever their valence or whichever practices they tell, be placed alongside diverse alternatives, all of which need to be listened to carefully, empathetically, and intersectionally.

Paying attention to temporality within these stories also raises questions about differences across experiences when the ostomy is temporary or permanent. I do not know with certainty whether ostomies were permanent or not for many of the storytellers I've featured thus far, specifically when it comes to stories beyond those told by my interview participants. However, some of the language in Julia's story suggests that her ostomy was temporary, and I do know that Jessica Grossman's ostomy is permanent based on information on Uncover Ostomy. Therefore, comparing the experiences of Julia and Grossman, with temporary/permanent in mind, indicates some additional ways that temporality is caught up in lived experiences of those with ostomies. Specifically, people who have temporary ostomies may be potentially less inclined to reflect on and interrogate their own compulsory nostalgia. When an ostomy is temporary, longing for the preostomy self is simultaneously a longing for a potential after-ostomy self that is *without* an ostomy. For people with temporary ostomies, unlearning and resisting ableist assumptions might seem less pressing as the possibility of an ostomy-less live remains viable. In contrast, for people who know with certainty that they have no future without an ostomy—that is, permanent ostomates—there may be more investment (and more at stake) in rejecting compulsory nostalgia. My intention here is not to paint with broad strokes and categorize temporary ostomates and permanent ostomates as distinct and stable groups that neatly align with doom-filled and bright-sided stories. Nevertheless, as this chapter has worked to analyze the rhetorical role of temporality within stigma stories, it is important to reflect on the possible role of permanence in lived experiences with ostomies and stigma.

Finally, disruptive stories do not only reveal important insights about the relationship among temporality, lived experiences, and stigma. They also serve as one example of how stories are actively challenging stigma and succeeding. Indeed, disruptive ostomy stories are making progress in increasing awareness of ostomies, shifting what it means to live with an ostomy, and dismantling stigma. These shifts are evidenced in the CDC's response to the backlash against Julia's video.[21] To its credit, the CDC did revise Julia's campaign materials. Her story still depicts her difficult ostomy experience, though some of the video's most negative ostomy depictions have since been edited out. Further, the CDC actually no longer features Julia's solo video—it has

---

21. The Cincinnati PD also issued a public apology. I have not seen evidence that the writers or producers at *Grey's Anatomy* responded to any ostomy-related petitions or protests.

been removed from both the Tips website and YouTube. It's almost as if her original video never existed, and perhaps for good, but certainly complicated, reasons. Removal of her video could be interpreted as the CDC's effort to remove the stigmatizing ostomy message from public discourse altogether. In place of the original video, Julia is featured in a collaborative one with another Tips participant, Mark, who also underwent ostomy surgery because of cancer. In their shared video, Julia no longer reports that what she hated most was her colostomy bag, and her "get over being squeamish" tip has been replaced with "keep your sense of humor. You're going to need it" (CDC, 2015b). While Julia and Mark still stage the ostomy as a negative consequence of smoking, the harshest part of Julia's message has been removed.

The CDC's revisions also illustrate the significant rhetorical labor required to fight stigma; only some of the ostomy-negative message has been removed, and, still, no mention of ostomy's lifesaving potential is included. Eleven thousand signatures, hundreds if not thousands of tweets, Facebook posts, emails, and letters all contributed to the CDC's temporary removal of and partial revision to their message regarding ostomies. Moreover, while it's clear that some of the protesters wanted Julia's story removed entirely, it's necessary to consider the implications of such a move. Many protestors made rhetorical efforts to clarify that it was not Julia's story itself that was problematic but rather the CDC's choice to advance a solely negative story of ostomies. Erasing Julia's story perhaps helps minimize stigmatizing ostomy messages, but it also silences Julia's experiences and leaves Julia and others who struggle with their ostomies to suffer in silence. Erasure privileges a different set of voices and experiences, namely of White ostomates who no doubt share common experiences with Julia but who do not share the same layers of marginalization and oppression that Julia has almost certainly endured. Eradicating stigma requires that all stories—doom-filled, bright-sided, and everything in between—be possible and heard. As many of the disruptive stories in this chapter suggest, destigmatization is not about silencing or ignoring the challenges of living with a disability, illness, or other chronic condition. Instead, it requires that no condition, disability, disease, or related lived experience render anyone "less-than-fully human" (Molloy, 2015, p. 159).

Attuning to temporality, specifically compulsory nostalgia, within ostomy stories insightfully highlights the ways in which ostomies are made to mean differently. For those, like Julia, whose before-ostomy and after-ostomy experiences transformed negatively, the ostomy is staged as a worst-case scenario and as undesirable. In contrast, for people like Jessica Grossman, Laura at Stomalicious, and many of my interview participants, whose after-ostomy experiences were desirable, even preferred over their before-ostomy experiences, the ostomy itself is staged as a lifesaver. Indeed, the language of "life-saving" is used in many disruptive ostomy stories and is evidenced by positive experiences like eating favorite foods, avoiding cancer, or simply feeling better. These experiences and the positive language used to describe them enact the ostomy as a lifesaving surgery and technology, which stands in stark contrast to the ostomy enacted in Julia's story, the Cincinnati PD's message, and the *Grey's Anatomy* episodes. Listening to these stories praxiographically, and with temporality in mind, demonstrates how the ostomy is done differently across experiences and can further allow us to recognize and resist the compulsivity of stigmatizing expectations or reactions.

CHAPTER 5

Managing Stigma

Visual Acts of Resistance

IN 2015 TLC,[1] the widely popular television channel known for its lifestyle reality-television shows including *My 600-lb Life, Say Yes to the Dress,* and *19 Kids and Counting,* announced its latest reality show for UK broadcast: *Too Ugly for Love?* This "observational documentary" followed ten adults with "extraordinary medical conditions . . . on their quest to find love" (TLC, 2017b). Each episode tracked the "ups and downs" of dating as an adult with "secret physical afflictions" such as alopecia, missing limbs, vitiligo, skin ulcers, hyperhidrosis,[2] and ostomies. The show was premised on the belief that these conditions make finding love "almost impossible" and therefore lured viewers with the drama of these "too ugly" people navigating the dating world. However, the supposed impossibility of finding love with an "extraordinary affliction" wasn't the only reason viewers were encouraged to watch. The show promised a look into "a whole world of dilemmas" surrounding the singletons' and their decisions to conceal or reveal their conditions. The show's promotional materials asked: "How can you find love when you are hiding your true self? . . . The longer you leave the truth, the harder it can be to come clean and the more dramatic the revelation" (TLC, 2017b). These tensions surrounding

---

1. Formerly known as The Learning Channel, in recent years TLC has become home to a range of reality shows ("a global leader in real life entertainment") aimed to "inspire, inform, and entertain" (TLC, 2020).

2. Hyperhidrosis is a condition characterized by uncontrollable, profuse sweating.

the ugly truth of finding love while living with embodied difference enticed viewers for three seasons, totaling twenty-two 45-minute episodes, several of which featured Antony, Marcia, Kieran, and Matt—four ostomates.

Too Ugly for Love? illustrates that illnesses and disabilities, including ostomies and chronic gastrointestinal (GI) conditions, are accompanied by specific visual expectations regarding attractiveness and disclosure. The show's very title implies that having a chronic condition or disability disqualifies people from being attractive and finding love. Further, the show emphasizes the relationship between visuality and stigmatizing practices. Specifically, it equates living with embodied difference with being ugly and romantically out of the question. By centering people living with "extraordinary physical afflictions," *Too Ugly for Love?* serves as a contemporary example of what Garland-Thomson (1997) might call "a spectacle of the extraordinary body." Indeed, "TLC's framing of the extraordinary body as a public spectacle," disability studies scholar Krystal Cleary (2016) has argued, "is both in keeping with the representational history of disability and the channel's investment in the shocking and unusual." The show explicitly positions each adult, including those with ostomies, as undesirably different and invites viewers to engage in evaluative visual work by watching the show and the extraordinary bodies it puts on display. Disabled bodies, particularly those visually on display, operate as the "vividly embodied stigmatized other" through "cultural dichotomies that do evaluative work: this body is inferior that one is superior; this one is beautiful or perfect and that one is grotesque and ugly" (Garland-Thomson, 1997, pp. 7–8). Participating in this evaluative economy, *Too Ugly for Love?* conflated ugliness and physical conditions and highlighted the precarity of visual practices for people living with disabilities and chronic conditions. In short, how you look and how you are looked at affect your worthiness and desirability.

Disability studies scholars and rhetoricians of health and medicine alike have shown that visuality is central to the lived experiences of people with a host of conditions and disabilities (see, e.g., Cleary, 2016; Garland-Thomson, 1997, 2009; Johnson & Kennedy, 2020; Moe, 2012; Quackenbush, 2011). Ostomies and chronic GI conditions are no exception. For the most part, these conditions can be hidden from others, kept invisible under clothes, and concealed in private spaces. Although concealing these conditions often allows those living with them to "pass" as normal[3] and avoid being stigmatized, the invisible nature of ostomies and chronic GI conditions also comes at a cost. As much research has demonstrated, the invisibility of chronic conditions

---

3. See Goffman (1963).

generally, and chronic GI conditions more specifically, often leads to doubt about the reality and severity of these conditions, which in and of itself serves to stigmatize these conditions in many contexts (Defenbaugh, 2013; Moore, 2013; Valeras, 2010; Vickers, 2000). At the same time, revealing an ostomy or chronic GI condition also opens up the possibility for stigmatization and judgment by making others aware of these conditions and thus creating opportunity for others to devaluate ostomy / chronic GI conditions and the people who have them.[4] For example, when Seven Charles's ostomy was made visible to his classmates, he was repeatedly harassed (see preface).

Although some visual practices can stigmatize and others run the risk of inviting stigmatization, visual practices are also used within the ostomy and chronic GI community to advocate, empower, and make public these conditions. Specifically, many people living with ostomies and/or chronic GI conditions currently work to resist ostomy stigma by posting pictures online (Frohlich, 2016; Frohlich & Zmyslinski-Seelig, 2016; Rademacher, 2018). Such visual practices (taking and posting photos publicly) not only help bring awareness to ostomies but also further work to destigmatize ostomies through public exposure. For instance, in response to Seven's death and in honor of his memory, thousands of people posted pictures of themselves revealing their ostomies using the hashtag #BagsOutForSeven.[5] These images at once eulogized Seven and countered stigma by making ostomies deliberately visible. Similarly, social media campaigns like #GetYourBellyOut have resulted in thousands of ostomy- and belly-revealing pictures posted to Twitter, Facebook, and Instagram in order to destigmatize and raise awareness of chronic GI conditions.

Overall, visual practices—revealing and displaying—as well as the visual practices they encourage—looking and staring—demonstrate how central visibility is to many of the stigma stories being told and heard about ostomies. This aligns with what scholars have noted about other disabilities and the visual entanglements of disabilities and stigmatized identities more broadly. Visual expectations regarding illness and disability are indeed complex and political. Johnson and Kennedy (2020) have pointed out:

> Visibility is strategic. Visibility is insistent. Visibility is an argument—for disabled people, an argument for recognition and rights, a demand to be part of the public and participants in public discourse, a call to be addressed in education and employment policies, seen in accessible spaces, and equi-

---

4. See, e.g., Rademacher (2018) and Leadley (2016).
5. Capitalization of each word added for accessibility.

tably represented in cultures that have discriminated against disabled people for millennia. Visibility is imperative. So imperative, in fact, that it is
easy to overlook the risks of visibility for minoritized populations. Visibility
is fraught. Visibility is not always voluntary. Visibility brings with it risks,
always demanding a calculation of the potential value of revealing oneself.
(p. 61)

Johnson and Kennedy make clear the conundrum facing people with disabilities including those living with ostomies and chronic GI conditions: visibility
is central to both empowerment and stigmatization.

As many scholars have shown, visual practices are deeply ensnared in
stigmatization vis-à-vis ableism. This is especially the case for ostomies and
chronic GI conditions. In her recent analysis of Tee Corrine's (2019) "Scars,
Stoma, Ostomy Bag, Portocath: Picturing Cancer in our Lives," art historian
Stefanie Snider (2019) summarized: "Western culture tends to rely on the
visual as a way of knowing, especially in terms of marking disability and illness" (p. 133). For this reason, people with disabilities and illnesses are often
charged with proving the existence of their conditions and the "truth" of their
bodies through visual practices, particularly when a marker of the illness or
disability (e.g., a wheelchair or white cane) might not be readily apparent to
outsiders. A range of visual practices or ways of looking have been identified as participating in this visual economy: the clinical or diagnostic gaze
(Calder-Dawe et al., 2020; Foucault, 1973; Johnson, 2010), the nondisabled
gaze (Hughes, 1999), the male gaze (Doane, 1982; Haraway, 1997; Mulvey,
1975), and staring (Garland-Thomson, 2009). Collectively, these ways of looking at disabled or ill bodies work to in/validate particular bodies (Hughes,
1999) and thereby perpetuate ideas of normalcy by "deciphering difference"
(Calder-Dawe et al., 2020, p. 141).

Each of these ways of looking participates in systems of power that not
only decipher differences but also police, objectify, and dehumanize people
with disabilities, including those with ostomies and chronic GI conditions, by
categorizing bodies according to "cultural dichotomies" like normal/abnormal,
attractive/repulsive, superior/inferior, sexual/asexual, able/disabled (Garland-
Thomson, 1997). For example, the clinical, diagnostic, and nondisabled gazes,
which participate in a medical model of disability, demand visual proof of an
illness or disability. This, in turn, pushes people to engage in what Calder-
Dawe et al. (2020) called "proofing practices" or "the range of strategies for
evidencing impairments" (p. 148). Importantly, too, proofing practices are
strongly influenced by stigmatization. Johnson (2010) asserts, "Stigma is . . .
active rhetorical propagation of community norms and values coupled with

the demand for visibility" (p. 475). Although stigmatization frequently leads people to conceal markers of disability or illness, it also often necessitates that people prove their disability or illness through visual displays. For instance, recall the story of Sam Cleasby from chapter 2. Cleasby was publicly criticized for using a disabled bathroom precisely because she failed to display a visual marker of disability with her ostomy hidden beneath her clothes.

Clearly, stigma's entanglement with the visual is complex, in some instances demanding that particular bodies make visible their difference and in others demanding that bodily difference be concealed to avoid stigmatization and discrimination. Therefore, people with illnesses and disabilities are required to visually manage their conditions, navigating the demands to reveal and conceal in different contexts, toward different goals, and with different repercussions (see Garland-Thomson, 2011, 2017; Rademacher, 2018). As Goffman (1963) described, individuals who "possess" a stigmatizing trait or identity must engage in "information control" practices as part of "stigma management"; they must decide "to display or not to display, to tell or not to tell; to let on or not let on; to lie or not to lie, and in each case, to whom, how, when, and where" (p. 57). These visual tensions and pressures are acutely active in the case of ostomies. Rademacher (2018) has argued:

> Anxiety among ostomates, therefore, is closely linked to fears that one's concealed ostomy may be discovered unintentionally due to a leak of one's ostomy appliance, frequent flatulence, or while one is emptying their pouch in the restroom, and as a result, face experiences of stigmatization. (p. 3861)

Indeed, people with ostomies and chronic GI conditions are paradoxically trapped, simultaneously required to visually prove their conditions and to conceal these same conditions to avoid being stigmatized. Ultimately, decisions to reveal or conceal are highly rhetorical.

Accordingly, this chapter examines the role of visual practices in stories that stigmatize ostomies as well as those that counter that stigma by querying how people with ostomies and chronic GI conditions navigate visual practices like revealing and concealing, as well as being looked at and stared at. In turn, the chapter argues that people with ostomies and chronic GI conditions rhetorically use visual practices to influence the meaning of ostomies and, in doing so, to actively resist stigmatization. Thus, this chapter reviews a range of stories that demonstrate the central and complex role of visual practices in the de/stigmatization of ostomies including *Too Ugly for Love?*, social media campaigns like #GetYourBellyOut and #AerieREAL, and stories of individual ostomates including Bethany Townsend, Jessica Grossman, and Sam Cleasby, whose ostomy-revealing photos have been circulated widely online. Through a discussion of these diverse cases, this chapter shows how stigmatization disciplines bodies across intersectional lines and, more specifically, how visibility-related ostomy stigmatization is deeply entangled with normalcy and normalization, particularly along axes of sexuality, beauty ideals, and gender norms. Moreover, the chapter shows how normalization, while pitched as a means to destigmatize ostomies, inadvertently reinscribes the enactment of stigma itself, particularly when studied intersectionally.

The chapter proceeds in the following way. First, I contextualize the analytic work of this chapter within conversations that have articulated the connections between stigma, normalization, embodiment, sexuality, and visuality. Then, I analyze how people with ostomies and chronic GI conditions capitalize on visual practices, especially on social media, as an act of resisting stigma. I detail how visual practices and textual practices come together to tell particular stories about living with ostomies and chronic GI conditions, specifically stories that work to normalize ostomies and chronic GI conditions through repeat, public displays that invite others to look, even stare, at ostomies. In doing so, I consider the rhetorical risks involved in participating in visual practices. I next trace how expectations regarding sexuality and gender work to control how, when, and why people living with ostomies and chronic GI conditions reveal and conceal their conditions. I end the chapter by contemplating what's at stake in the goal and practices involved in the normalization of ostomies and chronic GI conditions.

Normalcy, Norms, and the Impossibility of Normalization

To understand the rhetorical work and implications of visual practices for people with ostomies and chronic GI conditions, it's important to first discuss the role of normalcy and normalization in visuality, disability, and stigma. As I've mentioned, the idea of the "normal" is the conceptual opposite of the "stigmatized" (see Goffman, 1963). Scholars across fields invested in identity and embodied politics (e.g., disability studies, women's studies, queer studies, critical race studies) have compellingly and repeatedly shown how "normal" isn't so much a clear-cut identity or embodiment as it is a conceptual opposite, or an unmarked category rendered present only through the identification of what *isn't* normal. For instance, disabled bodies help define normalcy because disabled bodies (supposedly) aren't it. As Titchkosky and Michalko (2012) put it, "normal bodies need no explanation" (p. 127). Disabled bodies, on the other hand, are always "requiring explanation—what went wrong, how can it be fixed and brought back to normalcy?" (p. 127). As Goggin et al. (2017) have summarized, "Normality is a privileged, yet strikingly vacant and difficult to define category which gains its existence and status from its relationship to the constitutive disavows of abnormality" (p. 337).

Importantly, the stigmatization of disability through rhetorics of "normal is natural" (Cherney, 2019) is intersectional, making multiple normalizing demands at once. As Garland-Thomson (2017) explained, "gender, race, ethnicity, sexuality, class, and ability . . . exert tremendous social pressures to shape, regulate, and normalize subjugated bodies" (pp. 366–367). Recall that Goffman (1963) speculated that the "normal" body is actually White, male, cisgender, heterosexual, athletic, wealthy, and attractive. Thus, any bodies that deviate (read: basically, all bodies) are subject to stigmatization in one context or another, and often multiple contexts simultaneously. This, of course, is foundational to the idea of intersectionality (see Cho et al., 2013; Crenshaw, 1993). Each stigmatized and marginalized identity/embodiment multiplies, resulting in exponential oppression, harm, and subjugation of people who occupy several marginalized identities at once. Ultimately, these (multiply) marginalized identities and embodiments are subject to the pressures and policing of normalcy, and these pressures are acutely active in contexts of ostomies and chronic GI conditions (Hood-Patterson, 2020; Leadley, 2016; Manderson, 2005; Vidali, 2013).

Normalcy, as part of its rhetorical work to characterize disability as abnormal and thus stigma-worthy, manifests through cultural norms (which are then perceived to be violated by abnormal bodies). Norms operate in conjunction with normalization—the social, material, and rhetorical process of becoming normal[6]—that every body is expected to desire and adapt to. These norms range from obvious to insidious. And, importantly, they are "less a condition of human nature than a feature of a certain kind of society" (Davis, 1997, p. 3). In other words, norms, like their counterpart stigmas, are expansive arguments that cultural majorities (implicitly and sometimes explicitly) agree on and enforce. Take, for example, norms regarding the evacuation of waste; people generally agree that there are places where you pee and shit (bathrooms) and places where you don't (literally anywhere else). Ostomies and ostomates violate this norm in that they don't require (and in most cases can't abide by) specific physical places where waste evacuation happens. Ostomies excrete waste whenever there is waste to be excreted. Of course, it is into an ostomy bag, so it's not really the same as shitting in the street, but it's often

---

6. For more on normalization, see Coleman-Brown (1986), Gibbons (1986), and Wolfensberger (1972).

stigmatized as such. Ultimately, ostomies' proximity to and relationship with feces is frequently cited as a justification for stigmatization. As Yergeau (2018) has argued, shit is a "precondition for rhetoricity" (p. 20). In other words, shit influences meaning-making and, in the case of ostomies, shit's rhetoricity is preconditioned toward stigmatization.

In addition to cultural norms regarding shit, and more directly relevant to the stories in this chapter, are cultural norms regarding sexuality and gender. "Normal" sexuality is heterosexual and able-bodied (McRuer, 2003, 2011). Therefore, disabled people are required to address and explain their sexuality to others because it challenges the norm. As McRuer (2011) has explained, "'What exactly do you do?'" in relation to sex is about as frequent a question for disabled people as it historically has been for many queer people (p. 107). Curiosities and assumptions that disabled people inherently have abnormal sexuality and sexual practices is demonstrative of deeply entrenched ideas about disabled bodies, the practices they can and should participate in, and the way those embodiments and practices are presumed to be inherently outside the norm. Even when disabilities have little or nothing to do with sexual function, disabled people are subjected to what Harlan Hahn (1988) has called "asexual objectification," or the systematic assumption that people with disabilities are "inherently asexual, undesirable, or impotent" (Leadley, 2016, p. 26). The widely held stereotype that ill or disabled people always are (or should be) asexual[7] is tied up in a range of other stigmatizing stereotypes and assumptions about disability (see Cleary, 2016; Kafer, 2003; Kim, 2011; Leadley 2016; McRuer & Mollow, 2012; Sandahl, 2003; Santos & Santos, 2018; Shakespeare, 1996). As Cleary (2016) explains, "Because people with disabilities are assumed to be eternally dependent, they are frequently presumed to be infantile and asexual." In response, disability scholars and activists have countered the convergence of asexuality and disability, advocating that many disabled have fulfilling sexualities and sexual lives.

Importantly, I do not mean to say that asexuality[8] is inherently problematic or abnormal, as a sexual identity with related practices that defines heteronormativity, asexuality is itself stigmatized and often discussed as a form of sexual deviance. Outright rejection of the possibility of asexuality for disabled people or the positioning of asexuality as inherently abnormal can inadver-

---

7. When I use the term *asexual,* I follow Eunjung Kim (2011), who defines asexuality "broadly to a relative absence or insufficiency of sexual interest, biologically and socially described function, and interpersonal sexual engagement" (p. 481).

8. The Resources section at the Trevor Project (2020) is one helpful starting place to learn more about asexuality.

tently reinscribe problematic assumptions and erase disabled people who are proudly asexual. As Eunjung Kim (2011) has asserted,

> the universalizing claim that all disabled people are sexual denies that asexuality can be positively experienced by any subjects with a disability, thus displaying the tendency to negatively generalize about asexuality as unnatural and indeed impossible. (p. 482)

This complex entanglement of a/sexuality, disability, norms, and stigma reminds us that universalizing assumptions are nearly always problematic. Space for all lived experiences and identities is key, and I don't intend to recapitulate those frequently stigmatizing perspectives of asexuality here. Instead, I recite this scholarship regarding the asexualization of disabled people to highlight the highly problematic ways in which asexuality is often forced onto disabled bodies. Some disabled people no doubt are asexual, which is, of course, queerfully normal[9] and none of my or anybody's business. In fact, Eunjung Kim (2011) has compellingly shown how, for some, disabilities uniquely afford nonsexual sensualities and pleasures. However, the problem arises when that asexuality is demanded of disabled people. The a/sexualization[10] of disabled bodies is especially harmful given its histories in eugenics (see Davis, 1997; see also Kim, 2011). Disabled people have historically been rendered asexual as a means to advance "the notion of progress, human perfectibility, and the elimination of deviance, to create a dominating hegemonic vision of what the human body should be" (Davis, 1997, p. 8).

Further, the a/sexualization of disability intersects with gendered expectations, particularly related to beauty and desire (Calder-Dawe et al., 2020; Cleary, 2016; Loja et al., 2013; Mohamed & Shefer, 2015; Sandahl, 2003). That is, a/sexuality stereotypes and related stigmatization are imbricated in related norms regarding beauty, desire, and sexual attractiveness. Asexual bodies are incongruent with attractiveness and beauty, at least when it comes to sexualization. Garland-Thomson's (2017) feminist disability theory is instructive for further understanding appearance-related norms that regulate and evaluate disabled bodies. Specifically, Garland-Thomson asserted that normalcy and beauty are "twin ideologies" that "posit female and disabled bodies, particu-

---

9. I'm playing discursively on the concept of "perfectly normal" here in two ways: first by subbing in the term *queerfully* to signal resistance to heteronormativity; second, by using the word *normal* to queer the concept altogether.

10. Desexualization, the process that divides disability from sexuality and renders sexuality an irrelevant identity, discourse, and practice for disability people, is also tied up in eugenics, stigmatization, and disability. See Kim (2011) for a richer discussion.

larly, as not only spectacles to be looked at, but as pliable bodies to be shaped indefinitely, so as to conform to a set of standards called the 'normal' and the 'beautiful'" (p. 367). Normalcy and beauty norms, in tandem with sexuality expectations, police disabled bodies, especially disabled women, demanding that those bodies conform to the ever-shifting beauty norms of any given cultural moment.[11]

Of course, many disabled women can never fully conform to Western society's (impossible) beauty norms, leaving those bodies perpetually abnormal and stigmatized through the mere practices of existing. Ostomates find themselves in this impossible position, though they can mitigate the stigmatization by engaging in concealing practices (e.g., wearing clothes that mask the presence of the ostomy, using belts or other holsters to obscure the full visibility of an ostomy, or, in extreme cases, hiding in private spaces). This is the power of normalcy and normalization. Disabled people, including ostomates, are expected to indefinitely normalize—that is, work to be normal—despite never being allowed to reach normalcy. It is an impossible achievement that disabled people are demanded to work toward but forbidden from achieving.[12] As Jean Bessette (2016) has argued in the context of queer rhetorics, "normalization produces bodies, polices desire, privileges the powerful, classifies and punishes the perverse, and remains resistant to intervention" (p. 150).

With the social, personal, and physical pressures that accompany normalcy and thus disability, many ostomates and people living with chronic GI conditions have turned to visual practices to impede stigmatization. Importantly, many of these individuals leverage the visual, especially in online pub-

11. Western beauty ideals have, unsurprisingly, shifted over time. Leaving women in particular with an ever-moving and almost universally unachievable target.

12. An important semi-exception to this are supercrips, who are publicly perceived to "overcome" their disability through superhuman accomplishments like becoming Olympians or celebrities (see Booher, 2011, 2010), in which case the disability is a source of extraordinary strength and ability. The idea that a disability elevates a disabled person to superhuman status has been theorized extensively in disability studies under the "supercrip" trope. See, for example, Hardin and Hardin (2004), Booher (2010), and Gutsell and Hulgin (2013). Many disability studies scholars have shown the negative and damaging effects of the supercrip trope. Specifically, this work has shown how supercrip stories tend to be the *only* if not the most visible disability stories circulated in the public sphere. Too, supercrip stories tend to valorize disability as something that extraordinary individuals can overcome, thus setting an unreasonable and harmful expectation for other disabled people who cannot or do not live up that expectation. While some recent work has attempted to recuperate the supercrip as a helpful analytical and critical device, its role within disability discourse is complex and fraught (see Schaulk, 2017). Both Vicky Mulholland and Gut Girl animate the supercrip narrative in their own stories (in the next section). Supercrip stories, while positive on the surface, are problematic in that they set an impossible standard for disabled people and further entrench the idea that disabilities are something that can and should be defeated in service of becoming normal.

lic spaces, to "normalize" ostomies, which often seems to be in an effort to shake stigma. As Kristina Gupta (2019) has argued, "in a white supremacist capitalist patriarchy, normalization can be a survival strategy, it can alleviate suffering (including the suffering causes by the system in the first), and it can make bodies, minds, and lives more livable" (p. 3). However, the distinction between destigmatization and normalization is significant, and as my analysis will show, the nuances between the terms are not often clear in the lived experiences and stories of ostomates. Normalization might initially appear to be a reasonable goal; deviance from normalcy is, after all, a primary source of stigmatization for disabled people. However, as the visual stories in the next sections show, normalization as a potential or already achieved goal for (people living with) ostomies and chronic GI conditions not only relies on privilege (racial, gendered, heteronormative, economic) but also recapitulates the normal/stigmatized system that ostomates and other disabled people are working to dismantle.

Displaying Ostomies and Soliciting Stares

One primary way that visual practices participate in the de/stigmatization of ostomies is through the posting of photographs and selfies[13] online. Previous research on the relationship between online photos and the ostomy community has illustrated that "many members of the ostomy community are using . . . blogs and social media accounts (e.g., YouTube and Facebook) to challenge ostomy stigma" (Rademacher, 2018, p. 3859; see also Frohlich, 2016). My own investigation into lived experiences, ostomies and chronic GI conditions, and stigma confirm Rademacher's findings. During interviews, when I asked participants whether and how they are individually working to resist stigma, many reported participating in social media efforts to educate others about ostomies through posting and sharing pictures online. For example, one interview participant, Stacy, explained that the space in which she has felt "most stigmatized" is the beach or pool, where her ostomy is made visible. In response to this, Stacy said she shares photos of herself online in her swimsuit to help mitigate this stigmatization and actively promote products designed to support ostomates with fashionable garments like StealthBelt—a "stylish" belt/wrap designed to support and conceal the ostomy—during activities like

---

13. To be clear, *selfies* are defined by the *Oxford English Dictionary* (2013) as "a photograph that one has taken of oneself, typically with a smartphone or webcam and uploaded to a social media website." I distinguish between photos and selfies here because both play an important role in the visual practices of the ostomy community. However, they tend to operate in similar ways.

"sleeping, intimacy, swimming, and intense physical exercise" (StealthBelt, 2020).

Stacy is among thousands of people who have taken and shared photos and selfies online as acts of resistance against stigma. For example, in a tweet (2017) featuring a picture of herself lifting her shirt to reveal her ostomy, a woman named Vicky who frequently posts about life with her ostomy tweeted: "#myillnessisnotyourinsult my stoma makes me superwoman, has given me my life back and makes me awesome. think before you make a joke." Vicky's tweet, as part of the #myillnessisnotyourinsult social media initiative, resisted stigmatization specifically through what Sandahl (2003) called "cripping," or practices that "spin mainstream representations or practices to reveal able-bodied assumptions of exclusionary effects . . . expose the arbitrary delineation between normal and defective . . . and disarm what is painful with wicked humor" (p. 37). Vicky's image revealed her ostomy, and she used the caption to explain that her life is possible because of her ostomy, and, even more, that her ostomy makes her self "awesome." Vicky cripped the practices that use her ostomy as insult by using visual and discursive practices to argue that her ostomy "makes her superwoman." That is, she used the practice of displaying her ostomy to embody the positive, celebratory relationship she has with her ostomy.

Vicky is not the only ostomate who has used visual practices to prove superhuman status and fight stigma. For instance, consider Gut Girl, a self-proclaimed inflammatory bowel disease (IBD) superhero, who, while wearing an ostomy pouch, "fights IBD" and gives others the "tools" to do so, too (Ringer, 2012). To establish this superhero identity, Gut Girl shares photos of herself dressed in typical superhero attire, including a spandex leotard and shiny blue cape, as well as some supercrip special features, including underwear briefs on the outside of the spandex and, most important, a glitter-filled ostomy bag (Ringer, 2012). Like Vicky, Gut Girl wears and displays her ostomy specifically as part of her superhero armor and, in doing so, celebrates her ostomy. By integrating her ostomy as part of her tools to fight IBD, Gut Girl showcases it as part of her superhero self, making the ostomy meaningfully positive. Both Vicky and Gut Girl use visual practices—posting pictures online, revealing their ostomies, and visually highlighting their ostomies by focusing on them in the photos—to evince not only their ostomate identities but also their (super)human or supercrip statuses. The ostomy, according to Vicky and Gut Girl, is both empowering and elevating; it empowers them as women with ostomies and chronic GI conditions to be "awesome" and support others *and* it elevates them from abnormal to extraordinary.

While individuals like Vicky and Gut Girl work visually to dismantle ostomy stigma, there are also massive online campaigns working toward the same goal. Among the most popular is the #GetYourBellyOut (or #gybo) campaign, which has garnered thousands of Facebook posts, tweets, and Instagram posts. At the time of this writing, a search for #GetYourBellyOut on Instagram returned over 20,000 posts and thousands more on Twitter and Facebook. #GetYourBellyOut (n.d.) "encourage[s] people to take a photograph of their belly and post it to social media." Shortly after the #gybo campaign began in 2014, one of its founders explained that "what started out as a campaign to raise awareness of an invisible illness that so many people suffer with in silence has turned in to a campaign of INSPIRATION and UNITY!" (Fleetwood-Beresford, 2014). Further, a promotional video on the GetYourBellyOut website explains that the purpose of the campaign is "to raise awareness of inflammatory bowel disease . . . as well as trying to remove the stigma around these conditions" ("GetYourBellyOut," n.d.). #GetYourBellyOut ultimately asks people with ostomies and chronic GI conditions to deliberately reveal their bellies in order to challenge stigma and draw attention to these conditions.

True to these descriptions of the campaign, the photographs and selfies posted as part of #GetYourBellyOut include photos of ostomies, photos of abdomen scars presumably from surgeries and other procedures, as well as photos that show "no visible signs" of illness or disability (GetYourBellyOut, n.d.). As the campaign explains, "[#GetYourBellyOut] has helped put a visual aid on what is an invisible illness and has helped start the conversation to educate the public" (GetYourBellyOut, n.d.). With this explicit purpose, the #GetYourBellyOutCampaign actively calls on those in the ostomy and chronic GI community to engage in "proofing practices" to help make otherwise invisible illnesses visible (Calder-Dawe et al., 2020). The thousands of photos and selfies shared as part of this campaign suggest that visibly displaying these conditions is an activist effort to collectively respond to stigma through awareness and education.

For the campaign to succeed at these efforts, however, the visual practices at work in a campaign like #GetYourBellyOut require interaction. #GetYourBellyOut directly prompts participants to engage in visual practices, which, in turn, invite outsiders to participate in visual practices as they view the photos. In other words, the #GetYourBellyOut campaign both encourages displays and invites stares by circulating images of bellies and ostomies in the public sphere. As Garland-Thomson (2009) has argued, staring is "a communicative gesture," led by curiosity and discomfort that can readily transform into oppression (p. 185). However, Garland-Thomson clarified that this discomfort "can be positive . . . a stare is a response to someone's distinctiveness, and a staring exchange can thus beget mutual recognition, however fleeting" (p. 185). #GetYourBellyOut works to solicit this very kind of positive stare—stares that create an "empathetic exchange" in which "starers imagine what it is like to be" the starees (p. 92). Of course, starees cannot completely control starers or their stares. Staring and being stared at involves a relationship that neither side can fully control. That is, by displaying their ostomies online, ostomates can work to encourage empathetic exchanges, but they cannot guarantee them.

Garland-Thomson (2009) does suggest, though, that there are ways starees can work to exert influence during a staring exchange. She suggests that starees can "coach the public eye" (p. 188) to empathetically stare by including stories that help starers situate what they see within particular stories rather than within public stories that might be implicated in ableism, stigma, and other stereotypes and forms of oppression. We can see this work of sharing stories alongside ostomy images in various posts within the #GetYourBelly-Out campaign. Given the volume of posts with #gybo, a complete analysis of the campaign's posts is beyond the scope of my project. However, I have been following the campaign since it started in 2014 and have analyzed approximately 1,500 of the posts. Here, I focus on just two representative examples.

In an Instagram post, a woman I'll refer to as Petra[14] shared three different images. The first photo shows Petra standing outside what looks like a public place in jeans and a sweater; she smiles for the camera and does not appear to display any obvious sign of illness or disability. The second photo shows Petra again smiling for the camera, only this time her shirt is pulled up slightly to reveal a black ostomy bag affixed to her abdomen. Finally, the third photo shows Petra yet another time, fully covered by jeans and a blouse, still smiling, and taking a selfie in what looks like a bathroom. Included beneath these three photos is the following caption:

> I am still the same person despite my IBD. First picture was taken 7 years ago. I had no signs of illness that I knew of, no stoma and had very little knowledge of IBD. The next two pictures are my most recent. I live with a stoma, no colon, no rectum and an illness that I will have for the rest of my life . . . But I'm still the same person as I was in that first picture. I still have the same qualities I had before I got poorly[15] and if anything, being poorly has made me more strong and more confident than I was then.

---

14. I chose to anonymize this post in an effort to protect the woman's identity. This post was shared publicly; however, since it is on her personal account, I mask her identity here.

15. Here, I read *poorly* to mean *sick*.

#ostomy #ostomate #stomasquad #ibdsuperheros #invisibleillness #noco-
lonstillrollin #ilesotomy #ileostomywarrior #ileostomybag #crohnsdisease
#ulcerativecolitis #ibd #ibdawarness #noteverydisabiliyisvisible #ittakes-
guts #butyoudontlooksick #countdowntosurgery #sickbutinvisible #post-
operativerecovery #barbiebutt #getyourbellyout

This text provides a broader story in which public viewers can situate the
images and the display of Petra's ostomy. As Garland-Thomson (2009) might
put it, the text caption helps "coach the public eye" as it views and evaluates
Petra's photos. By explicitly telling viewers that she is "the same person" across
these images, Petra works to persuade viewers that her ostomy did not change
who she is, even though it did change her body. In other words, Petra insists
that she is the same person, identity unchanged, despite the addition of her
ostomy and chronic GI condition. In this way, Petra's post works to normalize[16] ostomies by situating the ostomy within an otherwise normalized story
and on an otherwise normal-looking body. This post also actively disrupts
the process of her identity becoming totalized by her ostomy through the
collective work of the caption and series of images. Petra's choice to include
pictures before her ostomy, with her ostomy revealed, and with her ostomy
concealed, emphasizes to viewers that she has maintained the same qualities
and sense of self throughout time and over the course of receiving her ostomy.
Taken together, the multiple images and caption work to control the story that
viewers create from these visual and discursive practices. Rather than allow
viewers to rely only on assumptions, stereotypes, or previously heard stories
about ostomies, Petra provides viewers her story and experiences to shape
how viewers make meaning of her photos.

Another post in the #GetYourBellyOutCampaign points to the campaign's
empowering and destigmatizing effect. Many posts in the campaign have been
shared through participants' personal accounts; however, many organizations,
including GetYourBellyOut as well as Crohn's and Colitis UK[17] and Ostomy

---

16. Goffman (1963) might actually call this process "normification," which he distinguishes
from normalization. Normification, according to Goffman, is "the effort on the part of a stigmatized person to present himself as an ordinary person, although not necessarily making a
secret of his failing" (p. 30). Despite Goffman's effort to distinguish between these two processes, the vast majority of disability studies and rhetorical scholarship in which I situate my
work does not separate these two terms or processes as distinct. Therefore, following this work,
I use the term *normalization*.

17. Crohn's and Colitis UK is "the leading charity for Crohn's and Colitis" in the UK
(Crohn's & Colitis UK, n.d.).

Awareness,[18] have encouraged people to submit photos and captions to be shared on these highly public accounts. For example, a post shared on both Twitter and Instagram by Ostomy Awareness features a man with his shirt off, revealing his ostomy as he looks away from the camera. The caption reads:

> Meet Ste! He says, "Many people still are disgusted by the fact that I wear my stoma with pride, I get it out without thinking about it, it's posted all over the internet, I wear no shirt when it's warm out, etc. Why should I not do these things, why should I hide away? Because I poop in a bag? Well I'm still breathing; that bag saved my life." Thanks for helping to spread ostomy awareness! #ostomyawareness #ostomy #ostomy bag #getyourbellyout #nocolonstillrollin

Much like Petra's post, this photo and caption collaboratively work to shape how viewers stare at and read ostomies and the people who have them. The caption directly calls out the stigmatization of ostomies by revealing the ostomy and explaining that people find it "disgusting" when they see ostomies, and by supplanting that reaction with an alternative way of seeing ostomies: as lifesaving. Together, these two #GetYourBellyOut posts exemplify how people with ostomies use visual practices to destigmatize ostomies, particularly when those visual practices are paired with stories that help contextualize and situate the images within lived experiences with ostomies.

Each individual post in #GetYourBellyOut collaboratively resists stigmatization through visual displays and coaching public onlookers to see the ostomy in specific ways and thus figure ostomies within positive, rather than stigmatizing, stories. In this way, #GetYourBellyOut, in combination with individual posts like Vicky Mulholland's and the work of Gut Girl, enact the ostomy not as negative, disfiguring entities, but as empowering embodiments that can and should be publicly visible. Central to this work is another layer of visibility—publicity. For individuals like Mulholland, the scope of impact can be limited to personal social media networks even when the posts are made openly public. To overcome this limitation, organizations leverage the affordances of social media, specifically hashtags, to consolidate images and posts and consequently increase their public visibility. However, there are also instances in which individual ostomy photos have gone viral. The next stories I share are three such examples. The first features Bethany Townsend, a UK woman and ostomate whose ostomy-revealing photos went viral (Birch, 2014;

---

18. Ostomy Awareness is an Instagram account with the explicit goal to "normalize colostomies, ileostomies, and urostomies." Ostomy Awareness accomplishes this goal by featuring ostomates who share photos and captions.

Morgan, 2014). In contrast, the second story, from Sam Cleasby, whom I first introduced in chapter 2, demonstrates how norms related to women's bodies are enforced problematically at the intersection of sexuality, beauty, and disability. Finally, I explore Kieran's story within the *Too Ugly for Love?* series, in which Kieran shows viewers the intricacies of dating with an ostomy through highly visual TV episodes. Kieran's story further complicates and nuances the visual complexities layered onto norms of dating, sexuality, and disabilities.

Visual Rewards and Risks: Sexualizing Disability

In 2014 Bethany Townsend, a UK model and ostomate, used social media to share an image of herself sunbathing in a bikini with her two ostomy bags revealed.[19] Within a matter of days, Townsend's images went viral, receiving over 12.4 million views (Rademacher, 2018; Walker, 2014). When asked about the image, Townsend reported, "It was just a picture that I got my husband to take on holiday and it was just for me and him really" (ITV, 2014). After receiving positive feedback from her husband and others, Townsend shared the image with Crohn's and Colitis UK, transforming it far beyond a personal picture for her husband. Not long after, Townsend was featured on a variety of news and pop culture broadcasts in the UK, explaining her picture and her ostomies and advocating for ostomy positivity.

Since then, Townsend's posting of the image has been championed as a heroic act that inspires confidence in herself and others with ostomies and chronic GI conditions, specifically IBD. In fact, *Cosmopolitan* (2014) called Townsend "the ultimate body confidence queen." Townsend's rationale for taking, posting, and sharing this image aligns with her reputation. In the time since her photo went viral, Townsend has explained that she was working to resist stigma both by wearing her bikini in public and by sharing online a photo from that day. Townsend also acknowledged that, in the three years leading up to this photo, she did not wear a bikini or reveal her ostomies in public, because she lacked confidence (Blumm, 2014). However, with the encouragement of her husband, Townsend decided that her ostomies are "nothing to be ashamed of" (Blumm, 2014), which led her to take and post the

---

19. Though I don't know with certainty the specifics of Townsend's ostomies, it is not uncommon for people to have two abdominal ostomies for a variety of reasons. For example, people may have a colostomy or ileostomy to reroute their digestive tracts *and* a urostomy to reroute their urinary tract. In other cases, they might have an ostomy in their lower abdomen (digestive or urinary) as well as a gastrostomy, which is an opening in the stomach used for feeding.

picture publicly. In response to her photo and story, thousands of other people with ostomies and IBD tweeted to support her and call her an inspiration for the IBD and ostomy communities. One Twitter responder, for instance, wrote that Townsend is "such an inspiration, especially in a world that's so judgmental about how a woman should look in a bikini" (Walker, 2014).

Although many of the responses to Townsend were positive, some were "less supportive, and sometimes outright negative" (Rademacher, 2018, p. 3873). In his analysis of Townsend's case and the public comments left in response to Townsend's image, Rademacher (2018) indicates that despite their destigmatizing efforts, images like Townsend's are still criticized by some. For example, his analysis compellingly shows how sometimes displays of ostomies can't fully be controlled and can elicit stares and responses that are oppressive and stigmatizing. Specifically, Rademacher analyzed several comments posted in response to various articles that covered Townsend's story, including this one:

> Seriously, is there no end to the stuff that people want to shove in other people's faces for the sake of a few minutes of infamy? For God's sake, keep it to yourself. I got a toe that looks really nasty—want to see it? My hemorrhoids have also really been acting up. For the love of God people. (p. 3872)

Despite Townsend's display being largely viewed as an empowering act, it still existed within a public, ableist rhetorical ecology in which ostomies are predominantly stereotyped and stigmatized. In other words, Townsend's intention to normalize her ostomy through a visual display could not completely ensure how others would see and stare at her. What was perceived as empowering and destigmatizing by some was considered "nasty" by others.

Collectively, Townsend, #GetYourBellyOut, Gut Girl, and Vicky Mulholland illustrate how people living with ostomies and chronic GI conditions both individually and collaboratively work to destigmatize these conditions by participating in visual practices like displays, especially in digital, social spaces. These visual stories and their visible ostomies also suggest that displaying, posting, and sharing photos also (attempt to) call public viewers to engage in visual work by looking and staring at images of ostomies, chronic GI conditions, and bodies that are often considered abnormal. Unfortunately, however, these cases also stress that despite their intent, visual practices do not always or directly lead to destigmatization. Publicly inviting others to stare at ostomies, even while coaching those stares toward empathy, doesn't guarantee destigmatization. It may help normalize ostomies, but more normal isn't the same as fully normalized (and, as I discuss later, normalization is a complicated end goal). In other words, making disability—in this case, ostomies and chronic GI conditions—visible is a risky endeavor (Johnson & Kennedy, 2020). Sam Cleasby's visual stories with her ostomies, as I explore next, showcase these risks, especially when contrasted with Bethany Townsend's story. While visual practices can productively "resymbolize" (Eiesland, 1994; Garland-Thomson, 2017) life with an ostomy or chronic GI condition, and in doing so, work to normalize these conditions, visual practices are not without risk (Johnson & Kennedy, 2020). When ostomies are revealed with bodies that do not meet other embodied norms related to beauty, sexuality, or gender, those ostomies and bodies become especially vulnerable to stigmatizing stares.

To illustrate this, I turn to Sam Cleasby. Cleasby has become a well-known figure in the ostomy and chronic illness communities as she catalogs her experiences with a range of chronic GI conditions and an ostomy on her website SoBadAss. In 2014 several photos of Cleasby went viral in the UK (Cleasby, 2014, 2015b) but became visible and well known within US ostomy and IBD communities as well. These photos capture Cleasby revealing her ostomy and stoma in a series of color and black-and-white images. Some of the images are close-up shots focused on Cleasby's abdomen, featuring her ostomy or stoma,[20] and a scar that runs from her rib cage to below the waistband of her black skirt. Other photos show Cleasby boudoir-style, in lingerie, lying on a couch, red high heels and legs propped up in the air. Together, the images display a confident-looking Cleasby, smiling and posing for the camera.

Describing the reason she decided to have her husband take these images and her own motivation for posting them, Cleasby (2015b) wrote in a blog post that accompanied the photos that she "wanted to show that [her] stoma didn't remove [her] from [her] femininity, sexuality, or who [she] was before." In an interview about the images, Cleasby elaborated:

> My husband is a photographer and we were talking about the lack of great images [of ostomies] out here. They were usually very medical and there wasn't really that many snapshots that people had taken of themselves at that time . . . I thought it was an old person's disease and I was just 32; I couldn't find any images that I could relate to . . . I wanted to do something completely different and show that this surgery hasn't removed my femininity or my sexuality—it was just a very small part of me and it didn't define me. (Saul, 2015)

---

20. In some of the images, Cleasby has removed her ostomy bag in order to reveal the stoma itself. Recall that stomas are the opening on the abdomen, which in the case of GI ostomies expose an end of the intestine on the abdomen.

Similarly, in the original blog post sharing these images, Cleasby (2014) clearly articulated that she wants to "show that people living with an ostomy can be sexy, fun, and cheeky . . . that this little bag doesn't define who I am." The images were originally shared on her personal blog and website but were eventually circulated and viewed across a variety social media and news outlets (Cleasby, 2014; Saul, 2015). Cleasby's explanation countered the idea that the person and disability "are synonymous" (Fine & Asch, 1988, p. 8). Cleasby explicitly asserted that her ostomy does not "define" her and offered these photos showing herself being "sexy, fun, and cheeky" to visually demonstrate that her ostomy is just a "small part" of who she is. These reasons for taking and sharing the photos align directly with reasons people have offered for participating in the #GetYourBellyOut campaign, like Petra's Instagram post analyzed earlier in this chapter.

However, when these images were circulated online, they were not received positively by all audiences. In fact, Cleasby (2015b) wrote a separate blog post specifically to address the criticism she received for sharing them. Cleasby explained that she was critiqued for sexualizing disability in her photos. She opened her blog post by tracing the core of the critiques against her photos: "I have been subject to a few comments about sexualizing disability (and some just telling me that ostomies are gross and I should put it away, but that is a WHOLE other story!!!)." She then considered whether she is "guilty" of sexualizing disability and concluded: "The short answer is fuck yeah! And you know why? Because my sexuality, my femininity, and the person I am didn't get removed along with my colon." By fully embracing the idea of "sexualizing disability," Cleasby cripped[21] (Sandahl, 2003) her criticisms and purposefully agreed that she is sexualizing her disabled self through her revealing photos.[22] It's clear in reading Cleasby's blogs and viewing her images together that her decision to display her disabled, female, sexualized self is an act of resistance against how ostomies had been visually represented in other spaces. She insisted that "looking at images [of ostomies online]" left her feeling "terrified" because she repeatedly found images of "stomas that were infected or

---

21. Sandahl (2003) describes cripping as practices that "spin mainstream representations or practices to reveal able-bodied assumptions of exclusionary effects . . . expose the arbitrary delineation between normal and defective . . . and disarm what is painful with wicked humor" (p. 37).

22. Cleasby's rhetorical reversal of the criticisms she received about sexualizing disability remind me of Shiri Eisner's discussions of "so what" versus "not true" rhetorics. While Eisner's work is not specifically related to disabilities or ostomies, there are interesting parallels here that are important to acknowledge and amplify. See Eisner's *Bi: Notes for a Bisexual Revolution* (2013).

prolapsed or photographs of smiling old ladies" (Cleasby, 2015b).[23] In response, she took photos of herself displaying her ostomy so that others who "are feeling lost in their illness" can find her photos and feel empowered by them.

Cleasby (2015b) went on to stress that the full answer requires an examination of "how disability is seen in our society *and* also how women are viewed in society" (emphasis added). Here, Cleasby explicitly called readers' attention to the way disability, sexuality, and gender intersect, particularly in visual ways. What Cleasby seemed to be getting at is the intersection of the male gaze (which visually polices women's bodies through patriarchal norms) and the ableist gaze (which visually polices disabled bodies through ableist norms). Caught at the intersection of these gazes, Cleasby argued that she was unfairly critiqued because disabled women are not expected or allowed to be sexualized. Specifically, Cleasby questioned why women are viewed and judged differently from men.

> It's so easy to use a woman's body against them, to suggest that showing flesh
> is in some way a dart in the heart of feminists everywhere . . . It is odd isn't it
> that when we see semi-naked photographs of men that there is no backlash,
> no one suggesting they are belittling the campaign by showing their bodies.

In this response, Cleasby called out the role and implications of the male gaze directed at her body. Cleasby went on to consider how sexuality, gender, and ostomy are compounded in the backlash her photos received. She directly rejected being "slut shamed" for choosing "to show [her] sexuality alongside her disability," and she recommended that anyone who finds her sexuality "uncomfortable" "step away."

Over the course of this blog, Cleasby (2015b) reflected on the oppressive practices and systems that contributed to the backlash her photos received. And, by the end of the blog, she revisited her initial answer to the question: did her photos sexualize disability? Her revised answer clarified:

> I wouldn't say I sexualize my disability, I would say I normalize it. I show
> photographs from every part of my life, there are photos of me playing with
> the chickens, hanging out with my kinds, with my husband, my mum, in my
> gym gear, at the beach . . . I show all parts of my life because my illness and
> my disability do not change all those parts of me.

---

23. Cleasby's comments about "old ladies" hark back to Clara's comments from the *Grey's Anatomy* episode discussed in chapter 3, in which Clara claims ostomies are only for older people. The resonance here demonstrates the pervasiveness of the ostomy/elderly/disability trope.

Cleasby's corrective move from sexualizing disability to normalizing disability is an important one. Much like Townsend's photos or the photos participating in the #GetYourBellyOut campaign, Cleasby's photos rhetorically display the ostomy in particular ways to encourage the normalization of ostomies. That is, according to Cleasby, she deliberately displayed her ostomy in nonmedical-ized, sexualized ways so that viewers see her ostomy as normal. Too, Cleasby resisted her ostomy becoming her defining identity.[24] Instead, her disability is minimized as one "small" dimension of her identity and she took, posted, and shared photos of herself revealing her ostomy because, as she put it,

> The facts are that I am a woman. I have a stoma. And I live in a country where I have free speech and the freedom to show images of myself. The facts are that I make a difference. I help many people and I do it in my own way. The facts are that I am so badd ass, and I will carry on raising aware-ness, supporting people and kicking ass!

As these passages indicate, expectations and norms regarding female bodies and disabled bodies intersectionally impacted the response to Cleasby's pho-tos. Cleasby confronted assumptions that people with disabilities are asexual and relatedly unattractive and undesirable, as well as demands that female bodies are expected to meet specific westernized beauty ideals. Therefore, Cleasby's sexualized images disrupt both sets of norms—she is at once dis-abled, female, and sexual. Put another way, Cleasby's body actively resists the scrutiny of male and ableist gazes, especially as these multiple systems of oppression lead to the condemnation of her photos.

Importantly, however, Cleasby fuses normalization with destigmatization, a common but precarious move, through her images and blog posts, particu-larly the above two passages. By buttressing normalization and destigmatiza-tion, Cleasby's images have to first accept and then espouse norms related to sexiness, femininity, and ability. That is, Cleasby first moves to equate being sexy with revealing her female body; she then minimizes her ostomy and situ-ates it within a series of presumably normal activities that demonstrate how normal her disability really is. By positing normalization as the goal of her self-described "sexualized" images, Cleasby inadvertently fortifies the very system of normalcy she is trying to dismantle by suggesting that ostomies and ostomates can be made normal so long as they conform to other gendered and beauty norms.

---

24. See Shakespeare (1996) for more on disability as a definitive or all-encompassing identity.

At the same time, despite the clear intention of sexualization in Cleasby's photos, her story and the visual practices involved within it illustrate how people with disabilities and illnesses are often presumptively positioned as asexual. It seems that part of the vitriol in response to Cleasby's pictures stems from the perspective that Cleasby couldn't and shouldn't be sexual because she has an ostomy. Such thinking pushes questions about Cleasby's sexuality and disability into criticisms and policing of her body and her (in)ability to conform to norms. In this way, the critiques she experienced could be traced to stigmatizing assumptions about disability, gender, and sexuality. However, the show *Too Ugly for Love?* opens a different set of questions. Cleasby's photos and responses both align with disability studies scholarship that has repeatedly demonstrated the asexualization of people with disabilities; however, other examples from within the ostomy community complicate this understanding. To explore the complex sexualization of people with ostomies, I turn now to the case that opened this chapter: *Too Ugly for Love?*

The very premise of a show like *Too Ugly for Love?* is that people with disabilities and illnesses are sexual, or desire to be sexual, but that their sexuality is potentially stunted by the ugliness that disabilities and illnesses cast on particular bodies. In addition, *Too Ugly for Love?* not only perpetuates stigmatizing stereotypes regarding sexuality and ostomies but also potentially destigmatizes ostomies through what Cleary (2016) has called a "discourse of extraordinary normalcy" or the way people with disabilities are figured as extraordinary *because* they are "profoundly ordinary," especially through reality television.[25] Examples of this discourse might look like congratulating an ostomate for how normal they look or praising them because their ostomy isn't even noticeable, the message being: passing as normal is a feat worthy of celebration. As mentioned in the introduction of this chapter, *Too Ugly for Love?* included four[26] different people living with ostomies, Marcia, Antony, Kieran, and Matt, over the course of its three seasons. In the show's promotional materials, these ostomates are depicted as "nervous" and "anxious" about dating with an ostomy and filled with concern about how others will react when they find out about their "condition" (TLC, 2017b). For instance, Antony's biography on the show's website admitted that he is

---

25. Cleary theorizes "the discourse of extraordinary normalcy" through an analysis of another TLC reality show, *Abby & Brittany,* which starred conjoined twins, Abby and Brittany Hensel.

26. At the time of writing, I am aware of four people who were featured on the show. Because this show is on TLC's UK broadcast, the show is neither available in the US nor fully available online. The analysis presented here is based on what is available online via YouTube, Vimeo, TLC's website, and the WayBack Machine internet archive.

"afraid [his ostomy] may scare women off," and Marcia's described that she finds dating "nerve-racking," especially as she has to navigate decisions about disclosing her ostomy (TLC, 2017b). These biographies provide some initial context that frames these ostomates and their ostomy experiences in particular for the show's viewers. Specifically, ostomies are staged, from the outset, through these descriptions and throughout the show's narration, imagery, and storylines, as embodied entities that invoke nerves, fear, and anxiety, particularly related to appearance and attractiveness. Extending the initial biographies and ostomates' descriptions, the show episodes pick up these stories as viewers watch Antony, Marcia, Matt, and Kieran date and navigate whether, when, and how to reveal their ostomies to their potential partners. A discussion of all four ostomates' depictions on the show is beyond the scope of this chapter; therefore, I focus on episodes that feature Kieran in the show's final season.

Viewers are first introduced to Kieran a few episodes into the series' third season.[27] The show's narrator begins Kieran's story by explaining that after nearly a year of being single, Kieran wants to return to the dating scene. He is briefly shown eating dinner with friends as they discuss the idea of Kieran dating again, but it's not immediately clear why Kieran is "too ugly for love," as he appears to have no immediately visible condition. I suspect this is an attempt to build tension; it's a strategy commonly used in the show to reiterate the stressful decision-making process that orbits dating while "afflicted" with a disability and accompanying ugliness. We next see Kieran in his apartment bathroom as the narrator explains, "dating isn't easy for Kieran" (Nicholson, 2016a). Kieran then narrates, as he unbuttons his shirt and reveals his ostomy to the camera, "I suffer from Crohn's disease and as a result, I've had to have surgery which has left me with having to wear an ileostomy bag" (Nicholson, 2016a). He then briefly defines *ostomy* for viewers while removing his ostomy bag to reveal his stoma. With his bag removed, viewers have the chance to see Kieran's stoma and ostomy site. Unfortunately, Kieran has developed a skin condition where his ostomy bag adheres to his skin, so his stoma appears red, inflamed, and painful. The narrator clarifies that while Kieran's stoma itself is not painful, the skin condition is severe and challenging for Kieran. Throughout this scene, the camera remains focused on Kieran's abdomen, giving viewers nearly a minute to stare at Kieran's stoma and ostomy. On one hand, the introduction to ostomies and stoma provided by and through Kieran successfully depicts the complex realities of living

---

27. For context, the show toggles between two storytellers: the show's omniscient narrator and each "too ugly" person. As I recount Kieran's story, I work to make clear who the storyteller is within each event and unfolding.

with an ostomy that include changing and cleaning the bag and managing skin conditions surrounding the ostomy site. In this sense, the show provides somewhat of an educational experience for the many people who may have never seen an ostomy or understood their function. On the other hand, it is important to remember the context in which viewers are gaining this exposure to ostomies: on a show that fundamentally judges Kieran (and people like him) as "too ugly for love" explicitly because of his ostomy.

With this introduction to ostomies and Kieran's experiences, Kieran's story next picks up as he prepares for his first date on the show and the narrator builds tension: "Today, Kieran has his first proper date in twelve years, and it requires some careful planning." Standing in his bedroom with clothes on his bed, Kieran anxiously jokes, "I'm going to put my battle armor on, which is my waistcoat and pocket watch. It keeps everything in check and it's a little, just a little bit of comfort thing to keep everything in check." Here viewers observe a common practice for people with ostomies: choosing clothes that deliberately conceal the ostomy and help keep it in place.[28] Then, after we watch Kieran nervously get dressed for his date, the narrator declares, "but, before heading out, Kieran has one final thing on his to-do list." Kieran is shown packing ostomy bags, gauze, a tube of ointment, and other supplies into a paper bag that he carefully places inside a leather satchel. Kieran clarifies: "This is backup, just in case, you know, the worst-case scenario happens, and my bag leaks or tears and you have that dreaded feeling, which has happened on several occasions so from experience just, yeah, pack a spare" (Nicholson, 2016a). Again, Kieran's practice of packing extra ostomy supplies in case he needs to perform a bag change while on a date is a practice that many ostomates I've spoken to have described. Although Kieran does seem concerned about "the worst-case scenario" of a leak, he looks calm as he packs the supplies and self-assured as he places the supplies in his bag and heads off on his date. This is, of course, an extra step that people *without* ostomies do not need to consider, and it does seem that the show includes Kieran's packing of supplies to build drama. However, seeing Kieran as he describes this practice could visually communicate to the audience that there are ways to manage these "worst-case scenarios" and leaks and, consequently, shows viewers that ostomies can be manageable, not life-ending. To this point, I can't help but

---

28. During my initial ethnographic observations of a weekend-long event for women living with ostomies and chronic GI conditions, attendees spent an entire afternoon sharing a variety of tips for dating, having sex, and managing close, sexual, and romantic encounters while having an ostomy. This day came to be known as "Sexy Sunday," and much of the discussions focused on lingerie, belts, and other products that could help conceal and/or secure the ostomy.

wonder how seeing Kieran in this way may have potentially helped someone like Julia not feel so "stuck at home" (see chapter 3; CDC, 2015a).

In contrast, viewers operating within ableist ideologies are primed to see Kieran's get-ready routine as a series of undesirable, extra experiences dictated by an ostomy—packing supplies, worrying about leaks, dressing to conceal, and even changing ostomy bags while experiencing painful-looking skin conditions. All these lived experiences displayed don't necessarily encourage an empathetic stare from viewers so much as a sympathetic or even abjectifying stare. Together, these experiences could easily be viewed as evidence that life with an ostomy is abnormal and stigmatizing. Kieran's discursive practices, along with the narrator's, do provide some guidance for viewers regarding how to make meaning of the ostomy practices made visible through the show. For example, the narrator clarifies that Kieran's stoma itself isn't painful, which helps viewers differentiate Kieran's painful skin condition from assumptions that ostomies and stomas themselves are inherently painful. Additionally, Kieran's comments about how and why he selects his particular date outfit coach viewers to understand those practices in particular ways. Kieran's tone in those moments is upbeat and nervous, but those nerves are presented more as typical predate jitters than distress over the difficulty of concealing his ostomy. In these ways, the show simultaneously confronts and complicates stigmatizing stereotypes, and while it doesn't paint life with an ostomy as universally positive and easy, it doesn't suggest that it is unequivocally terrible, either.

After an unsuccessful first date,[29] Kieran is shown later in the series meeting up with a friend to discuss his dating strategy. During this conversation, viewers witness Kieran contemplating an online dating profile. With the encouragement of his friend, Kieran decides to go for it, and he quickly begins to scroll through the photos on his phone to consider various images for his profile picture. Kieran swipes to a photo of himself on the beach, arms and legs outstretched in what looks like joy as his ostomy bag is revealed. In reaction to the photo, Kieran exclaims, "Ah! This is the one, with the bag out. Do I? Do I? Do I?" His friend replies, laughing, "So, do you bag or not bag?" The two continue to laugh as Kieran smirks but then turns serious: "To bag or not to bag? . . . You know if someone doesn't want to date someone with this sort of condition, then they're not the right person so do me a favor. They'll know what to expect physically" (Nicholson, 2016a). Ultimately, he decides to

---

29. To be clear, when I say *unsuccessful* here, I mean to say that the first date Kieran is shown going on in the show ends with Kieran ultimately deciding he is not romantically interested. The date is depicted as going well in terms of Kieran's ostomy, which remains hidden and undisclosed to his date.

use the ostomy-revealing picture for his profile, which the show and Kieran insinuate is a high-stakes decision.

Toward the end of the episode, Kieran pursues another date, this time with a man named Matt, whom Kieran met through his online profile that featured his ostomy-revealing photo. The two decide to go rock climbing, and Kieran is shown again packing his "emergency kit" of extra ostomy supplies in preparation. After successfully rock climbing, Kieran privately debriefs to the camera and joyfully reports: "The date went really well, no issues with the bag whatsoever rock climbing. It just went really smoothly." Kieran and Matt are next shown grabbing a drink, where they get into a conversation about what each other is looking for in a romantic partner. Matt offers that he "really wanted to meet [Kieran] because of how much [he] opened up really, you know . . . that takes quite a lot of strength . . . that's a really admirable character in a person." Kieran appears both flattered and relieved and replies, "Well thank you. But, physically, did my bag freak you out, or? Be honest." Matt pauses momentarily before responding, "Well, it is a bit like [sigh] you know, because it is a bit different. I couldn't really just be like 'ew!' you know, all of a sudden. All the things I think about you, I couldn't just dismiss it. It kind of made me a bit more intrigued actually because you were so open about it and that just made me respect you quite a lot." After the date, Kieran is clearly excited. Smiling profusely, he energetically tells the camera that the date went "just brilliantly."

Though the show never acknowledges this complexity, Kieran's dating life, sexuality, and disability present an often overlooked and underdiscussed intersection of ostomy experience. As a queer man with an ostomy, Kieran faces many similar but also many different circumstances and potential challenges compared with ostomates like Sam Cleasby or Bethany Townsend. The similar first. Although Kieran, as a man, doesn't face the same gendered norms that women with ostomies do, there are several similarities between beauty norms for queer men and for heteronormative ciswomen. As Nathan Wheeler, a gay man with an ostomy wrote in a 2020 blog post:

> Stigma in the gay community is very high because many people (not everyone, but a lot of people) think that gay men have to be body beautiful. They should have clear skin, abs, hairless bodies, and be over six feet tall. If this is what you base a person on, chances are—you are probably going to be single for a long time!

The specific physical characteristics Wheeler described as norms for queer men mostly parallel those for women: be thin, athletic (but not too muscular); have clear, blemish-free, and hairless skin. This is not to say that gay men and women are socially expected to look the same way but that there are some similarities in the normative expectations for attractiveness and that these similarities evaluate and policy ostomy bodies across differences in sexuality and gender. Wheeler went on to note that these norms related to appearance are "very apparent online and on social media," much the same for women ostomates as evidenced by stories earlier in this chapter.

At the same time, there are important differences between the norms Kieran faces and those discussed so far in this chapter. Namely, when it comes to sexuality and the ways in which ostomates can and do meet those expectations, queer men face an entirely unique set of challenges. As Wheeler (2020) explained:

> Gay stigma with an ileostomy is even harder because there are certain things a gay man can no longer do if they have an ileostomy and a barbie butt (total removal of the rectum), like myself. Instead the gay community in terms of sex, there are a few options that a man can take. A *top*, is usually the guy doing the penetrating. A *bottom* is a male that receives the penetration and a *versatile* is something who doesn't mind which role they take; they can be either. Obviously, with an ileostomy and having the rectum removed, this is one of the things that can open you up to stigma. People that have had their rectum removed cannot be a *bottom* or a *versatile* anymore because there is nowhere to be penetrated. That function is removed from sex. You can, however, be a *top*. This is just something you have to work around with an ileostomy. (emphasis original)

The considerations and challenges that Wheeler described are made invisible in Kieran's storyline on *Too Ugly for Love?* However, that doesn't mean that they were not factors in his dating experiences depicted on the show, particularly in his anxiety about finding a partner or in the ways his two different dates responded to his ostomy. To be clear, Kieran does not disclose whether he underwent barbie butt surgery.[30] Nevertheless, there are additional norms at work and potentially being defied by Kieran at the intersection of queerness, masculinity, sex, attractiveness, and ostomies. This particular intersection is underdiscussed in general within the ostomy and IBD communities and underrepresented in my research. However, I discuss it now because it further complicates the connections between asexuality and disability. As Kim

---

30. The language of *barbie butt* is extremely common throughout the ostomy community. For those unfamiliar with Barbies, Barbie dolls are manufactured with no genitalia or anus. Thus, when the rectum and anus are removed, ostomates often call it *barbie butt surgery* because their anus is removed, and that opening is surgically closed.

(2011) noted, disability can present opportunities to explore new, alternative, or different ways to experience pleasure, sexual or otherwise, and perhaps these are an affordance to ostomies and surgeries to remove the rectum and anus for some individuals. My point here is that asexuality is not the only way that sexuality-related norms and assumptions are forced onto ostomates' identities and experiences. Kieran's story, and the specific nuances it manifests, helps showcase how an intersectional approach focused on the practices and lived experiences with ostomies is both important and necessary for a deep understanding of ostomies as well as stigmatization.

Despite the show's title and the intersectional experiences that go unexplored in Kieran's time on the show, the ways in which Kieran *is* depicted on the show ultimately communicate that dating with an ostomy is not only possible but can be successful. Kieran is never shown navigating a negative response to his ostomy, though the show's title and premise suggest that negative experiences are the rule, not the exception, for people like Kieran. It's unclear how the show would have rhetorically managed a negative reaction to Kieran's ostomy during a date, but the lack of negative experiences has a potentially empowering effect for people living with ostomies. It is possible, given how Kieran and his experiences are displayed on the show, that viewers might conclude that people with ostomies are not indeed "too ugly for love" but are instead fully capable of being loved, going on dates, and managing their ostomies at the same time. In Kieran's final appearance in the show, several episodes later, the status of Kieran and Matt's relationship is unclear, but Kieran ends by saying, "It's been the best experience actually, to go on a date and meet someone. Before I had all this self-doubt but the thing I've realized actually is that I have the right to find love" (Nicholson, 2016b).

Kieran's overall portrayal on *Too Ugly for Love?* focuses on the potential risks of revealing an ostomy. Viewers watched Kieran navigate whether, when, and how to tell and/or show dates his ostomy—that this decision was contemplated at all suggests that revealing and displaying are risky endeavors for people with ostomies. Further, as Kieran weighs whether to reveal his ostomy on his online dating profile or not, the risks of revealing become clearer and the stakes potentially higher. Revealing his ostomy could scare off potential dates before they even get to know Kieran, or it could make Kieran ugly or less attractive. Additionally, Kieran's decision to front his ostomy on his online dating profile further risks soliciting dehumanizing stares that could enable viewers of his profile to see Kieran as his ostomy instead of as a person with an ostomy. For Kieran, the decision to visually reveal his ostomy pays off because it allows him to find Matt, who then praises him for his courage in revealing it.

At the same time, Kieran is included under the guise of being too ugly for love and therefore is made a spectacle (Garland-Thomson, 1997, 2009). Audiences are encouraged to stare at and consequently objectify and judge the people featured on the show, including Kieran and the other ostomates. The show's title and framing place Kieran and the other adults on the show under rhetorical and visual scrutiny in which bodies are valued along binaries including inferior/superior, beautiful/grotesque, attractive/ugly (see Garland-Thomson, 1997, pp. 7–8). Consequently, the inclusion of Kieran and other ostomates on *Too Ugly for Love?* invites us to question the sexualization of ostomies. The show raises a variety of questions: Do ostomies disqualify people from being seen as sexy? Attractive? Loveable? Can disabled people make themselves attractive enough to find love? What happens when a person with a disability or other physical condition reveals their "true" self (TLC, 2017a)? If Kieran serves as the only evidence, then the answer appears to be no, ostomies do not render people too ugly for love. However, including ostomates on the show positions ostomies and the people who have them in a state of sexual contingency in which their sexuality and attractiveness are bound up directly in their ability to find partners who are willing to love them *despite* the ostomies. Too, the show encourages viewers to grapple with the risks of living with an ostomy, including those that accompany decisions to conceal and reveal as well as risks like skin breakdown (as when Kieran shows his ostomy to the camera during his introduction on the show) and the potential of ostomy leaks while on a date. These risks are no doubt real, and, in my estimation, the show does a fair job displaying both the existence of these risks and how people living with ostomies can successfully manage them in a way that could potentially destigmatize ostomies, despite the show's problematic positioning. Nevertheless, although Kieran ultimately does find someone who is "willing to accept his ostomy," the show simultaneously implores viewers to see living with an ostomy as a risk that could negate any chance at finding love and acceptance.

Showing Off Ostomies and Arriving at the Destination of Normal

The stories in this chapter have so far stressed two things: (1) displaying ostomies and being seen as a person with an ostomy can be a risky practice, and (2) a common goal of and/or justification for revealing ostomies, especially online, is normalization. To further interrogate the relationship between visual practices, stigmatization, and normalization, I end this chapter by examining two final examples that demonstrate the complexity of displays: Gaylyn Henderson's participation in the #AerieREAL campaign, and Jessica Grossman and her online advocacy organization/campaign, Uncover Ostomy.[31] My analysis of Henderson's and Grossman's highly public visual displays extends the discussions I have explored thus far in this chapter, specifically by considering a different set of rhetorical risks and rewards that emerge at the nexus of disability, visuality, sexuality, and gender, particularly when "normalizing" ostomies is the goal.

People with ostomies and chronic GI conditions around the world have been celebrating Aerie, an apparel company that mostly sells lingerie and athletic wear for young women. In 2014 Aerie launched its "Aerie Bras Make You Feel Real Good" campaign, coinciding with a variety of bra collections designed and advertised for "real women," which includes women of "all shapes, sizes and colors" (Callahan, 2018). Now called #AerieREAL Life, this campaign works to "spread the brand's mission to love your real self—inside and out" and to "empower and inspire the Aerie community to be the change they want to see in the world through leadership, advocacy, workshops and philanthropic partnerships" (Owens, 2020) by featuring #AerieREAL Role Models. These role models have included a breadth of women, such as Aly Raisman, a former Olympic gymnast and advocate against sexual abuse,[32] and the Tony Award–winning actor Ali Stroker, who was the "first person using a wheelchair to appear on Broadway" (Aerie, 2020a). Alongside these famous women are several noncelebrities chosen to participate in the campaign for their "passion and positive influence" and to "represent and embody" real, relatable women (Aerie, 2020c). Notably, several of these women "proudly display" disabilities, conditions, and illnesses, ranging from Down syndrome and insulin pumps to feeding tubes to, you guessed it, ostomies (Callahan, 2018).

Specifically, #AerieREAL featured Gaylyn Henderson, founder of the online advocacy organization and social media campaign Gutless and Glamorous (Gutless and Glamorous, n.d.). Like the other role models in Aerie's campaign, Henderson submitted a short video application in hopes of being selected for inclusion as one of the campaign's models. Once selected, Henderson participated in a photoshoot, where she sported various Aerie bras and underwear and, in most images, clearly displayed her ostomy. These photos not only serve as display photos for a variety of products on Aerie's website;

---

31. Readers might recall Grossman from chapter 4, where I discussed her response to Julia's Tips from Former Smokers video.

32. Raisman famously led the charge against former USA Gymnastics doctor Larry Nassar, who was accused and convicted of raping and sexually assaulting over 200 young women and girls during his tenure as the team's doctor.

they have also been featured in larger poster displays in Aerie stores across the US. When asked about her participation in the campaign, Henderson said:

> I think it is absolutely a step in the right direction. In mainstream media, it's often referenced as having an ostomy in a negative way. It may seem trivial to some, but popular cultural beliefs can be very impressionable to others. Society can make a drastic impact on a person's decision to receive an ostomy and can have a drastic impact on a person living with an ostomy. Even though ostomy is a lifesaving surgery many are reluctant to receive them because of the negative stigma. All of these factors combined makes it that much more significant that Aerie recognized how having a model with an ostomy has the ability to change and save lives! (IBD Editorial Team, 2018)

Henderson's participation in this campaign exemplified the role of visual practices in thwarting stigma. Importantly, too, Henderson is a Black woman with an ostomy and therefore resists not only ostomy stigma but also racialized notions and norms of beauty through her participation in #AerieREAL. Her participation celebrates the beauty of being an ostomate, of being a woman, and of being Black, all of which are entangled in opposition to whitestream[33] beauty norms. Unlike *Too Ugly for Love?* the Aerie campaign celebrates embodied differences (in fact, many of the same conditions featured on the TLC show have been featured in the Aerie initiative). The #AerieREAL campaign and Henderson's participation in it benchmark an important public moment because women with disabilities are not just included for token representation; they are celebrated as representations of beauty, leadership, and what "real" women look like.[34]

Of course, this campaign and the company endorsing it are ultimately geared toward selling clothes and making a profit through displays of wom-

---

33. I deliberately use *whitestream* instead of *mainstream* here, following Cedillo (2018) and Grande (2003). In doing so, I'm signaling the racialized dimensions of mainstream. Inherent in the idea of "mainstream" is the majority and thus systems of power and oppression that subjugate minoritized people. Cedillo (2018), citing Grande (2003), explained, "Whitestream . . . [is] the version of reality 'principally structured on the basis of white, middle-class experience.'"

34. This discussion of "real" women is not without problems. In implying that Aerie women are real women, they suggest that, somewhere, not-real women exist. Such opposition is nearly always problematic. That said, it seems that the goal of this language for Aerie and its campaign is to challenge westernized beauty norms, which are often manufactured through unrealistic or extreme practices (e.g., extreme dieting, cosmetic surgery, waist-training) or through digital alteration like photoshopping images and falsifying women's bodies to further instantiate problematic and unattainable beauty norms.

en's bodies, and I do not mean to suggest that this kind of marketing campaign is without flaw. However, not only has Aerie included disabled women as models, it has also begun to sell products that are specifically designed for disabilities. For example, Aerie now sells products from Abilitee Adaptive Wear, a company focused on "creating adaptive apparel for people with disabilities and medical needs that's both fashionable and empowering" (Aerie, 2020b). Among Abilitee's products are undergarments designed specifically for ostomies. The company has claimed that they created ostomy covers after hearing about experiences with leaks from ostomates. For instance, the brand makes water-resistant ostomy covers with phrases like "OH SHIT" and "HOT SHIT" that "are designed to retain leaks, should they occur, so the wearer doesn't have to worry about staining their clothing" (Aerie, 2020b). This language, paired with products responsive to ostomates' lived experiences and concerns, is another example of practices that crip and resist stigmatization. In this case, shit puns visibly and boldly displayed on ostomy covers crip the negative affiliation between ostomies and feces. As Yergeau (2018) has argued, similar to visceral emotions described by Johnson (2016), shit talk is often characterized by the need to do something, to fix, cure, or distance ourselves from feces and whatever problem has put feces in proximity. Putting language like "hot shit" on ostomy covers is a comical act of resistance that crips by combining sexiness with shit itself through a play on the common phrase *hot shit,* in which shit is not really shitty at all.

Ultimately, #AerieREAL raises important questions at the nexus of normalization, visual practices, and stigma. Garland-Thomson (2017) has argued that "disabled fashion modeling," such as Henderson's modeling for Aerie, is "at once liberatory and oppressive" (p. 376). On one hand, images that might be categorized as disabled fashion modeling participate in "capitalism's appropriate of women as sexual objects"; on the other hand, they "produce politically progressive counter images" that integrate "a previously excluded group into the dominant order" (p. 377). Embracing this complexity, Garland-Thomson proposed that disabled fashion modeling can serve as an activist response in which disabled women persist as "embodied paradoxes," at once beautiful and disabled. I'd like to end by forwarding Garland-Thomson's insights here to suggest that visual displays, including Henderson but also the many visual practices discussed in this chapter, can do the complex work of "bringing disability as a human experience out of the closet and into the normative public sphere" (p. 376) through repeatedly "refusing to normalize" (p. 377). #AerieREAL, thus, seems to offer one example of how visual practices can crip (Sandahl, 2003) the very practices and systems that subjugate people with ostomies, particularly women with ostomies. Although the campaign could be read as objectifying the bodies of disabled women, there has been extensive public support for the campaign, particularly from within the ostomy community.[35] For instance, one ostomate tweeted, "This is just another reason I LOVE @Aerie. Like I am crying y'all don't understand. As an ostomate who has been self-conscious about my colostomy, this is just so amazing to see. I'll never be over how much this means to me." Another tweeted, "This new campaign by American Eagle [Aerie's parent company] is incredible. Representation is important. Models of all colors, sizes, and models using mobility assistance devices, all looking amazing! Shout out to Gaylyn (and her ostomy!)." And, even those outside the ostomy community have praised Gaylyn's inclusion and display of her ostomy: "I can't express how happy it made me feel the first time I was online shopping & saw an Aerie model with a colostomy bag. As a person with a feeding tube, to see a beautiful woman wearing her disability like a fashion statement is so empowering" (Aerie, 2020c). In reflecting on the response overall, the advocacy organization Ostomy Connection (2019) said, "people" "went totally off-the-wall ecstatic" when Henderson's pictures began circulating as part of the campaign.

While displaying ostomies comes with many risks, the #AerieREAL campaign, and the many visual displays and stories presented in this chapter, illustrate that along with these risks can come important rewards. In fact, #AerieREAL testifies to the possibilities that can be generated when visual practices are deployed in the public sphere. Visual practices like those of Gaylyn Henderson refuse to normalize (and perhaps are prohibited from doing so), and they embrace dissent through visual displays. In other words, these visual practices undermine negative ostomy stories and resist stigma. Rather than conceal their ostomies and conform to the pressures of normalcy, ostomates like Henderson, and also Townsend and Cleasby, crip selfies by revealing their ostomies and stake claim to their right to not only exist but also celebrate their full embodiments and identities. They take normalized social media practices and spin them into something new and political, a platform for displaying ostomies, increasing ostomy awareness, and destigmatizing life with and bodies with ostomies.

However, public visual practices, as this chapter has repeatedly emphasized, participate in a rhetorical ecology where ostomy stigma, gender norms, sexuality, and normalcy intersect. As disability theorist Lennard Davis (2013) has contended, "The mythos of the normal body has created conditions for the emergence and subjection of the disabled body, the raced body, the gen-

---

35. Research has further confirmed the positive response to and implications of the Aerie campaign. See Rodgers et al. (2019) and Convertino et al. (2019).

dered body, the classed body, the geriatric body—and so on" (p. 2). Kieran's inclusion in *Too Ugly for Love?*, accusations against Cleasby for sexualizing disability, and the celebration of Henderson's inclusion as an underwear model all point to the rhetorical complexities that people with embodied differences must navigate when it comes to revealing or concealing their difference. Too, these diverse cases raise important questions about how normalcy and normalization rhetorically impact visual practices themselves. Therefore, I turn now to one final case, with Jessica Grossman, that illuminates the rhetorical impact of normalcy and normalization for disabled, gendered, raced, and sexualized bodies.

Grossman is the founder of Uncover Ostomy, a website designed to educate about ostomies and fight ostomy stigma. On the site's landing page, the first thing viewers see is a collage of six photos of Grossman. In all six photos Grossman looks directly into the camera, which has the effect of engaging viewers through what feels like direct eye contact. Two of the photos show Grossman naked, which displays her ostomy, as her hair and hands cover her breasts. In another photo, Grossman lies on a bed with a sheet that covers her breasts and the area from her hips to her knees, while strategically revealing her ostomy. In the other three photos, Grossman is partially or fully clothed, and in only one of the photos is the ostomy partially visible. The other pages on Uncover Ostomy, including a blog, calendar of events, and contact information, also feature images of Grossman displaying her ostomy. Grossman has become a well-known advocate and ostomate, in part, through revealing images like these. When Uncover Ostomy first began, an initial series of images showing Grossman displaying her ostomy by lifting her white tank top and lowering her unbuttoned jeans helped garner the attention that put Uncover Ostomy on the map.[36]

In a blog post from 2018, Grossman reflects on her decision to start Uncover Ostomy and specifically, to share photos of herself and her ostomy:

> 9 years ago, when you Googled "ostomy," you would have wished you didn't.
> It was full of very graphic pictures of stomas—not even healthy stomas—
> clear ostomy bags, bleeding scars, and just a whole whack of photos you

---

36. Not all responses to Grossman's images have been positive in the eleven years since she started Uncover Ostomy (Frohlich & Zmyslinski-Seelig, 2016; Leadley, 2016). Responses to Grossman's photos have sparked an important debate regarding how and when ostomies should be displayed publicly. On one hand, many have celebrated Grossman's choice to publicly share such images. Onlooking ostomates, people living within chronic GI conditions, and others have praised Grossman for her bravery and willingness to make her ostomy visible. Other researchers have studied Grossman and Uncover Ostomy, specifically to ask questions about visuality, ostomies, and sexuality.

would have wanted to see if you were trying to convince yourself not to have surgery. Not ideal for those who had no choice but to get an ostomy bag.

Grossman's rationale for posting her photos that reveal her ostomy matches Cleasby's. Both women were unsatisfied with the images online of ostomies, specifically because many of these images were graphic and unhelpful. Therefore, Grossman spent nearly a decade displaying her ostomies in photos shared online and encouraging others to do the same. Uncover Ostomy is defined by these photos.

However, nearly ten years after starting Uncover Ostomy, Grossman began to publicly reflect on the work she was doing and what she had planned for Uncover Ostomy moving forward. In reflecting on how Grossman wants Uncover Ostomy to evolve and grow in the coming years, Grossman (2018) stressed:

I'm posting more about my life with an ostomy on Instagram, instead of writing entire blog posts. I will continue to write blogs (even though my life is pretty boring these days), but I am going to shift more of my awareness efforts to platforms where society is used to absorbing a lot of information quickly and in visual form. After all, the ostomy is very visual, so might as well capitalize on that, right?

In making this move to share more images, particularly on Instagram because it is visual-focused, Grossman recognizes the important role that visual practices can play in normalizing ostomies and resisting ostomy stigma. Additionally, she seems committed to using visual practices to promote ostomy awareness and "chang[e] the way the world views the ostomy" (Uncover Ostomy, n.d.).

In 2019 Grossman announced big changes for the tenth anniversary of Uncover Ostomy. In a three-minute video posted to the Uncover Ostomy Instagram profile, she announces that she has "an important message" for the ostomy community. That important message? "It's time to stop showing off your ostomy." She then unpacks why she is advocating this message and further why it is important for the entire ostomy community to hear:

These past ten years, I've worked hard building Uncover Ostomy to break the negative stigma surrounding ostomy surgery. And so have you. Together we've come to accept ourselves and we've made the ostomy known through social media posts to news articles to companies showcasing people with stomas. The word ostomy has become better understood and incorporated into everyday terminology. That said, we've done a great job highlighting what makes us different. But I don't want to be different. I'm not different. And neither are you. We're normal, everyday people who just happen to have to use the bathroom in a unique way. Other than that, we're just like everyone else.

Grossman's message argues that displaying ostomies is no longer necessary or helpful in the effort to raise ostomy awareness, empower ostomates, or fight stigma. Specifically, she insists, people with ostomies are "normal, everyday people"; thus, showing off ostomies in photos online serves to differentiate ostomies rather than normalize them. She adds, "We've done such a great job at setting ourselves apart from the crowd, but we put ourselves in a category of people with different needs and it's time to stop that." One interpretation of Grossman's argument here is that she is suggesting that people with ostomies need to stop identifying as different and, more specifically, it seems, as disabled. As Garland-Thomson (2017) might explain, Grossman was advocating for the ostomy body to become the "unobtrusive body" that "may pass unnoticed" (p. 367) in society and thus go unmarked as abnormal and stigmatized. While she does not use that language directly, her contention that people with ostomies have "put [themselves] in a category of people with different needs" does raise the question of who exactly she means by "people with different needs" and why exactly it is problematic to have different needs. To justify her call for people with ostomies to stop showing them off, Grossman focuses on ostomies' practical function—to excrete waste. She asks viewers, "I mean, how many other times have you seen someone else flash their butt? Hopefully not a lot."

Despite her charge to the ostomy community, Grossman (2019) explains that she will continue to release photos "unlike" ones she has previously shared. These new photos, Grossman says, are different in that they do not draw attention to her ostomy bag but instead focus on *her* because the Uncover Ostomy movement is "about living normally with an ostomy, as if it wasn't such a big deal because it's not." Grossman ends the video with the following directive for viewers:

Don't stop talking about your ostomy. Don't stop telling people how it saved your life. But maybe stop voluntarily showing people where you shit from. Instead, show them how awesome you are as a whole. That's what these photos are meant to represent, and this is the message that I want to take forward. I hope you'll join me because it's time to stop showing off your ostomy and it's time to start showing off you.

Much like Cleasby and the #GetYourBellyOut campaign examples, Grossman rejects her ostomy becoming her sole or total identity. She further argues that people with ostomies should engage in particular discursive and visual practices (those that de-emphasize or conceal ostomies) to normalize ostomies. Notably, Grossman's comments here enact what Linton (1998) has called the "rhetoric of overcoming" in which disability itself isn't overcome (for most, this isn't possible) but instead social stigma is overcome, thus eliminating the problem with disability. Such rhetoric is often extremely problematic, especially when leveraged by individuals who otherwise benefit from privilege. In the case of Grossman, her announcement that ostomies no longer need to be amplified because they put ostomates in "a category of people with different needs" is not only ableist in that it suggests that being a person with different needs is abnormal; it also relies on racial, sexuality, and gendered privilege that many ostomates are not advantaged by. That is, as a White-presenting, cisgender, heterosexual woman with access to healthcare, resources, and support (as evidenced by other posts on her blog), Grossman has little authority to speak on behalf of *all* ostomates. Many ostomates are Black, Indigenous and people of color (BIPOC); many cannot so readily conceal their ostomies (because of placement of the ostomy itself on the abdomen, access to clothes that conceal, or access to resources that help them manage the ostomy itself); and many across genders do not conform to beauty and appearance norms in the ways that Grossman does.

My analysis here is not intended to belittle Grossman's ostomy positivity, nor to suggest that Grossman hasn't faced stigma or challenges with her ostomy. Grossman's individual lived experiences may very well suggest to her that ostomy stigma has been dismantled enough that ostomies too can join the ranks of unmarked, unnoticed normal embodiments. My point is that Grossman's call for all other ostomates to "join her" in de-emphasizing ostomies, and embrace being "normal, everyday people," only works (and even then, not with any amount of certainty) for ostomates who share her identities and lived experiences. Moreover, her assessment that "the word ostomy has become better understood and incorporated into everyday terminology," partnered with the contrasting statements that the ostomy community has devoted the last ten years to fighting ostomy stigma, suggests that this battle is over. Ostomy stigma solved; normalcy achieved. This assessment, though, can only be made by ignoring or isolating other intersecting experiences and identities that are not represented by Grossman and by assuming that Grossman's individual experiences can speak for all ostomy and chronic GI experiences. In sum, the normalization that Grossman suggests has been achieved for ostomies and ostomates is a fraught accomplishment that belies the intersectional oppression and lived realities of many ostomates.

In step with my analysis, several commenters challenged the story Grossman was presenting about ostomies and the recommendations she was making for other ostomates. That is, not everyone in the ostomy community supported Grossman's message and her suggestion that the ostomy community had eclipsed the need to raise awareness and resist stigma through displaying the ostomy. Of the eleven comments that were left in response to the video, five challenged Grossman's evaluation of the ostomy community and its needs. In response to Grossman's post, one commenter addressed the never-ending fight against stigma, and specifically the self-centeredness the commenter felt was apparent in Grossman's comments:

> These pics are therefore just modelling photos of you, posted to your "ostomy themed & named" blog that you don't want to be ALL about the ostomy but how you live life . . . I'm kinda confused [to be honest]. *The awareness is never finished, erasing the stigma still has so far to go, teaching those that are vulnerable and scared about the mechanics of living with an ostomy is still vital.* Yes we can live a normal life & yes we don't want to feel singled out as "different" but that doesn't mean we have to stop sharing knowledge, experience, negatives & images of our bags. Sadly, I think this 10yr anniversary campaign feels as though it's more about you, than anything ostomy related. (emphasis added)

Another comment articulated the complexity of Grossman's mandate for the community:

> I agree that when it comes to awareness we can certainly do that and keep our shirts on . . . but I'm torn with the negative vibe you kinda threw out there towards those of us who choose to show "where we shit from." I show my bag because it is part of me . . . I show my bag because I want to show other woman they don't have to hide themselves to make society comfortable, I show my bag because it helps me accept myself, I show my bag because it DOES NOT define me.

Both responses to Grossman emphasize that there is critical rhetorical value in continuing to share images that reveal the ostomy. Building community, empowering ostomates, resisting stigma, educating others—these are the reasons commenters argue that displaying ostomies has been and continues to be an important rhetorical practice.

Conclusion

Ultimately, the complexity of visual practices, particularly along axes of gender, disability, and sexuality, raised by Grossman's video, its responses, and the other visual stories presented in this chapter remind me of a line from Garland-Thomson's (2009) *Staring: How We Look*: "Normality is the destination to which we all hasten and the stick used to drive us there" (p. 31). While Grossman (2019) argues that the ostomy community has arrived at the destination of normal and should consequently work to stay there, it's clear that many others in the community still feel pressured by the stick to get there. The many stories and experiences explored in this book evidence that not everyone in the ostomy community feels that ostomies have been successfully normalized, nor that normalization is the ultimate goal. Indeed, the responses to Grossman's video and the ongoing #GetYourBellyOut campaign provide just two examples that attest to the ongoing need for acts, like sharing pictures and telling stories, that resist stigma, empower people living with ostomies and chronic GI conditions, and shape how ostomies are made to mean in the everyday experiences of individuals who live with these conditions *and* in the public sphere.

The visual practices and stories explored in this chapter signal that "normalization" is, at the very least, a complex goal. On one hand, thousands of people have worked and are working to destigmatize and subsequently normalize ostomies through visual practices. People living with ostomies and chronic GI conditions are retooling visual practices like taking selfies to place ostomies within the public, social sphere and thus position ostomies as normal and ordinary. On the other hand, normalization is the very process by which ostomies have been deemed abnormal and problematic in the first place, which raises the question whether normality is actually the best destination. Too, normalization, as a manifestation of the interlocking systems of power that minoritize, leaves many ostomates behind in our contemporary moment. Normalization requires an embracing of privilege, when people with ostomies and chronic GI conditions, along with other minoritized groups and privileged allies, might instead work to dismantle systems of oppression altogether. For many people with ostomies and chronic GI conditions, to work toward normality is to strive for invisibility, which is perhaps what Grossman was advocating for. If normalization is the goal, then posting images that reveal ostomies and chronic GI conditions is a step toward making ostomies so ordinary that they can be simultaneously visible and invisible, seen but not stared at. Moreover, it is the collective pressure to be normal that demands that people look, act, evacuate waste, and live in particular ways.

As this chapter has also argued, normality is caught up in an array of norms and expectations, related not just to disability but also to gender, sexuality, and, no doubt, class and race. As Foucault (1995) summarized, "The judges of normality are present everywhere" (p. 304). Making sense of the visual practices being deployed as acts of resistance against stigma requires intersectional considerations that attune to the multiple systems of norms at work. As Leadley (2016) reminds us, "When one speaks of 'normal' bodies, one must take into account not only ability, but also the assumed cis male, heterosexual assumptions implicitly linked to thinking of the so-called 'normal' body" (p. 26). Indeed, arriving at normality in one capacity does not guarantee residence there.

CHAPTER 6

Thinking with Stories

Toward Stigma Interventions

EACH OF THE CHAPTERS in this book tells a different story—many different stories, in fact—and each story illuminates what it is like to deal with stigma, live with chronic conditions, and navigate these experiences through and within stories. These stories bring to light not only the complexities of living with chronic conditions but also the myriad ways in which stigma is done and undone. From the outset, I aimed to listen to these stories and to theorize stigma as an act of care because, as others have argued, care can orient us toward what matters most to our participants and their embodied lived experiences (Dolmage, 2014; Scott & Gouge, 2019). In this book, acting in care has motivated me to listen and retell many stories. Yet, I know that I've told only a few of the many stories and experiences worth telling about ostomies, chronic gastrointestinal (GI) conditions, stigma, and lived experiences more broadly. As Johnson (2014) poignantly reminds me:

> There is something missing . . . tens of thousands of stories that will never
> be told. Those stories, and the faces, voices, and lives behind them, haunt
> this story, as they haunt all histories. Histories are intrinsically rhetorical.
> They select and interpret a certain reality for their audiences and each
> time something is made present, something is made absent by default.
> (p. 178)

Johnson's sentiment here speaks to a type of historical story that this book does not tell; however, the insight remains relevant. I've included many stigma stories in this book—stories of ostomy leaks and lifesaving stomas, stories of being stigmatized and fighting back, stories of bathroom stalls and selfies. In telling these stories, I've left many others untold; thus, the insights offered through a rhetorical investigation of stigma stories are incomplete but nevertheless important. In collaboration with the people I observed, interviewed, and listened to throughout this project, I aimed to make visible the rich possibilities for both disciplinary insight and intervention in the domains of chronic illness, stigma, disability, and embodiment through a study of stories and lived experiences.

Through a rhetorical praxiographic approach, I have argued that the stories people tell about experiences with stigma and conditions that are frequently stigmatized, like ostomies, have something important to teach us about stigma's rhetoricity. I've also argued for a particular approach to listening to these stories—that is, to listen to the stories and the lived experiences that are shared within them as if they tell about the events of what it is like to live with stigma, an ostomy, or chronic GI conditions (see Mol, 2002). Practicing such listening has allowed me to consider how a variety of rhetorical forces—fear, ableism, social media, racism, medical institutions, beauty norms, disability stereotypes, television shows, histories, feces, and temporality—all participate in stigmatization; and, of course, this list is incomplete. Nonetheless, the praxiographic approach I've used to study stigma has demonstrated the material, discursive, affective, social, institutional, and individual actors and practices implicated in stigma. In closing this book, I reflect on the scholarly, interventional, and personal insights that emerge from in this analysis.

The Value of a Praxiographic Approach to Stories

I began this book by acknowledging the complex and diverse ways that stigma has been studied across disciplines. Specifically, I entered the scholarly arena of stigma by laying groundwork from previous research in rhetoric, disability studies, and sociology, and, in doing so, I positioned the rhetorical study of stigma undertaken in this book as something to add to these conversations. I advocated for a praxiographic approach to stigma through stories that (1) treats people as their own ethnographers, and (2) studies stigma as a set of practices rather than an inherent property of particular entities, individuals, or conditions. This move, I argued, is not just methodological but ethical, in that it attempts to theorize stigma while looking for ways to intervene in stigma, which requires first that we see stigma not as something that is given in the world but as something that is done through practices and made meaningful through those practices along with the systems and logics that orient us in the world. Accordingly, this praxiographic approach to stigma stories invites researchers to recognize the rhetorical processes, experiences, and practices in which stigma is enacted or countered, instead of placing stigma as a psychological phenomenon or as an attribute inherent in particular individuals, conditions, or bodies.

More broadly, such praxiographic listening enables rhetoric of health and medicine (RHM) to simultaneously capitalize on its commitments to rhetorical analysis, lived experience, and advocacy/intervention. Lived experiences are caught up in the stories we tell just as much as the stories are caught up in lived experience—the two richly inform each other, for better or worse. In advocating for a praxiographic approach, I have attempted to demonstrate how praxiography can complement critical and rhetorical analyses, particularly by orienting researchers, in RHM and beyond, to the embodied lived experiences that profoundly engage in meaning-making of bodies, disabilities, chronic conditions, and experiences. "The stories people tell," as Mol (2002) put it, "do not just present grids of meaning. They also convey a lot about legs, shopping trolleys, or staircases. What people say in an interview doesn't only reveal their perspective, but it also tells us about the events they have lived through" (p. 15).

Applying this praxiographic approach to stigma stories, I then spent chapters 3, 4, and 5 focusing on a variety of stories—public, personal, visual—in which stigma was enacted, resisted, and otherwise imbricated in the ways people spoke, moved through the world, acted toward others, and experienced chronic GI conditions and ostomies. I thus praxiographically listened to many stories as a means of following stigma. In doing so, I first listened to public stories about ostomies that consistently stage the ostomy as a leaky worst-case scenario. These stories, told by institutions perceived as credible, like the CDC, police officers, and a prized medical TV show, demonstrated that stigma emerges through the complex entanglement among key entities, including histories of ostomies, negative ostomy experiences, visceral publics, and systems of power (ableism, sexism, and racism) that steer audiences to participate in meaning-making about ostomies that stigmatizes through fear and rejection of particular bodies and experiences.

In recognition that a single public story of ostomies does not tell the whole story, in chapter 4 I listened to disruptive ostomy stories, stories, and experiences that do not align with the dominant public ostomy story. These disruptive stories suggested that the experiences of many people living with ostomies are not solely defined by leaks, fear, isolation, and a compulsive desire for life before the ostomy. Instead, for many ostomates, the experiences that define their ostomies are positive: leaving the hospital, healing from debilitating disease, and returning to desired activities like exercise, dating, and traveling. Through these positive experiences, the ostomy is staged as lifesaving and empowering, not a worst-case last resort. And, in turn, these positive experiences enable many ostomates to fully embrace life with or after receiving their ostomies, rather than miss their before-ostomy life. In sharing these alternative experiences, these ostomates challenge the idea that the ostomy is a "single passive object" and show that what an ostomy *is* depends on how an ostomy *is done* (Mol, 2002, p. 5). These disruptive stories, and the experiences shared within them, further challenge ableist assumptions about what life with a disability should be; that is, they tell us that life with an ostomy can be and often is better than life without one.

Finally, chapter 5 asserted not only that stigma is caught up in ableism but that sexism and gendered expectations are also strongly at work within the experiences of ostomates and the de/stabilization of stigma. Through discussions of various visual practices within the ostomy and chronic GI conditions community, this chapter argued that such practices, though risky, operate as acts of resistance against stigma. Specifically, displaying ostomies and evidence of chronic GI conditions in public contexts provides one avenue for resisting norms of sexuality, beauty, ability, and gender while offering a way for individuals to bring their conditions and related experiences into the "normative public sphere" (Garland-Thomson, 2017, p. 376). This analysis of visual practices as complex acts of resistance interrogated the complexity of normalization as a solution to stigma.

Collectively, this praxiographic approach has revealed three key takeaways regarding stigma's rhetoricity. The following sections summarize how the specific insights of this book might influence or motivate future work on stigma.

Stigma as a rhetorical practice, not an inherent quality. On its most basic level, this book argues that stigma is not an inherent quality, mark, or property of entities; instead, stigma is better understood as the product of rhetorical practices. In the context of this book, positioning stigma as a rhetorical practice has revealed that ostomies are not inherently scary, dehumanizing, or gross; instead, ostomies are *made to mean* in these negative ways through oppressive practices like staring and stereotyping and through focusing on solely negative experiences like experiences with leaks and social isolation. In other words, the stories in this book demonstrate that stigma is not inherent in ostomies but is instead a manifestation of rhetorical forces. Stories and the lived experiences within them, in other words, operate like arguments that persuade others about what to think and feel about ostomies. The lived experiences with ostomies shared through stories stage the ostomy as a leaking bag or a surgery that enables freedom from debilitating disease while communicating to listeners what those experiences mean: positive, negative, demeaning, empowering, de/stigmatizing, or otherwise. Listening to stigma stories as if they "tell about events" and experiences with stigma, accordingly, (1) foregrounds practices that de/stabilize stigma, and (2) reminds us that there are multiple ways to live with and experience ostomies and thus multiple ostomies (e.g., worst-case scenarios and lifesaving technologies). These findings are obviously ostomy-specific; however, the foundational insight that stigma surfaces in rhetorical, material-discursive practices is applicable beyond ostomies and chronic GI conditions. Future rhetorical studies of stigma might extend and complicate my findings to develop richer understandings of how rhetorical practice participates in the stigmatization of any range of conditions or lived experiences. As chapter 1 pointed out, there is, unfortunately, no shortage of conditions that are stigmatized. Therefore, I offer the insights of my work as an invitation for RHM to apply and adapt my praxiographic approach to theorize and intervene in the stigmatization of other conditions.

Stigma is imbricated in multiple, intersecting systems of power. In addition to making an ethical argument about how to study stigma and, therefore, an argument about what stigma is, this book advocates for attuning to how stigmatization is enabled by a variety of norms rooted in ableism, sexism, racism, gendered expectations, medicalization, and ageism. And although the stories in this book and my analysis of them did not overtly address them, I've no doubt that the enactment of classism, homophobia, transphobia, and many other forces are enmeshed in stigmatization. Recognizing stigma as a product of these systems is key to not only understanding stigma but intervening in it. Thus, this book argued that disability studies, especially a political/relational model of disability, and RHM can mutually inform each other. The productive overlaps across disability studies and RHM are complex but nevertheless highly generative for understanding how power circulates and participates in the meaning-making of embodied experience and difference. Work in this area, of course, has been ongoing, but recently there have been calls for additional scholarship at the intersections of disability and RHM (Reed & Meredith, 2020; Scott & Melonçon, 2019). My hope is that this book contributes to these conversations and brings disability studies to the fore for other rhetoricians of health and medicine.

Stigma acts across a spectrum of rhetorical activity. In chapter 1, I proposed that stigma actively operates through individuals and individual interactions, as well as across the public sphere including institutional, cultural, and social spaces. Various stigma stories in this book exemplified the enactment and resistance of stigma across this spectrum. For instance, my own story that opens chapter 2 showcased how stigma is enacted in interpersonal exchanges. In contrast, the highly public stories in chapter 3 illustrated how stigma moves from individual experiences to the institutional level and into the public culture; and the stories in Chapter 4 showed how individuals work independently and collectively to nuance and complicate singular public narratives that become dominant. The visual stories in chapter 5 further indicate how digital interactions and circulation can both resist and fortify stigmatization. Too, all these stories are in dialogue with each other as they circulate in the public sphere, collaboratively curating the meaning(s) of ostomies and chronic GI conditions. Accordingly, the stories across this book, while grounded in their commonality of ostomies and chronic GI conditions, can serve as examples for where future rhetorical examinations of stigmatization of other conditions, illness, and disabilities might look for stigma's subtle and overt manifestations. Stigma stories as a concept and the praxiographic approach I took to investigate them also offer one set of tools for future work interested in exploring the webs of rhetorical activities in which stigma emerges, operates, and de/stabilizes.

Interventional Insights

While the insights of my investigation into the rhetoricity of stigma have pointed to a variety of conclusions for RHM and allied scholars, I'd like to also explicate the practical, interventional implications that might emerge from this book. In particular, this rhetorical investigation of stigma has the potential to intervene in the practices and experiences for people living with ostomies and chronic GI conditions, healthcare providers, and public institutions such as the CDC. I offer two interrelated strategies—thinking with stories and embodying empathy—that a variety of stakeholders, including scholars in RHM and allied fields, as well as healthcare providers, institutions like the CDC, or any individual person, might adopt to dismantle stigma. In these final sections, I define these strategies and elucidate how they might be helpful and just responses to stigma.

In the opening of his oft-cited book *Wounded Storyteller,* Arthur Frank (2013) advocated that we move away from thinking *about* stories and instead begin to think *with* stories. Clarifying this distinction, Frank outlined: "To think *about* a story is to reduce it to content and then analyze that content.

Thinking *with* stories . . . is to experience it affecting one's own life" (p. 23; emphasis added). Frank (2010) further discerned that to think with stories is to get "caught up" in them, to allow them to "get under [our] skin" and "affect the terms in which [we] think, know, and perceive" (p. 28). These lines from Frank also evoke Candice Rai's (2016) concept of rhetoric offered in the opening chapter, in which she argued that rhetoric too "gets under our skin" (p. 7). To bring Frank and Rai together, I advocate for thinking rhetorically with stories as a strategy that affords empathy and an opportunity for intervention motivated by reflection. With this book, I have attempted to think rhetorically with stories that at once tell us what it is like to live with an ostomy or chronic GI condition and how stigma is done and undone. Therefore, as a way of both concluding and generating future work, I'd like to think with the stigma stories presented throughout this book and consider how these stories can affect practices moving forward and shape the practices and experiences that matter most to people.

A perhaps obvious but nevertheless important conclusion of my investigation of stigma stories is that stories are profoundly important, especially when we think with them. Stories are not only descriptive; they can also be prescriptive. In other words, they can tell how others have lived or are living with disability or illness, which affords us the opportunity to reflect on how our own lived experiences might be changed. Specifically, for people living with ostomies and chronic GI conditions, listening to others' stories can help others change and manage their own lives. Indeed, telling and sharing stories is as much for ourselves as it is for others; these practices enable us to bear witness to what others experience in their own day-to-day lives (Frank, 2013). As one interview participant told me:

> People need to realize that we need to be real with each other and share our stories authentically with each other so we can learn to have a heart for people in our lives. I don't always have to be happy about dealing with [my ostomy]. There are days that it breaks me down . . . it's not fun. But I have this life, and I'm going to make it amazing and that's fine. And, at least you know who I am, I don't have to act anymore. That's my message more than anything: we all have a story to tell. Tell the real one and people will love you for it . . . together we can empathize a lot more when we know each other's stories.

Heeding this participant's call, I am actively collaborating with an organization called Girls with Guts to help others think with stories and learn from others' stories and experiences. The organization's mission is to "support and empower women with inflammatory bowel disease (Crohn's disease & ulcerative colitis) and/or ostomies through the building of sisterhood and self-esteem" (Girls with Guts, 2020). Over the course of writing this book, I have worked with and talked to many women affiliated with Girls with Guts and thus turned to this organization with initial findings from my research in hopes of identifying useful interventions. As a result of these discussions, I am working with Girls with Guts and its current president, Alicia Aiello, to create a digital storytelling archive that highlights the stories of women with ostomies and chronic GI conditions. To date, we have recorded the stories that five women offered in response to this question: If you could tell other people one story about what it is like to live with your condition, what would that story be? These five initial videos feature stories from women living with permanent and temporary ostomies as well as Crohn's disease, ulcerative colitis, and a j-pouch. The goal of this project is to create an archive that patients, providers, caregivers, family members, and the general public can use to learn more about lived experiences with these conditions. It is one way to add nuance to the public story/ies about ostomies and chronic GI conditions. Moving forward, we hope to incorporate additional stories from diverse perspectives (including but not limited to women) that can speak to the many ways to live with an ostomy or chronic GI conditions.

This digital storytelling archive not only provides access to stories; it further can serve as a repository for the ways that ostomates and people living with chronic GI conditions respond to stigmatizing experiences. Each of the first five videos we have collected addresses both triumphs and challenges of living with these conditions as well as how the storyteller responded to these experiences. In this way, these stories provide potential strategies and practices that others can learn from. Stories enable others "to construct new maps and new perceptions of their relationships to the world" (Frank, 2013, p. 3). Thus, this storytelling archive can support others living with, considering, or caring for ostomies and chronic GI conditions by providing a window into the ways people already living with these conditions navigate the world. Overall, the Girls with Guts video project is one practical way I am using this research to intervene in stigma and advocate for people living with these conditions. My hope is that this project will encourage others to think with these stories, allowing the stories and experiences shared within them to affect the ways ostomies and chronic GI conditions are understood and engaged.

Thinking with the stories I heard over the course of my research points to a variety of additional interventions. During interviews, I asked participants what they thought the best strategies for dismantling stigma are. In their responses, I was surprised to hear the same answers over and over: educate and raise awareness. Participants consistently stressed that many of their stigmatizing experiences were the product of "ignorance." People just "do not understand what an ostomy is," one participant told me as she sighed, sounding both frustrated and exhausted. Another participant summarized, "So much of the fear about ostomies is just that people don't know what they are or why people have them. People just know it's a bag full of poop." These comments and others like them indicate just how important ostomy stories are in the public sphere, as chapters 3 and 4 also argued. People learn from the stories told about living with an ostomy or chronic GI condition; thus, it is critical that those stories show the diversity of lived experiences, not just negative ones. In line with this suggestion, participants proposed a range of strategies to raise awareness of ostomies and chronic GI conditions specifically strategies that make them visible (literally and socially) and foreground ostomies' lifesaving and empowering potential. One participant remarked that "being honest" about living with an ostomy, showing others her ostomy through pictures, and revealing it during interpersonal encounters have been strategies she has personally used to destigmatize:

> I think the more honest I've been . . . posting pictures of my ostomy even just like a week after my [ostomy] surgery with my stomach all poofy and with some pretty intense incisions. It helped destigmatize it. The more I show people or people have seen it, the less afraid they get. So I think it's really important and cool to do that. Everybody's stomach looks different and I think it's great to show that.

Like the displays in chapter 5, this participant felt that visual practices are one way individuals can intervene in stigma on both personal and public levels. Other people I spoke with also advocated for being open and honest in personal interactions and for telling others about living with a GI condition. These suggestions signal the importance of telling, listening to, and thinking with stories.

In addition to these strategies, many participants pointed out that destigmatization needs to occur not only in the public sphere but also within healthcare spaces. Several interview participants expressed frustration and disappointment with healthcare providers' lack of education and awareness. Here we can also recall Hilary's story from chapter 2 that detailed interactions with nurses as some of the "most stigmatizing" experience she had ever had. Adding to Hilary's experiences, another interview participant, Keisha, lamented, "Most of my providers don't know anything about ostomies. I'm their only patient with an ostomy so that's been a little difficult . . . it's very stressful." Elaborating on this stress, Keisha said that none of her local health-care providers are able to help her when she has issues with skin breakdown, despite repeatedly reporting these as issues to her providers. Instead of her providers seeking the necessary information to properly care for Keisha, she said, she travels several hours to see an ostomy- and wound-care nurse and otherwise relies on other ostomates via social media groups and digital communities to help her manage her own ostomy.

Moreover, when I asked interview participants whether their providers had ever discussed stigma with them, not one of my twenty participants said yes. Every interview participant, instead, told me that their healthcare providers didn't talk to them about stigma or what it might mean to live with an ostomy beyond medically related experiences. One participant said that when she brought up concerns related to stigmatizing experiences she had, a provider shrugged and casually offered to refer her to a therapist. To be fair, this provider may have been well intentioned and, by suggesting the referral, acknowledging the limitations of their own expertise. Nonetheless, it is alarming that any provider whose practice includes caring for current ostomates and helping patients contemplate decisions about whether to undergo ostomy surgery or not may not see stigmatizing experience as even somewhat within their purview. Another interview participant's response echoes similar concerns:

> My GI hasn't ever brought up stigma. I don't know. I guess we don't have a ton of time to talk during appointments anyway. But what immediately popped into my head when you asked that question [has a provider ever talked to you about stigma?] was this time when my provider kept saying that my body failed me and that's why I needed to get an ostomy. Like who says that? My body isn't a failure. This stupid disease is and the fact that medicine has no cure is a failure. Ugh. That crushed me.

This participant's story and experience confirm just how impactful healthcare providers and their practices are when it comes to stigma. Notably, this participant later explained that she was overall "pretty happy" with the care she has received from her medical team, but her comments about embodied failure showcase that stigma can creep up where it is least expected and perhaps most powerful.

Encouraging healthcare providers to listen to and think with stories is, therefore, another interventional pathway illuminated by this book. Indeed, this finding aligns well with work already underway across medicine, though, as I'll explain, this finding also complicates this ongoing work. Empathy has been identified as an important dimension of chronic illness care (Jerant et al., 2005; Weed, 2012). In acknowledgment of the key role that empathy plays in care, medical schools, nursing programs, and physical therapy programs, among others, have begun to integrate training designed to foster empathy in future healthcare providers. For instance, many medical school programs have incorporated "standardized patient programs," which bring in trained individuals (often actors) to act as patients in live-action clinic simulations. Additionally, courses and programs in medical humanities[1] and narrative medicine have begun popping up across the country in response to an increased desire to provide insight into the lived experiences of patients. Such medical humanities and narrative medicine programs are grounded in the idea that stories are not only informative but interventional.

One concrete way these programs aim to foster empathy is through simulation experiences in which students physically engage in scenarios designed to emulate real clinical scenarios. In addition to providing students the opportunity to develop technical literacies in cognitive and embodied capacities, nursing simulation experiences have specifically been used to blend "kinesthetic actions and deliberate reflection" (Díaz et al., 2015, p. 513) in order to "enhance empathy" and "create caring and empathetic nurses" (Maruca et al., 2015; see also Díaz et al., 2015). In other words, such simulations work to make empathy core to the identity of nursing professionals through embodied experiences.

One specific type of nursing simulation is especially relevant within the context of this book: the ostomy simulation—in which prospective nurses wear an ostomy pouch through their regular daily routines for a day. It is heartening that nursing schools have recognized both the likelihood that nurses will interact with an ostomate and the important role nurses play in the care of these patients. Often, nurses are the *only* people ostomates have to teach them how to live with this new, long-term condition and technology. However, Gemmill et al. (2011) found that although nurses are a primary educator and care provider for new patients with ostomies, many nurses are uncomfortable caring for ostomate patients. In response to these findings, nursing programs have begun to include ostomy simulation experiences to address what has been called "empathy gaps" as well as educational gaps in ostomy care (Weed, 2012). By requiring nursing students to physically wear an ostomy pouch (i.e., use adhesive or a belt to physically attach the ostomy pouch to their bodies), these simulation experiences attempt to teach

---

1. See Campbell (2018) for a more thorough discussion of the role that medical humanities curriculum plays in medical education.

the embodied reality of living with a long-term condition and technology. Ostomy simulations therefore present a rich site for investigating empathy as an embodied healthy literacy.

Although ostomy simulations are geared toward fostering empathy, many of my interview participants questioned the effectiveness of such experiences. For instance, many were pleased that nursing programs were emphasizing ostomy education, and many responded positively to the idea of ostomy simulations, particularly for helping nurses understand the embodied dimensions of changing an ostomy bag—a skill often necessary when caring for an ostomate. However, several pointed out that a simulation experience cannot fully replicate the chronic and embodied challenges of ostomies, including leaks and stigma, as well as the often chronic nature of living with an ostomy. Indeed, interview participants expressed concern that these simulations had the potential to backfire, engendering apathy or callousness toward ostomates' experiences and concerns if the simulations simplified the complexity of life with an ostomy. One interview participant reflected:

> I think it's really cool . . . I've seen a lot of people on social media who will have their partner wear an ostomy for World Ostomy Day. It's really important . . . but I think it's really hard to fully simulate the experience because they don't get the experience of the bag filling up or walking around with a full bag on your stomach. Or like oh, I ate and then thirty minutes later it starts filling up . . . I think it's a step in the right direction but it is by no means what it is actually like wearing an ostomy for a day.

Another participant provided similar feedback:

> Well, obviously [nursing simulations] are not very accurate, I mean it's good that they are doing it, but if you don't wear it long term you don't have the skin breakdown and if you don't have the output you don't have the concern for leakage, so I mean I guess it's good that they learn how to put it on, but they don't anything to work with what's real . . . it's kind of fake learning.

While wearing an ostomy for a day can *begin* to foster empathy, as this interview participant noted, a single-day simulation is not sufficient to capture what it is like to live with an ostomy long term. It's clear from these comments that living with an ostomy is more than simply wearing an ostomy pouch for a day. According to my interview participants, a richer, deeper engagement with lived experiences of having an ostomy is necessary to understand and care for ostomates.

I followed up with participants who shared these cautions regarding ostomy simulations and encouraging empathy. What would be better? I asked, and in response I heard the same answer repeatedly: bring ostomates in and listen to the stories they share. One participant said, "Have actual ostomates be in the classroom with them for a day or have actual ostomates come in for hands-on, so they can see the different kinds of stomas and ostomies and hear about what it's actually like to live with them." Living with an ostomy is more than simply affixing a pouch to the abdomen. As many interview participants recommended, listening to the lived experiences of ostomates is more important than pretending to be an ostomate for a day. These reactions to ostomy simulations point to the value of listening to stories and engaging lived experiences. In particular, these responses clearly articulate that there is more living with an ostomy or any chronic condition than any simulation can attempt to recreate.

Moreover, it is not just healthcare providers who might benefit from listening to and thinking with stigma stories. Health-related institutions like the CDC or the National Center for Chronic Disease Prevention and Health Promotion may also learn from stories. For instance, the Julia controversy exposes a place where diverse and even disruptive stories and lived experiences might be especially informative. The insights garnered through listening to stigma stories help showcase the value in understanding the rhetorical ecology in which public stories circulate. In particular, the analysis presented in chapters 3 and 4 illustrates the continued need for health organizations and other authoritative voices to more effectively and comprehensively engage with diverse patients and their stories. The CDC clearly had a particular audience (current and potential smokers) and purpose (decrease smoking) in mind as they crafted the Tips from Former Smokers campaign, which obscured the complexity of communicating within the public sphere. The CDC's reliance on the negative ostomy metanarrative failed to consider that ostomy experiences and stories might go beyond what any single person can offer.

Overall, thinking with these stories and the recommendations for intervention offered within them identifies at least some initial intervention pathways that include increasing public and institutional knowledge and awareness through micro-level and macro-level visibility, including visual displays, storytelling, and media representations, and expanding healthcare-provider education into ostomies and ostomy management by more fully collaborating with patients and engaging their stories and experiences. Listening to stories as informant accounts that tell about events (Mattingly, 1998; Mol, 2002, p. 20) can further enable us to listen *with* those stories and the events within them as a way of identifying ways to move forward. Indeed, Frank

(2010) argued, "Stories do not simply report past events. Stories project possible futures" (p. 10). In these ways, a praxiographic approach to stigma stories further supplemented by thinking with those stories is akin to the kind of rhetorical listening that Krista Ratcliffe (2005) has called for. Following these calls, I advocate for thinking with stories as one way that a rhetorical investigation into stigma stories can shape possible futures and eradicate stigma.

Conducting Entangled Research

I want to end this book by briefly reflecting on what it was like to study the stigmatization of a condition that I live with. Specifically, I offer reflections regarding my patient/researcher identities throughout the research and writing of this book. These reflections speak to the complexities of conducting entangled[2] research, and I hope my work draws attention to what I consider one of the key questions in rhetorical studies of health and medicine: how do we attend to our personal identities and entanglements? It is not uncommon for rhetoricians of health and medicine to study and theorize about conditions that scholars are personally connected to (see Molloy et al., 2018). Often in their work rhetoricians simultaneously occupy many roles, including patient, caretaker, spouse, parent, and even healthcare provider. Thus, our field must hold thorough and sustained methodological and theoretical conversations regarding how these positions specifically shape our work and our discipline (Molloy et al., 2018). As many other rhetoricians of health and medicine find themselves in similar entangled positions, I hope this project might add to the ongoing conversation about how we attend to our identities and how we manage the insights they foster.

Perhaps most importantly, my patient identity alerted me to how personal and sensitive living with chronic GI conditions can be, how difficult it is to deal with stigma, and how intimate it can feel to share stories about navigating illness and stigma. Though it may not seem like it, given that I disclosed my patient identity within the first few pages of this book and proceeded to share a deeply personal bathroom story in chapter 2, it feels difficult and risky to talk publicly about my experiences with Crohn's. In fact, for the first two years after I was diagnosed, I actively hid my disease to the extent that I can count on one hand the number of people who knew about my diagnosis and the lived experiences that led to it. It wasn't until I was hospitalized for the first time that I began to tell others about Crohn's, and it took nearly three

---

2. Here, I draw on Ginsburg and Rapp's (2013) "entangled ethnography" methodology.

years of studying chronic GI conditions before I publicly disclosed my patient identity as a researcher. I have found that it is often easier to pretend that I don't have Crohn's than to attempt to unpack all the intricate ways in which Crohn's impacts my life.

That said, my own experiences are the very reason I began searching for a methodology that would allow me to study stigma and connect with people living with ostomies and chronic GI conditions on their own terms. My patient identity and personal lived experiences are also the very reason I so strongly disagree with classifying some stigma experiences as "perceived" and others as "enacted" (see chapter 2) and thus the reason I sought to determine how a nuanced rhetorical understanding of stigma might add something important to ongoing stigma research. Without my own patient experiences, I don't know that I would have pursued stigma stories or a praxiographic approach that helped place stigma as done in practice. Even more, I don't know that I would have ever studied chronic GI conditions and ostomies. I certainly would have been more inclined to consider other research topics after receiving harsh, stigmatizing reviewer feedback had I not been personally invested in acknowledging and countering such stigmatization. Undoubtedly, my patient experiences enabled me to recognize that people living with ostomies and chronic GI conditions have much to teach us about stigma and the rhetoricity of chronic illness and motivated me to find an approach that would allow me to respect, care for, and listen to participants in my research on their own terms.

Additionally, my patient identity significantly influenced my ability to recruit and work with many of my research participants. A few even disclosed that they had agreed to talk to me specifically *because* I am "one of them" and I "get it." Being part of the IBD community helped at least some of my participants feel comfortable sharing their stories because I have demonstrated through my engagement online and in-person discussion, events, and community-building as a patient that I am committed to improving the lives of people living with ostomies, GI diseases, and chronic illnesses more generally, and to dismantling stigma. To be clear, I did not aim to use my patient identity to coerce participants into participating in my research efforts. Instead, I honestly disclosed my motivations for my research and attempted to articulate the ways in which my research was and is committed to caring for those living with chronic conditions. These practices, motivated by both my patient and my research identities, enabled me to build trust and connections within the ostomy and chronic GI communities.

That said, it's also important to recognize that disclosing my patient identity to potential participants did come with some costs. Earlier in this conclusion, I described how important it can be for people living with chronic conditions to hear others' stories. Along with the potential benefits I earlier described, it can also be challenging to hear others' stories, especially when those stories describe side effects, surgical complications, or other experiences that materialize the risks and difficulties of living with chronic conditions. I experienced both these benefits and challenges as I conducted the research for this book. During one interview, in particular, a participant repeatedly insisted that he knew exactly what it was like for me to live with Crohn's, even though what he described was dramatically different from my own actual experiences (which I never shared with him). This participant's comments likely were an effort to connect with me, but I couldn't help but think *you have no idea what it is like to be me,* and I not only struggled to finish the interview but found it incredibly difficult to listen to that recording as I worked to transcribe and analyze it. This experience illustrated for me that my patient and researcher identities are not only mine to navigate; participants were also faced with grappling (consciously or not) with my entanglements as they participated in my research. I've no doubt that my patient identity influenced how my participants spoke to me and the kinds of stories they were willing to tell. This doesn't make the stories any less real or important; it did, however, require extra care during analysis and reporting. Moreover, this experience reminded me how, despite common diagnoses, lived experiences with chronic conditions are highly individualized, and while my patient identity helped me relate to many of my participants, it did not grant me full access to or total understanding of their experiences.

I was surprised, during both interviews and observations, to find myself struggling to listen to some of the stories I heard. When it comes to being a patient, sometimes it can honestly be easier to not know what a future with a chronic condition might look like. This is not to say that I buy into what Kafer (2013) called "a future of no futures" for people with illnesses and disabilities. Instead, this is a recognition that life with a chronic condition or disability can simultaneously be positive, worth living, *and* difficult. It would be dishonest for me to say that it was always empowering or uplifting to hear others' stories about living with ostomies or chronic GI conditions. Sometimes it just reminded me of how unpredictable life with a chronic illness can be, a fact that I, as a patient, often try to forget. To help account for my own embodied and emotional responses, I began to take personal notes[3] in addi-

---

3. In such notes I would write things like "Hm . . . that is not how I feel about X" or "I am feeling really anxious listening to this story. I think it's because I'm nervous about my next scope." I worked to consciously record my emotions and opinions so that I could later try to account for them.

tion to collecting data so that when I later worked on data analysis, I could recall how my personal responses might have impacted what I noticed and documented as a researcher. This, of course, is not a flawless strategy, but it provided one mechanism through which I could account for my patient identity. Hearing stories—both those that aligned with my personal patient experiences and those I had trouble relating to—ultimately showcased the resilience and strength that often emerges in chronic illness experiences, and I am immeasurably grateful for the many people who shared their stories with me in hopes that doing so would help dismantle stigma.

Ultimately, I have come to see my patient identity and the experiences that accompany it as a strength of my research, not a liability. Working from the intersections of my patient and research identities is not difficult because I lack objectivity. Doing this research is difficult because being a researcher is an *embodied experience*.[4] When I sit down at my desk to write, I do not flip off my patient identity or magically erase my lived experiences. I am *always* a patient and researcher, whether or not I study Crohn's disease. As Jenell Johnson (2014) has argued, "We may not choose our emotions or our attachments, but once we recognize them, we can cultivate them in certain ways" (p. 177). I certainly did not choose to have Crohn's disease; nevertheless, I have cultivated my patient identity and experiences in an effort to acknowledge, understand, and intervene in stigma. I hope that by engaging in entangled research and encouraging readers to listen to and think with stigma stories, we can all identify ways in our own daily practices and lived experiences to resist stigma.

---

4. For another take on how research is embodied, see Johnson (2014, pp. 175–179).

REFERENCES

Active Guts. (2015, April 6). *An open letter to the CDC.* Active Guts. Retrieved September 19, 2019, from https://activeguts.wordpress.com/2015/04/06/an-open-letter-to-the-cdc/

Adichie, C. (2009, July). *The danger of a single story.* Ted. Retrieved September 28, 2020, from https://www.ted.com/talks/chimamanda_ngozi_adichie_the_danger_of_a_single_story?language=en

Aerie. (2020a, January 23). *Ali Stroker, Tony Award winning actor.* Retrieved September 28, 2020, from https://www.ae.com/aerie-real-life/2020/01/23/ali-stroker-tony-award-winning-actor/

Aerie. (2020b, January, 30). *Meet the change-making brand creating adaptive apparel.* Retrieved October 1, 2020, from https://www.ae.com/aerie-real-life/2020/01/30/meet-the-change-making-brand-creating-adaptive-apparel/

Aerie. (2020c, August 25). *Your new #AerieREAL ambassadors have arrived!* Retrieved October 1, 2020, from https://www.ae.com/aerie-real-life/2020/08/28/your-new-aeriereal-ambassadors-have-arrived/

Aerie. (2020d, September 15). *Watch changemaker Kendall Renee's inspiring music video.* Retrieved October 1, 2020, from https://www.ae.com/aerie-real-life/2020/09/15/watch-changemaker-kendall-renees-inspiring-music-video/

Afzali, A., & Cross, R. K. (2016). Racial and ethnic minorities with inflammatory bowel disease in the United States: A systematic review of disease characteristics and differences. *Inflammatory Bowel Disease, 22*(8), 2023–2040. https://doi.org/10.1097/MIB.0000000000000835

Ahmed, S. (2003). The politics of fear in the making of worlds. *International Journal of Qualitative Studies in Education, 16*(3), 377–398.

Ahmed, S. (2015). *The cultural politics of emotion* (2nd ed.). Edinburgh University Press.

Aikins, A. D. G. (2006). Reframing applied disease stigma research: A multilevel analysis of diabetes stigma in Ghana. *Journal of Community & Applied Social Psychology, 16*(6), 426–441.

American Cancer Society. (2020, June 29). *About colorectal cancer.* https://www.cancer.org/content/dam/CRC/PDF/Public/8604.00.pdf

Anderson, G. F. (2010). *Chronic care: Making the case for ongoing care.* Robert Wood Johnson Foundation.

Anyanwu, L. J., Mohammad, A., & Oyebanji, T. (2013). A descriptive study of commonly used postoperative approaches to pediatric stoma care in a developing country. *Ostomy Wound Management, 59*(12), 32–7.

Arduser, L. (2014). Agency in illness narratives: A pluralistic analysis. *Narrative Inquiry, 24*(1), 1–27.

Arduser, L. (2017). *Living chronic: Agency and expertise in the rhetoric of diabetes.* The Ohio State University Press.

Bailey, Z. D., Krieger, N., Agénor, M., Graves, J., Linos, N., & Bassett, M. T. (2017). Structural racism and health inequities in the USA: Evidence and interventions. *The Lancet, 389*(10077), 1453–1463.

Barad, K. (2003). Posthumanist performativity: Toward an understanding of how matter comes to matter. *Signs: Journal of Women in Culture and Society, 28*(3), 801–831.

Barad, K. (2007). *Meeting the universe halfway: Quantum physics and the entanglement of matter and meaning.* Duke University Press.

Baynton, D. C. (2017). Disability and the justification of inequality in American history. In L. Davis (Ed.), *The disability studies reader* (pp. 17–33). Routledge.

Bennett, J. A. (2019). *Managing diabetes: The cultural politics of disease.* New York University Press.

Berkenkotter, C. (2008). *Patient tales: Case histories and the uses of narrative in psychiatry.* University of South Carolina Press.

Berlant, L. G. (1997). *The queen of America goes to Washington City: Essays on sex and citizenship.* Duke University Press.

Bessette, J. (2016). Queer rhetoric in situ. *Rhetoric Review, 35*(2), 148–164.

Bhopal, R. (2001). Racism in medicine. *The British Medical Journal, 322,* 1503–1504.

Birch, J. (2014, July 3). *Why everyone is talking about this woman's brave bikini photo.* Women's Health. Retrieved April 7, 2021, from https://www.womenshealthmag.com/health/a19919732/bethany-townsend-colostomy-bag-selfie/

Bitzer, L. F. (1968). The rhetorical situation. *Philosophy & Rhetoric, 1*(1), 1–14.

Bivens, K. M. (2018). Rhetorically listening for microwithdrawals of consent in research practice. In L. Melonçon & J. B. Scott (Eds.), *Methodologies for the rhetoric of health & medicine* (pp. 138–156). Routledge.

Blumm, K. C. (2014, July 2). *Former model poses in bikini with colostomy bags.* People. https://people.com/celebrity/former-model-bethany-townsend-poses-in-bikini-with-colostomy-bags/

Booher, A. K. (2010). Docile bodies, supercrips, and the plays of prosthetics. *IJFAB: International Journal of Feminist Approaches to Bioethics, 3*(2), 63–89.

Booher, A. K. (2011). Defining Pistorius. *Disability Studies Quarterly, 31*(3). https://dsq-sds.org/article/view/1673/1598

Booth, E. T., & Spencer, L. G. (2016). Sitting in silence: Managing aural body rhetoric in public restrooms. *Communication Studies, 67*(2), 209–226.

Bos, A. E., Pryor, J. B., Reeder, G. D., & Stutterheim, S. E. (2013). Stigma: Advances in theory and research. *Basic and Applied Social Psychology, 35*(1), 1–9.

Brenner, B. (2016). *So much to be done: The writings of breast cancer activist Barbara Brenner*. University of Minnesota Press.

Brune, J., Garland-Thomson, R., Schweik, S., Titchkosky, T., & Love, H. (2014). Forum introduction: Reflections on the fiftieth anniversary of Erving Goffman's Stigma. *Disability Studies Quarterly, 34*(1). https://dsq-sds.org/article/view/4014

Burke, K. (1969). *A rhetoric of motives*. University of California Press.

Burns, S., Wingate, L., & Hastings, P. (2015, April 13). *An open letter to the Centers for Disease Control and Prevention* [Open letter]. United Ostomy Association of America.

Buttorff, C., Ruder, T., & Bauman, M. (2017). *Multiple chronic conditions in the United States*. RAND Corporation.

Calder-Dawe, O., Witten, K., & Carroll, P. (2020). Being the body in question: Young people's accounts of everyday ableism, visibility and disability. *Disability & Society, 35*(1), 132–155.

Callahan, C. (2018, July 13). *These joyful lingerie ads include models with disabilities and chronic illnesses*. Today. Retrieved October 1, 2020, from https://www.today.com/style/aerie-bra-ads-feature-models-disabilities-t133155

Campbell, L. (2018). The rhetoric of health and medicine as a "Teaching Subject": Lessons from the medical humanities and simulation pedagogy. *Technical Communication Quarterly, 27*(1), 7–20.

Card, D., Kessler, M. M., & Graham, S. S. (2018). Representing without representation: A feminist new materialist exploration of federal pharmaceuticals policy. In A. Booher & J. Jung (Eds.), *Feminist rhetorical science studies: Human bodies, posthumanist worlds* (pp. 183–204). Southern Illinois University Press.

Cataldo, P. A. (1999). Intestinal stomas: 200 years of digging. *Diseases of the Colon & Rectum, 42*(2), 137–142.

Cedillo, C. V. (2018). What does it mean to move? Race, disability, and critical embodiment pedagogy. *Composition Forum, 39*. https://compositionforum.com/issue/39/to-move.php

Centers for Disease Control and Prevention. (2015a). *Julia C.'s story*. https://www.cdc.gov/tobacco/campaign/tips/stories/julia.html

Centers for Disease Control and Prevention (2015b, May 5). *CDC: Tips from Former Smokers—Julia C. and Mark A.'s Ad* [Video]. YouTube. https://www.youtube.com/watch?v=3q8oUdOdP70

Centers for Disease Control and Prevention. (2017, January 13). *Tips from former smokers—Julia C.* [Audio podcast]. https://tools.cdc.gov/medialibrary/index.aspx#/media/id/303163

Centers for Disease Control and Prevention. (2019a, May 13). *Mission, role and pledge*. https://www.cdc.gov/about/organization/mission.htm

Centers for Disease Control and Prevention. (2019b, October 23). *About chronic diseases*. https://www.cdc.gov/chronicdisease/about/index.htm

Centers for Disease Control and Prevention. (2019c, October 23). *Health and economic costs of chronic diseases*. https://www.cdc.gov/chronicdisease/about/costs/index.htm

Centers for Disease Control and Prevention. (2020a, March 23). *Frequently asked questions about the Tips® campaign*. https://www.cdc.gov/tobacco/campaign/tips/about/faq/campaign-faq.html

Centers for Disease Control and Prevention. (2020b, March 23). *Tips impact and results*. https://www.cdc.gov/tobacco/campaign/tips/about/index.html

Centers for Disease Control and Prevention. (2020c, May 22). *Firearm violence prevention*. https://www.cdc.gov/violenceprevention/firearms/fastfact.html

Centers for Disease Control and Prevention. (2021a, March 1). *African Americans.* https://www.cdc.gov/tobacco/campaign/tips/groups/african-american.html

Centers for Disease Control and Prevention. (2021b, July 28). *Chronic disease center (NCCDPHP).* https://www.cdc.gov/chronicdisease/index.htm

Charmaz, K. (2000). Experiencing chronic illness. In G. L. Albrecht, R. Fitzpatrick, & S. C. Scrimshaw (Eds.), *Handbook of social studies in health and medicine* (pp. 277–292). Sage.

Charmaz, K. (2006). *Constructing grounded theory: A practical guide through qualitative analysis.* Sage.

Charon, R. (2006). *Narrative medicine: Honoring the stories of illness.* Oxford University Press.

Cherney, J. L. (2019). *Ableist rhetoric: How we know, value, and see disability.* Pennsylvania State University Press.

Cheselden, W. (1750). *The anatomy of the human body* [Book]. Medical Heritage Library (004908078, anatomyofhumanbo1750ches). Francis A. Countway Library of Medicine, Boston. Retrieved from Internet Archive https://archive.org/details/anatomyofhumanbo1750ches

Cho, H., & Witte, K. (2005). Managing fear in public health campaigns: A theory-based formative evaluation process. *Health Promotion Practice, 6*(4), 482–490.

Cho, S., Crenshaw, K. W., & McCall, L. (2013). Toward a field of intersectionality studies: Theory, applications, and praxis. *Signs: Journal of Women in Culture and Society, 38*(4), 785–810.

Chung, J. E. (2014). Medical dramas and viewer perception of health: Testing cultivation effects. *Human Communication Research, 40*(3), 333–349.

Cima, R. R., & Pemberton, J. H. (2004). Early surgical intervention in ulcerative colitis. *Gut, 53*(2), 306–307.

Clare, E. (1999). *Exile and pride: Disability, queerness and liberation.* South End Press.

Cleary, K. (2016). Misfitting and hater blocking: A feminist disability analysis of the extraordinary body on reality television. *Disability Studies Quarterly, 36*(4). https://dsq-sds.org/article/view/5442

Cleasby, S. (2014, May 7). *Ostomy photoshoot—50s pin up.* SoBadAss. Retrieved September 21, 2020, from http://www.sobadass.me/2014/05/07/ostomy-photoshoot-50s-pin-up/

Cleasby, S. (2015a, February 17). *To the woman who tutted at me using the disabled toilets.* SoBadAss. http://www.sobadass.me/2015/02/17/to-the-woman-who-tutted-at-me-using-the-disabled-toilets/

Cleasby, S. (2015b, April 14). *Sexualising disability or normalising life with an illness?* SoBadAss. http://sobadass.me/2015/04/14/sexualising-disability-or-normalising-life-with-an-illness/

Cleveland Clinic. (2020). *Familial adenomatous polyposis (FAP) management and treatment.* Retrieved September 29, 2020, from https://my.clevelandclinic.org/health/diseases/16993-familial-adenomatous-polyposis-fap/management-and-treatment

Coleman, L. M. (1986). Stigma. In S. C. Ainlay, G. Becker, & L. M. Coleman (Eds.), *The dilemma of difference: A multidisciplinary view of stigma* (pp. 211–232). Springer. https://doi.org/10.1007/978-1-4684-7568-5_11

Coleman-Brown, L. M. (2017). "Stigma: An Enigma Demystified." In L. Davis (Ed.), *The disability studies reader* (pp. 145–160). Routledge.

Conrad, S., Garrett, L. E., Cooksley, W. G. E., Dunne, M. P., & MacDonald, G. A. (2006). Living with chronic hepatitis C means "you just haven't got a normal life any more." *Chronic Illness, 2*(2), 121–131.

Convertino, A. D., Rodgers, R. F., Franko, D. L., & Jodoin, A. (2019). An evaluation of the Aerie Real campaign: Potential for promoting positive body image? *Journal of Health Psychology, 24*(6), 726–737.

Cosmopolitan. (2014, December, 3). *Our ultimate body confidence queen: Bethany Townsend.* Retrieved September 21, 2020, from https://www.cosmopolitan.com/uk/entertainment/news/a31657/ultimate-women-awards-bethany-townsend/

Courtwright, A. M. (2009). Justice, stigma, and the new epidemiology of health disparities. *Bioethics, 23*(2), 90–96.

Cragg, S. (Writer), & Rimes, S. (Director). (2010, May 20). Good mourning (Season 6, Episode 23) [TV series episode]. In S. Rimes (Executive Producer), *Grey's Anatomy.* American Broadcasting Company.

Crenshaw, K. (1993). Mapping the margins: Intersectionality, identity politics, and the violence against women of color. *Stanford Law Review, 43*, 1241–1299.

Creswell, J. W., & Creswell, J. D. (2014). *Research design: Qualitative, quantitative, and mixed methods approaches.* Sage.

Crohn's & Colitis Foundation of America. (n.d.). *Restroom access.* Retrieved September 27, 2020, from https://www.crohnscolitisfoundation.org/get-involved/be-an-advocate/restroom-access

Crohn's & Colitis UK. (n.d.). *About us.* Retrieved September 27, 2020, from https://www.crohnsandcolitis.org.uk/about-us

Davis, J. S., Svavarsdóttir, M. H., Pudło, M., Arena, R., Lee, Y., & Jensen, M. K. (2011). Factors impairing quality of life for people with an ostomy. *Gastrointestinal Nursing, 9*(Supplement 2), 14–18.

Davis, L. J. (1997). Constructing normalcy: The bell curve, the novel, and the invention of the disabled body in the nineteenth century. In L. J. Davis (Ed.), *The disability studies reader* (pp. 3–19). Routledge.

Davis, L. (2013). *The end of normal: Identity in a biocultural era.* University of Michigan Press.

Defenbaugh, N. L. (2013). Revealing and concealing ill identity: A performance narrative of IBD disclosure. *Health Communication, 28*(2), 159–169.

Díaz, D. A., Maruca, A. T., Kuhnly, J. E., Jeffries, P., & Grabon, N. (2015). Creating caring and empathic nurses: A simulated ostomate. *Clinical Simulation in Nursing, 11*(12), 513–518.

Doane, M. A. (1982). Film and the masquerade: Theorizing the female spectator. *Screen, 23*(3–4), 74–88.

Dolmage, J. (2014). *Disability rhetoric.* Syracuse University Press.

Doughty, D. B. (2008). History of ostomy surgery. *Journal of Wound Ostomy & Continence Nursing, 35*(1), 34–38.

Douglas, M. (1966). *Purity and danger: An analysis of concepts of pollution and taboo.* Routledge.

Druschke, C. G. (2017). The radical insufficiency and wily possibilities of RSTEM. *Poroi, 12*(2), 1–10.

Druschke, C. G., & McGreavy, B. (2016). Why rhetoric matters for ecology. *Frontiers in Ecology and the Environment, 14*(1), 46–52.

Druschke, C. G., & Rai, C. (2018). *Field rhetoric: Ethnography, ecology, and engagement in the places of persuasion.* University of Alabama Press.

Earnshaw, V. A., & Quinn, D. M. (2012). The impact of stigma in healthcare on people living with chronic illnesses. *Journal of Health Psychology, 17*(2), 157–168.

Edelman, L. (2004). *No future: Queer theory and the death drive.* Duke University Press.

Ehrenreich, B. (2001). Welcome to cancerland. *Harper's Magazine, 303*(1818), 43–53.

Ehrenreich, B. (2009). *Bright-sided: How positive thinking is undermining America.* Metropolitan Books.

Eiesland, N. (1994). *The disabled God: Toward a liberating theology of disability.* Abingdon.

Eisner, S. (2013). *Bi: Notes for a bisexual revolution.* Seal Press.

Ellingson, L. L. (2009). *Engaging crystallization in qualitative research: An introduction.* Sage.

Emery, S. L., Szczypka, G., Abril, E. P., Kim, Y., & Vera, L. (2014). Are you scared yet? Evaluating fear appeal messages in tweets about the tips campaign. *Journal of Communication, 64*(2), 278–295.

Erevelles, N. (2014). Thinking with disability studies. *Disability Studies Quarterly, 34*(2). https://dsq-sds.org/article/view/4248

Erevelles, N., & Minear, A. (2010). Unspeakable offenses: Untangling race and disability in discourses of intersectionality. *Journal of Literary & Cultural Disability Studies, 4*(2), 127–146.

Ewing, E. L. (2020, July 2). I'm a Black scholar who studies race. Here's why I capitalize "White." Zora. https://zora.medium.com/im-a-black-scholar-who-studies-race-here-s-why-i-capitalize-white-f94883aa2dd3

Falk, G. (2001). *Stigma: How we treat outsiders.* Prometheus Books.

Fight Colorectal Cancer. (2015, April 21). *Our response & action to the CDC's ostomy ads.* Retrieved January 1, 2019, from https://fightcolorectalcancer.org/blog/our-response-action-to-the-cdcs-ostomy-ads/

Fine, M., & Asch, A. (1988). Disability beyond stigma: Social interaction, discrimination, and activism. *Journal of Social Issues, 44*(1), 3–21.

Fleetwood-Beresford, S. (2014). *The rise of #GetYourBellyOut.* Crohn's & Colitis UK. Retrieved September 21, 2020, from https://www.crohnsandcolitis.org.uk/news/the-rise-of-getyourbellyout

Follick, M. J., Smith, T. W., & Turk, D. C. (1984). Psychosocial adjustment following ostomy. *Health Psychology, 3*(6), 505–517.

Ford, C. L., & Airhihenbuwa, C. O. (2010). Critical race theory, race equity, and public health: Toward antiracism praxis. *American Journal of Public Health, 100*(S1), S30–S35.

Foucault, M. (1973). *The birth of the clinic* (A. M. Sheridan, Trans.). Routledge. (Original work published 1963)

Foucault, M. (1995). *Discipline and punish: The birth of the prison* (A. M. Sheridan, Trans.). Random House.

Fountain, T. K. (2014). *Rhetoric in the flesh: Trained vision, technical expertise, and the gross anatomy lab.* Routledge.

Frank, A. W. (2010). *Letting stories breathe: A socio-narratology.* University of Chicago Press.

Frank, A. W. (2013). *The wounded storyteller: Body, illness, and ethics.* University of Chicago Press.

Freeman, E. (2007). Introduction: Theorizing queer temporalities: A roundtable discussion. *GLQ: A Journal of Lesbian and Gay Studies, 13*(2–3), 177–195.

Freeman, E. (2010). *Time binds: Queer temporalities, queer histories.* Duke University Press.

Freeman, E. (2019). The queer temporalities of queer temporalities. *GLQ: A Journal of Lesbian and Gay Studies, 25*(1), 91–95.

Frohlich, D. O. (2014). Support often outweighs stigma for people with inflammatory bowel disease. *Gastroenterology Nursing, 37*(2), 126–136.

Frohlich, D. O. (2016). The social construction of inflammatory bowel disease using social media technologies. *Health Communication, 31*(11), 1412–1420.

Frohlich, D. O., & Zmyslinski-Seelig, A. N. (2016). How *Uncover Ostomy* challenges ostomy stigma, and encourages others to do the same. *New Media & Society, 18*(2), 220–238.

Garcia, J. A., Crocker, J., & Wyman, J. F. (2005). Breaking the cycle of stigmatization: Managing the stigma of incontinence in social interactions. *Journal of Wound Ostomy & Continence Nursing, 32*(1), 38–52.

Garland-Thomson, R. (1997). *Extraordinary bodies: Figuring physical disability in American culture and literature.* Columbia University Press.

Garland-Thomson, R. (2009). *Staring: How we look.* Oxford University Press.

Garland-Thomson, R. (2011). Misfits: A feminist materialist disability concept. *Hypatia, 26*(3), 591–609.

Garland-Thomson, R. (2014). Roadkill truths. In Forum introduction: Reflections on the fiftieth anniversary of Erving Goffman's Stigma. *Disability Studies Quarterly, 34*(1). https://dsq-sds.org/article/view/4014

Garland-Thomson, R. (2017). Integrating disability, transforming feminist theory. In L. Davis (Ed.), *The disability studies reader* (pp. 360–380). Routledge.

Gemmill, R., Kravits, K., Ortiz, M., Anderson, C., Lai, L., & Grant, M. (2011). What do surgical oncology staff nurses know about colorectal cancer ostomy care? *The Journal of Continuing Education in Nursing, 42*(2), 81–88.

GetYourBellyOut. (n.d.). Retrieved September 21, 2020, from https://getyourbellyout.org.uk/

Gibbons, F. X. (1986). Stigma and interpersonal relations. In S. Ainlay, G. Becker, & L. M. Coleman (Eds.), *The dilemma of difference: A multidisciplinary view of stigma* (pp. 123–144). Springer.

Ginsburg, F. & Rapp, R. (2013). Entangled ethnography: Imagining a future for young adults with learning disabilities. *Social Science & Medicine, 99*, 187–193.

Girls With Guts. (n.d.). Retrieved September 30, 2020, from https://www.girlswithguts.org/

Goffman, E. (1963). *Stigma: Notes on the management of spoiled identity.* Simon and Schuster.

Goggin, G., Steele, L., & Cadwallader, J. R. (2017). Normality and disability: Intersections among norms, law, and culture. *Continuum, 31*(3), 337–340.

Graham, S. S. (2015). *The politics of pain medicine: A rhetorical-ontological inquiry.* University of Chicago Press.

Graham, S. S., & Herndl, C. (2013). Multiple ontologies in pain management: Toward a postplural rhetoric of science. *Technical Communication Quarterly, 22*(2), 103–125.

Grande, S. (2003). Whitestream feminism and the colonialist project: A review of contemporary feminist pedagogy and praxis. *Educational Theory, 53*(3), 329–346.

Grant, D. M. (2017). Writing Wakan: The Lakota pipe as rhetorical object. *College Composition and Communication, 69*(1), 61–86.

Graves, R. E., Cassisi, J. E., & Penn, D. L. (2005). Psychophysiological evaluation of stigma towards schizophrenia. *Schizophrenia Research, 76*(2–3), 317–327.

Green, A., _, A., Dura, L., Harris, P., Heilig, L., Kirby, B., McClintick, J., Pfender, E., & Carrasco, R. (2020). Teaching and researching with a mental health diagnosis: Practices and perspectives on academic ableism. *Rhetoric of Health & Medicine, 3*(2), Article 1.

Greenly, J. (n.d.). *Joseph Greenly* [YouTube Channel]. https://www.youtube.com/channel/UCiKnuW1hSS7duoZd1_CPnnQ

Grossman, J. (2015, April, 9). *Dear CDC. . . Uncover Ostomy*. Retrieved September 21, 2020, from https://uncoverostomy.org/2015/04/09/dear-cdc/

Grossman, J. (2018, October 3). *9 years of Uncover Ostomy*. Uncover Ostomy. Retrieved September 21, 2020, from https://uncoverostomy.org/2018/10/03/9-years-of-uncover-ostomy/

Grossman, J. [@uncoverostomy]. (2019, October 3). *It's time to stop showing off your ostomy | 10 years of Uncover Ostomy* [Photo]. Instagram. Retrieved September 27, 2021, from https://www.instagram.com/p/B3K7pu2AtHJ/

Grosz, E. A. (1994). *Volatile bodies: Toward a corporeal feminism*. Indiana University Press.

Gunn, J. (2006). Shittext: Toward a new coprophilic style. *Text and Performance Quarterly, 26*(1), 79–97.

Gupta, K. (2019). *Medical entanglements: Rethinking feminist debates about healthcare*. Rutgers University Press.

Gutless and Glamorous. (n.d.). *About—Founder, Gaylyn*. Retrieved September 28, 2020, from https://www.gutlessandglamorous.org/about-c1enr

Gutsell, M., & Hulgin, K. (2013). Supercrips don't fly: Technical communication to support ordinary lives of people with disabilities. In Lisa Melonçon (Ed.), *Rhetorical accessibility: At the intersection of technical communication and disability studies* (pp. 84–94). Baywood.

Guttman, N., & Salmon, C. T. (2004). Guilt, fear, stigma and knowledge gaps: Ethical issues in public health communication interventions. *Bioethics, 18*(6), 531–552.

Hafner, D. (2009, November 14). Letter to director of Grey's Anatomy [Open letter]. *North Central Oklahoma Ostomy Newsletter Index*. Retrieved from https://www.ostomyok.org/newsletter/news1001a.shtml

Hahn, H. (1988). Can disability be beautiful? *Social Policy, 18*(3), 26–32.

Halberstam, J. (2005). *In a queer time and place: Transgender bodies, subcultural lives*. New York University Press.

Hamilton-West, K. E., & Quine, L. (2009). Living with ankylosing spondylitis: The patient's perspective. *Journal of Health Psychology, 14*(6), 820–830.

Haraway, D. (1988). Situated knowledges: The science question in feminism and the privilege of partial perspective. *Feminist Studies, 14*(3), 575–599.

Haraway, D. J. (1997). Modest_Witness@Second_Millennium.FemaleMan©_Meets_ OncoMouse™. Routledge.

Hardin, M. M., & Hardin, B. (2004). The "supercrip" in sport media: Wheelchair athletes discuss hegemony's disabled hero. *Sociology of Sport Online, 7*(1). http://physed.otago.ac.nz/sosol/v7i1/v7i1_1.html

Harding, S. (2009). Standpoint theories: Productively controversial. *Hypatia, 24*(4), 192–200.

Harrington, A. (2008). *The cure within: A history of mind-body medicine*. Norton.

Himmelstein, M. S., Incollingo Belsky, A. C., & Tomiyama, A. J. (2015). The weight of stigma: Cortisol reactivity to manipulated weight stigma. *Obesity, 23*(2), 368–374.

Hood-Patterson, R. D. (2020). *A parent's dis-ease with marginalization following a gastrointestinal ostomy: Implications of abject theory and normalcy discourses on theological constructs and practices of care* (Publication No. 27838344) [Doctoral dissertation, Texas Christian University]. ProQuest.

Hubrig, A., Masterson, J., Seibert Desjarlais, S. K., Stenberg, S. J., & Thielen, B. M. (2020). Disrupting diversity management: Toward a difference-driven pedagogy. *Pedagogy: Critical Approaches to Teaching Literature, Language, Composition, and Culture, 20*(2), 279–301.

HuffPost. (2013, March 29). Jim Carrey: Fox News "a media colostomy bag that has begun to burst at the seams." https://www.huffpost.com/entry/jim-carrey-fox-news_n_2981222

Hughes, B. (1999). The constitution of impairment: Modernity and the aesthetic of oppression. *Disability & Society, 14*(2), 155–172.

Hughes, S. L., & Romo, L. K. (2020). An exploration of how individuals with an ostomy communicatively manage uncertainty. *Health Communication, 35*(3), 375–383.

Hurny, C., & Holland, J. (1985). Psychosocial sequelae of ostomies in cancer patients. *CA: A Cancer Journal for Clinicians, 35*(3), 170–183.

IBD Editorial Team. (2018, August 2). *American Eagle's new campaign spotlight—An interview with Gaylyn Henderson.* Retrieved September 25, 2020, from https://inflammatoryboweldisease.net/living/ae-campaign-interview-gaylyn-henderson/

ITV. (2014, July 7). *Dare to bare: Living with a colostomy bag.* https://www.itv.com/thismorning/articles/living-with-a-colostomy-bag-bikini-crohns-disease

Jacoby, A. (1994). Felt versus enacted stigma: A concept revisited. Evidence from a study of people with epilepsy in remission. *Social Science and Medicine 38*(2), 269–274.

Jain, S. L. (2007). Living in prognosis: Toward an elegiac politics. *Representations, 98*(1), 77–92.

Janis, I. L., & Feshbach, S. (1953). Effects of fear-arousing communications. *The Journal of Abnormal and Social Psychology, 48*(1), 78–92.

Jerant, A. F., Levich, B., Balsbaugh, T., Barton, S., & Nuovo, J. (2005). Walk a mile in my shoes: A chronic illness care workshop for first-year students. *Family Medicine, 37*(1), 21–26.

Joachim, G., & Acorn, S. (2000). Stigma of visible and invisible chronic conditions. *Journal of Advanced Nursing, 32*(1), 243–248.

Joachim, G. L., & Acorn, S. (2016). Living with chronic illness: The interface of stigma and normalization. *Canadian Journal of Nursing Research, 32*(3), 37–48.

Johnson, J. (2010). The skeleton on the couch: The Eagleton affair, rhetorical disability, and the stigma of mental illness. *Rhetoric Society Quarterly, 40*(5), 459–478.

Johnson, J. (2014). *American lobotomy: A rhetorical history.* University of Michigan Press.

Johnson, J. (2016). "A man's mouth is his castle": The midcentury fluoridation controversy and the visceral public. *Quarterly Journal of Speech, 102*(1), 1–20.

Johnson, J., & Kennedy, K. (2020). Introduction: Disability, in/visibility, and risk. *Rhetoric Society Quarterly, 50*(3), 161–165.

Jones, N. N. (2016). Narrative inquiry in human-centered design: Examining silence and voice to promote social justice in design scenarios. *Journal of Technical Writing and Communication, 46*(4), 471–492.

Kafer, A. (2003). Compulsory bodies: Reflections on heterosexuality and able-bodiedness. *Journal of Women's History, 15*(3), 77–89.

Kafer, A. (2013). *Feminist, queer, crip.* Indiana University Press.

Kafer, A. (2016). Other people's shit (and pee!). *South Atlantic Quarterly, 115*(4), 755–762.

Kato, A., Fujimaki, Y., Fujimori, S., Izumida, Y., Suzuki, R., Ueki, K., Kadowaki, T., & Hashimoto, H. (2016). A qualitative study on the impact of internalized stigma on type 2 diabetes self-management. *Patient Education and Counseling, 99*(7), 1233–1239.

Kelly, M. (1992). Self, identity and radical surgery. *Sociology of Health & Illness, 14*(3), 390–415.

Kessler, M. M. (2016). Wearing an ostomy pouch and becoming an ostomate: A kairological approach to wearability. *Rhetoric Society Quarterly, 46*(3), 236–250.

Kessler, M. M. (2020). The ostomy multiple: Toward a theory of rhetorical enactments. *Rhetoric of Health & Medicine, 3*(3), 293–319.

Kılınç, S., & Campbell, C. (2009). "It shouldn't be something that's evil, it should be talked about": A phenomenological approach to epilepsy and stigma. *Seizure, 18*(10), 665–671.

Kim, C. (2019, January 24). *Bullied over a colostomy bag or not, Seven Charles Thomas Bridges has died—born to love, tormented by hate.* OstomyConnection. Retrieved January 27, 2019 from https://ostomyconnection.com/news-and-culture/10-year-old-seven-bridges-bullied-dies-by-suicide?fbclid=IwAR0OmXZ8ii1WkTwza1RXr2YyWfA9mwQeYQyv_0

Kim, E. (2011). Asexuality in disability narratives. *Sexualities, 14*(4), 479–493.

King, S. (2006). *Pink Ribbons, Inc: Breast cancer and the politics of philanthropy.* University of Minnesota Press.

Kochanek, K. D., Murphy, S. L., Xu, J., Arias, E. (2019). Deaths: Final data for 2017. *National Vital Statistics Reports, 68*(9).

Kochanek, K. D., Xu, J., Murphy, S. L., Miniño, A. M., & Kung, H. C. (2011). Deaths: Preliminary data for 2009. *National Vital Statistics Reports, 59*(4).

Koerber, A. (2000). Toward a feminist rhetoric of technology. *Journal of Business and Technical Communication, 14*(1), 58–73.

Koerber, A., & McMichael, L. (2008). Qualitative sampling methods: A primer for technical communicators. *Journal of Business and Technical Communication, 22*(4), 454–473.

Kosenko, K., Winderman, E., & Pugh, A. (2019). The hijacked hashtag: The constitutive features of abortion stigma in the #ShoutYourAbortion Twitter campaign. *International Journal of Communication, 13*, 1–21.

Lawrence, H. L. (2020). *Vaccine rhetorics.* The Ohio State University Press.

Leadley, A. (2016). Babes and bags: Tensions within the (re)presentations of non-normative bodies and narratives of sexuality in Canada's Uncover Ostomy campaign. In A. Leadley (Ed.), *Theorizing sex and disability: An interdisciplinary approach* (pp. 25–34). Brill.

Leshner, G., Bolls, P., & Thomas, E. (2009). Scare 'em or disgust 'em: The effects of graphic health promotion messages. *Health Communication, 24*(5), 447–458.

Link, B. G., & Phelan, J. C. (2001). Conceptualizing stigma. *Annual Review of Sociology, 27*(1), 363–385.

Linton, S. (1998). Disability studies/not disability studies. *Disability & Society, 13*(4), 525–539.

Loja, E., Costa, M. E., Hughes, B., & Menezes, I. (2013). Disability, embodiment and ableism: Stories of resistance. *Disability & Society, 28*(2), 190–203.

MacDonald, S. M. (2007). Leakey performances: The transformative potential of the menstrual leak. *Women's Studies in Communication, 30*(3), 340–357.

Mack, K., & Palfrey, J. (2020, August 26). *Capitalizing Black and White: Grammatical justice and equity.* MacArthur Foundation. Retrieved April 9, 2021, from https://www.macfound.org/press/perspectives/capitalizing-black-and-white-grammatical-justice-and-equity

Malterud, K., & Ulriksen, K. (2011). Obesity, stigma, and responsibility in health care: A synthesis of qualitative studies. *International Journal of Qualitative Studies on Health and Well-Being, 6*(4). https://doi.org/10.3402/qhw.v6i4.8404

Manderson, L. (2005). Boundary breaches: The body, sex and sexuality after stoma surgery. *Social Science & Medicine, 61*(2), 405–415.

Martinez, A. Y. (2014). A plea for critical race theory counterstory: Stock story versus counterstory dialogues concerning Alejandra's" fit" in the academy. *Composition Studies, 42*(2), 33–55.

Martinez, A. Y. (2020). *Counterstory: The rhetoric and writing of critical race theory.* National Council of Teachers of English.

Maruca, A. T., Díaz, D. A., Kuhnly, J. E., & Jeffries, P. R. (2015). Enhancing empathy in undergraduate nursing students: An experiential ostomate simulation. *Nursing Education Perspectives, 36*(6), 367–371.

Mattingly, C. (1998). *Healing dramas and clinical plots: The narrative structure of experience.* Cambridge University Press.

McAfee, T., Davis, K. C., Alexander Jr., R. L., Pechacek, T. F., & Bunnell, R. (2013). Effect of the first federally funded US antismoking national media campaign. *The Lancet, 382*(9909), 2003–2011.

McCreery, P. (2008). Save our children/let us marry: Gay activists appropriate the rhetoric of child protectionism. *Radical History Review, 2008*(100), 186–207.

McKee, H., & Porter, J. (2012). The ethics of conducting writing research on the internet: How heuristics help. In L. Nickoson & M. P. Sheridan (Eds.), *Writing studies research in practice: Methods and methodologies* (pp. 245–260). Southern Illinois University Press.

McRuer, R. (2003). As good as it gets: Queer theory and critical disability. *GLQ: A Journal of Lesbian and Gay Studies, 9*(1), 79–105.

McRuer, R. (2011). Disabling sex: Notes for a crip theory of sexuality. *GLQ: A Journal of Lesbian and Gay Studies, 17*(1), 107–117.

McRuer, R., & Mollow, A. (2012). *Sex and disability.* Duke University Press.

Mehl-Madrona, L. (2007). *Narrative medicine: The use of history and story in the healing process.* Simon and Schuster.

Melonçon, L., & Frost, E. A. (2015). Special issue introduction: Charting an emerging field: The rhetorics of health and medicine and its importance in communication design. *Communication Design Quarterly Review, 3*(4), 7–14.

Melonçon, L., & Scott, J. B. (Eds.). (2018). *Methodologies for the rhetoric of health & medicine.* Taylor & Francis.

Middleton, M. K., Senda-Cook, S., & Endres, D. (2011). Articulating rhetorical field methods: Challenges and tensions. *Western Journal of Communication, 75*(4), 386–406.

Miller, E. (2019). Too fat to be president? Chris Christie and fat stigma as rhetorical disability. *Rhetoric of Health & Medicine, 2*(1), 60–87.

Moe, P. W. (2012). Revealing rather than concealing disability: The rhetoric of Parkinson's advocate Michael J. Fox. *Rhetoric Review, 31*(4), 443–460.

Moeller, M. (2015). Pushing boundaries of normalcy: Employing critical disability studies in analyzing medical advocacy websites. *Communication Design Quarterly Review, 2*(4), 52–80.

Mohamed, K., & Shefer, T. (2015). Gendering disability and disabling gender: Critical reflections on intersections of gender and disability. *Agenda, 29*(2), 2–13.

Mol, A. (2002). *The body multiple: Ontology in medical practice.* Duke University Press.

Mol, A., & Law, J. (2004). Embodied action, enacted bodies: The example of hypoglycaemia. *Body & Society, 10*(2–3), 43–62.

Molloy, C. (2015). Recuperative ethos and agile epistemologies: Toward a vernacular engagement with mental illness ontologies. *Rhetoric Society Quarterly, 45*(2), 138–163.

Molloy, C. (2019). *Rhetorical ethos in health and medicine: Patient credibility, stigma, and misdiagnosis.* Routledge.

Molloy, C., Beemer, C., Bennett, J., Green, A., Johnson, J., Kessler, M., Novotny, M., & Siegel-Finer, B. (2018). A dialogue on possibilities for embodied methodologies in the rhetoric of health & medicine. *Rhetoric of Health & Medicine, 1*(3), 349–371.

Montgomery, S. R. Jr., Butler, P. D., Wirtalla, C. J., Collier, K. T., Hoffman, R. L., Aarons, C. B., Damrauer, S. M., & Kelz, R. R. (2018). Racial disparities in surgical outcomes of patients with inflammatory bowel disease. *The American Journal of Surgery, 215*(6), 1046–1050.

Moore, I. S. (2013). "The beast within": Life with an invisible chronic illness. *Qualitative Inquiry, 19*(3), 201–208.

Morgan, S. (2014, July 1). *Beauty Beth's COLOSTOMY PIC bags her millions of fans.* The Sun. Retrieved April 7, 2021, from https://www.thesun.co.uk/archives/news/947896/brave-bethanys-pic-in-bikini-colostomy-bags/

Mukherjee, S. (2010). *The emperor of all maladies: A biography of cancer.* Simon and Schuster.

Mulholland, V. [@TheDazzleDoll]. (2017, December 23). #myillnessisnotyourinsult my stoma makes me superwoman, has given me my life back and makes me awesome[.] think before you make a "joke." [Tweet]. Twitter. https://twitter.com/TheDazzelDoll/status/812220637703966720

Mulvey, L. (1975). Visual pleasure and narrative cinema. *Screen, 16*(3), 6–18.

Murphy, S. L., Xu, J., Kochanek, K. D., Curtin, S. C., & Arias, E. (2017). Deaths: Final data for 2015. *National Vital Statistics Reports, 66*(6).

Murphy-Hoefer, R., Davis, K. C., Beistle, D., King, B. A., Duke, J., Rodes, R., & Graffunder, C. (2018). Impact of the Tips from Former Smokers campaign on population-level smoking cessation, 2012–2015. *Preventing Chronic Disease, 15.* https://doi.org/10.5888/pcd15.180051

National Center for Chronic Disease Prevention and Health Promotion. (2012, October). *Mental health and chronic diseases* [Issue Brief No. 2]. https://www.cdc.gov/workplacehealthpromotion/tools-resources/pdfs/issue-brief-no-2-mental-health-and-chronic-disease.pdf

Nichols, T. R. (2016, September 9). *We've come a long way.* Hollister. https://www.hollister.com/en/newslanding/OstomyPouchHistory

Nicholson, I. (Producer). (2016a). Episode 3 [TV series episode]. In *Too Ugly for Love?* TLC.

Nicholson, I. (Producer). (2016b). Episode 4 [TV series episode]. In *Too Ugly for Love?* TLC.

Nielsen, E. (2019). *Disrupting breast cancer narratives.* University of Toronto Press.

Oliver, M. (1996). *Understanding disability: From theory to practice.* Macmillan International Higher Education.

Ostomy Connection. (2018, July 12). *Aerie launched an amazing campaign with a diverse group of models . . . INCLUDING AN OSTOMATE.* Retrieved October 1, 2020, from https://ostomyconnection.com/news-and-culture/aerie-campaign-aeriereal-gayln-henderson

Owens, M. (2020, January 23). *Aerie introduces eight new #AerieREAL role models to inspire you to make 2020 the year of change.* Business Wire. Retrieved October 1, 2020, from https://www.businesswire.com/news/home/20200123005191/en/Aerie-Introduces-Eight-New-AerieREAL-Role-Models-to-Inspire-You-to-Make-2020-the-Year-of-Change

Oxford English Dictionary. (2013). *Word of the year.* Retrieved Octover 29, 2021, https://languages.oup.com/word-of-the-year/

Pastrana, A. (2004). Black identity constructions: Inserting intersectionality, bisexuality, and (Afro)latinidad into Black studies. *Journal of African American Studies, 8*(1), 74–89.

Pender, K. (2018). *Being at genetic risk: Toward a rhetoric of care.* Pennsylvania State University Press.

Penner, L. A., Eggly, S., Griggs, J. J., Underwood, W. III, Orom, H., & Albrecht, T. L. (2012). Life-threatening disparities: The treatment of Black and White cancer patients. *Journal of Social Issues, 68*(2), 328–357.

Pescosolido, B. A., Medina, T. R., Martin, J. K., & Long, J. S. (2013). The "backbone" of stigma: Identifying the global core of public prejudice associated with mental illness. *American Journal of Public Health, 103*(5), 853–860.

Pezzullo, P. C., & Cox, R. (2017). *Environmental communication and the public sphere*. Sage.

Pfau, M. W. (2007). Who's afraid of fear appeals? Contingency, courage, and deliberation in rhetorical theory and practice. *Philosophy & Rhetoric, 40*(2), 216–237.

Powell, M. (2012). 2012 CCCC chair's address: Stories take place: A performance in one act. *College Composition and Communication, 64*(2), 383–406.

Powers, A. (2020). *The ostomy guy*. Retrieved September 28, 2020, from https://www.theostomyguy.com/

Prendergast, C. (2001). On the rhetorics of mental disability. In J. C. Wilson & C. Lewiecki-Wilson (Eds.), *Embodied rhetorics: Disability in language and culture* (pp. 45–60). Southern Illinois University Press.

Pryal, K. R. G. (2010). The genre of the mood memoir and the ethos of psychiatric disability. *Rhetoric Society Quarterly, 40*(5), 479–501.

Quackenbush, N. (2011). Speaking of—and as—stigma: Performativity and Parkinson's in the rhetoric of Michael J. Fox. *Disability Studies Quarterly, 31*(3). https://dsq-sds.org/article/view/1670/0

Quick, B. L. (2009). The effects of viewing *Grey's Anatomy* on perceptions of doctors and patient satisfaction. *Journal of Broadcasting & Electronic Media, 53*(1), 38–55.

Quick, B. L., Morgan, S. E., LaVoie, N. R., & Bosch, D. (2014). *Grey's Anatomy* viewing and organ donation attitude formation: Examining mediators bridging this relationship among African Americans, Caucasians, and Latinos. *Communication Research, 41*(5), 690–716.

Rademacher, M. A. (2018). "The most inspiring bikini photos you'll see this summer": A thematic analysis of mass audiences' interpretations of ostomy selfies. *New Media & Society, 20*(10), 3858–3878.

Rai, C. (2016). *Democracy's lot: Rhetoric, publics, and the places of invention*. University of Alabama Press.

Ratcliffe, K. (2005). *Rhetorical listening: Identification, gender, whiteness*. Southern Illinois University Press.

Reed, A. R., & Meredith, S. (2020). Shaping contexts and developing invitational ethos in response to medical authority: An interview study of women Down syndrome advocates. *Rhetoric of Health & Medicine, 3*(3), 258–292.

Reynolds, J. M. (2017). "I'd rather be dead than disabled"—The ableist conflation and the meanings of disability. *Review of Communication, 17*(3), 149–163.

Ringer, Sara. (2012, July 22). *Meet Gut Girl, the IBD superhero!* Inflamed and Untamed. https://inflamedanduntamed.org/gut-girl/

Riome, P. (2018, June 10). *Paul Riome shares the story about his Grandma Mabel's ostomy surgery in 1938*. Ostomy Connection. https://ostomyconnection.com/news-and-culture/grandma-mabels-ostomy-surgery-in-1938

Rodgers, R. F., Kruger, L., Lowy, A. S., Long, S., & Richard, C. (2019). Getting Real about body image: A qualitative investigation of the usefulness of the Aerie Real campaign. *Body Image, 30*, 127–134.

Rohde, J. A., Wang, Y., Cutino, C. M., Dickson, B. K., Bernal, M. C., Bronda, S., Liu, A., Priyadarshini, S. I., Guo, L., Reich, J. S., & Farraye, F. A. (2018). Impact of disease disclosure on stigma: An experimental investigation of college students' reactions to inflammatory bowel disease. *Journal of Health Communication, 23*(1), 91–97.

Rosman, S. (2004). Cancer and stigma: Experience of patients with chemotherapy-induced alopecia. *Patient Education and Counseling, 52*(3), 333–339.

Ross, A. (2019, January 23). *Louisville mom blames bullying at JCPS for suicide of her 10-year-old*. Courier Journal. https://www.courier-journal.com/story/news/education/2019/01/22/louisville-mom-blames-jcps-bullying-sons-death-suicide/2643320002/

Rothfelder, K., & Thornton, D. J. (2017). Man interrupted: Mental illness narrative as a rhetoric of proximity. *Rhetoric Society Quarterly, 47*(4), 359–382.

Rund, R. (2015). Remove tobacco colon cancer advertisement. Change.org. Retrieved August 17, 2020, from https://www.change.org/p/centers-for-disease-control-and-prevention-remove-tobacco-colon-cancer-advertisement

Sandahl, C. (2003). Queering the crip or cripping the queer? Intersections of queer and crip identities in solo autobiographical performance. *GLQ: A Journal of Lesbian and Gay Studies, 9*(1), 25–56.

Santos, A. C., & Santos, A. L. (2018). Yes, we fuck! Challenging the misfit sexual body through disabled women's narratives. *Sexualities, 21*(3), 303–318.

Saul, H. (2015, April 9). *The inspirational photos that show surgery doesn't remove femininity*. Independent. Retrieved September 21, 2020, from http://www.independent.co.uk/life-style/health-and-families/stomaselfie-woman-posts-images-stoma-and-ileostomy-bag-challenge-taboos-around-ibd-10165203.html

Saunders, B. (2014). Stigma, deviance and morality in young adults' accounts of inflammatory bowel disease. *Sociology of Health & Illness, 36*(7), 1020–1036.

Scambler, G. (1989). *Epilepsy*. Tavistock.

Scambler, G. (2004). Re-framing stigma: Felt and enacted stigma and challenges to the sociology of chronic and disabling conditions. *Social Theory & Health, 2*(1), 29–46.

Schalk, S. (2016). Reevaluating the supercrip. *Journal of Literary & Cultural Disability Studies, 10*(1), 71-86.

Scott, B., Segal, J. Z., & Keranen, L. (2013). The rhetorics of health and medicine: Inventional possibilities for scholarship and engaged practice. *Poroi, 9*(1), 1–6.

Scott, J. (1989). "Cyborgian socialists?" In E. Weed (Ed.) *Coming to terms: Feminism, theory, politics.* (pp. 215-217). Routledge.

Scott, J.-A. (2018). *Embodied performance as applied research, art and pedagogy.* Palgrave Macmillan.

Scott, J. B., & Gouge, C. C. (2019). Theory building in the rhetoric of health and medicine. In A. Alden, K. Gerdes, J. Holiday, & R. Skinnell (Eds.), *Reinventing (with) theory in rhetoric and writing studies: Essays in honor of Sharon Crowley* (pp. 181–195). Utah State University Press.

Scott, J. B., & Melonçon, L. (2018). Manifesting methodologies for the rhetoric of health & medicine. In L. Melonçon & J. B. Scott (Eds.), *Methodologies for the rhetoric of health & medicine* (pp. 1–23). Routledge.

Scott, J. B., & Melonçon, L. (2019). Caring for diversity and inclusion. *Rhetoric of Health & Medicine 2*(3), iii–xi. https://www.muse.jhu.edu/article/736838

Segal, J. Z. (2005). *Health and the rhetoric of medicine*. Southern Illinois University Press.

Segal, J. Z. (2012). Cancer experience and its narration: An accidental study. *Literature and Medicine, 30*(2), 292–318.

Sewell, J. L., Inadomi, J. M., & Yee, H. F. Jr. (2010). Race and inflammatory bowel disease in an urban healthcare system. *Digestive Diseases and Sciences, 55*(12), 3479–3487. https://doi.org/10.1007/s10620-010-1442-8

Shakespeare, T. (1996). Disability, identity and difference. In C. Barnes & G. Mercer (Eds.), *Exploring the divide* (pp. 94–113). Disability Press.

Shakespeare, T. (2017). The social model of disability. In L. Davis (Ed.), *The disability studies reader* (pp. 195–203). Routledge.

Shanklin, S. (2019, January 22). *The heartbreak of suffering in silence*. WHAS11 ABC. Retrieved January 24, 2019, from https://www.whas11.com/article/features/the-heartbreak-of-suffering-in-silence/417-c7a30302-4894-4243-96ee-19824c50fd5f

Sharp, S. P., Ata, A., Chismark, A. D., Canete, J. J., Valerian, B. T., Wexner, S. D., & Lee, E. C. (2020). Racial disparities after stoma construction in colorectal surgery. *Colorectal Disease, 22*(6), 713–722.

Sheets, D. (2005). Aging with disabilities: Ageism and more. *Generations, 29*(3), 37–41.

Shildrick, M. (1997). *Leaky bodies and boundaries: Feminism, deconstruction and bioethics.* Routledge.

Siebers, T. (2008). *Disability theory.* University of Michigan Press.

Simbayi, L. C., Kalichman, S., Strebel, A., Cloete, A., Henda, N., & Mqeketo, A. (2007). Internalized stigma, discrimination, and depression among men and women living with HIV/AIDS in Cape Town, South Africa. *Social Science & Medicine, 64*(9), 1823–1831.

Smith, D. M., Loewenstein, G., Rozin, P., Sherriff, R. L., & Ubel, P. A. (2007). Sensitivity to disgust, stigma, and adjustment to life with a colostomy. *Journal of Research in Personality, 41*(4), 787–803.

Smith, R. A. (2007). Language of the lost: An explication of stigma communication. *Communication Theory, 17*(4), 462–485.

Smith, R. A. (2014). Testing the model of stigma communication with a factorial experiment in an interpersonal context. *Communication Studies, 65*(2), 154–173.

Snider, S. (2019). Visually representing lesbian sexuality and disability in Tee Corinne's *Scars, stoma, ostomy bag, portocath: Picturing cancer in our lives*. In A. Wexler & J. Derby (Eds.), *Contemporary art and disability studies* (pp. 133–145). Routledge.

Soames Job, R. F. (1988). Effective and ineffective use of fear in health promotion campaigns. *American Journal of Public Health, 78*(2), 163–167.

Spaeth, G. L. (2015). Treat the patient—not just the dieases. Review of Ophthalmology. Retrieved September 20, 2020, from https://www.reviewofophthalmology.com/article/treat-the-patient-not-just-the-disease

StealthBelt. (2020). *Best ostomy support belts & wraps: Colostomy pouch covers*. Retrieved September 21, 2020, from https://www.stealthbelt.com/

Stomalicious. (2015a, May 11). *About me*. https://stomalicious.wordpress.com/aboutme/

Stomalicious. (2015b, May 11). *About Stomalicious*. https://stomalicious.wordpress.com/about-stomalicious/

Swain, J., & French, S. (2000). Towards an affirmation model of disability. *Disability & Society, 15*(4), 569–582.

Taft, T. H., Ballou, S., & Keefer, L. (2012). Preliminary evaluation of maternal caregiver stress in pediatric eosinophilic gastrointestinal disorders. *Journal of Pediatric Psychology, 37*(5), 451–460.

Taft, T. H., & Keefer, L. (2016). A systematic review of disease-related stigmatization in patients living with inflammatory bowel disease. *Clinical and Experimental Gastroenterology, 9*, 49–58.

TallBear, K. (2017). Beyond the life/not-life binary: A feminist-indigenous reading of cryopreservation, interspecies thinking, and the new materialisms. In J. Radin & E. Kowal (Eds.), *Cryopolitics: Frozen life in a melting world* (pp. 179–202). MIT Press.

Teston, C. (2017). *Bodies in flux: Scientific methods for negotiating medical uncertainty*. University of Chicago Press.

Teston, C. B., Graham, S. S., Baldwinson, R., Li, A., & Swift, J. (2014). Public voices in pharmaceutical deliberations: Negotiating "clinical benefit" in the FDA's Avastin Hearing. *Journal of Medical Humanities, 35*(2), 149–170.

Titchkosky, T., & Michalko, R. (2012). The body as the problem of individuality: A phenomenological disability studies approach. In D. Goodley, B. Hughes, & L. Davis (Eds.), *Disability and social theory* (pp. 127–142). Palgrave Macmillan.

TLC. (2017a). *Too Ugly for Love? Bibliographies*. Retrieved January 17, 2020, from http://www.uk.tlc.com/shows/too-ugly-for-love/bibliographies

TLC. (2017b). *Too Ugly for Love? New series starts Wednesday 13th January 9pm*. Retrieved January 17, 2020, from http://www.uk.tlc.com/shows/too-ugly-for-love

TLC. (2020). *About*. https://www.tlc.com/general/about

The Trevor Project. (2020, October 07). *Asexual*. Retrieved April 7, 2021, from https://www.thetrevorproject.org/trvr_support_center/asexual/

Turner, B. S. (2003). Social fluids: Metaphors and meanings of society. *Body & Society, 9*(1), 1–10.

Uncover Ostomy. (n.d.). *About us*. Retrieved September 21, 2020, from https://uncoverostomy.org/about-us/

United Ostomy Association of America. (2016, February 26). *Living with an ostomy*. https://www.ostomy.org/wp-content/uploads/2018/12/UOAA_Living_with_An_Ostomy_Pamphlet.pdf

Valeras, A. (2010). "We don't have a box": Understanding hidden disability identity utilizing narrative research methodology. *Disability Studies Quarterly, 30*(3/4). https://dsq-sds.org/article/view/1267

Van Amsterdam, N. (2015). Othering the "leaky body." An autoethnographic story about expressing breast milk in the workplace. *Culture and Organization, 21*(3), 269–287.

Van Brakel, W. H. (2006). Measuring health-related stigma—A literature review. *Psychology, Health & Medicine, 11*(3), 307–334.

Vernoff, K. (Writer), & D'Elia, B. (Director). (2009, September, 24). Good mourning (Season 6, Episode 2) [TV series episode]. In S. Rimes (Executive Producer), *Grey's Anatomy*. American Broadcasting Company.

Vernoff, K. (Writer), & Ornelas, E. (Director). (2009, September, 24). Good mourning (Season 6, Episode 1) [TV series episode]. In S. Rimes (Executive Producer), *Grey's Anatomy*. American Broadcasting Company.

Vickers, M. H. (2000). Stigma, work, and "unseen" illness: A case and notes to enhance understanding. *Illness, Crisis & Loss, 8*(2), 131–151.

Vidali, A. (2010). Out of control: The rhetoric of gastrointestinal disorders. *Disability Studies Quarterly, 30*(3/4). https://dsq-sds.org/article/view/1287/1313

Vidali, A. (2013). Hysterical again: The gastrointestinal woman in medical discourse. *Journal of Medical Humanities 34*(1), 33–57.

Walker, D. (2014, July 7). *Bethany Townsend reveals colostomy bag bikini pictures have changed other Crohn's sufferers lives*. Mirror. http://www.mirror.co.uk/tv/tv-news/bethany-townsend-reveals-colostomy-bag-3823608

Warren, J. (2013, September 28). *Colostomy comment by Cincinnati police lieutenant offends; opens dialogue*. https://www.wcpo.com/news/local-news/colostomy-comment-offends-opens-dialogue

Washington, H. A. (2006). *Medical apartheid: The dark history of medical experimentation on Black Americans from colonial times to the present*. Doubleday Books.

Weed, M. A. (2012). A cure for the empathy gap? Experience and perspective of a chronically ill and disabled medical educator. *Archives of Ophthalmology, 130*(2), 263–264.

Wendell, S. (1989). Toward a feminist theory of disability. *Hypatia, 4*(2), 104–124.

Wendell, S. (1996). *The rejected body: Feminist philosophical reflections on disability.* Psychology Press.

Wendell, S. (2001). Unhealthy disabled: Treating chronic illnesses as disabilities. *Hypatia, 16*(4), 17–33.

Wheatley, K. (2019, January 22). *Parents of 10-year-old boy who committed suicide plan to sue JCPS.* WDRB. https://www.wdrb.com/in-depth/parents-of—year-old-boy-who-committed-suicide-plan/article_c8a75bde-1dc0-11e9-a655-571c9e9b9a1e.html

Wheeler, N. (2020). *Stigma as a gay man with a stoma.* SecuriCare Medical. Retrieved April 7, 2021, from https://www.securicaremedical.co.uk/blog/stigma-as-a-gay-man-with-a-stoma

Wilson, J. C. (2002). (Re)writing the genetic body-text: Disability, textuality, and the Human Genome Project. *Cultural Critique, 50,* 23–39.

Winderman, E., Mejia, R., & Rogers, B. (2019). "All smell is disease": Miasma, sensory rhetoric, and the sanitary-bacteriologic of visceral public health. *Rhetoric of Health & Medicine, 2*(2), 115–146.

Witte, K. (1992). Putting the fear back into fear appeals: The extended parallel process model. *Communications Monographs, 59*(4), 329–349.

Wolfensberger, W. (1972). *The principle of normalization in human services.* National Institute on Mental Retardation.

Wu, J. S. (2012). Intestinal stomas: Historical overview. In V. W. Fazio, J. M. Church, & J. S. Wu (Eds.), *Atlas of intestinal stomas* (pp. 1–37). Springer.

Wu, S. Y., & Green, A. (2000). *Projection of chronic illness prevalence and cost inflation.* RAND Health.

Xu, J., Kochanek, K. D., Murphy, S. L., & Tejada-Vera, B. (2010). Deaths: Final data for 2007. *National Vital Statistics Reports, 58*(19).

Xu, J., Murphy, S. L., Kochanek, K. D., Bastina, B., & Arias, E. (2018). Deaths: Final data for 2016. *National Vital Statistics Reports, 67*(5).

Yergeau, M. (2018). *Authoring autism.* Duke University Press.

Zola, I. K. (1993). Self, identity and the naming question: Reflections on the language of disability. *Social Science & Medicine, 36*(2), 167–173.

INDEX

www.ingramcontent.com/pod-product-compliance
Lightning Source LLC
Chambersburg PA
CBHW020702270326
41928CB00005B/231